Chihuahuas

FOR

DUMMIES

2ND EDITION

Chihuahuas For Dummies, 2nd Edition

Cheat Sheet

Selecting a Chihuahua Puppy

Follow these suggestions to help choose a Chihuahua with your head as well as your heart (and check Chapter 4):

- **Trust your instincts.** Does one puppy catch your eye immediately? First impressions are important, and love at first sight can last a lifetime. But take time to ensure that your furry favorite is healthy and has a pleasing personality.

- **Be observant.** Watch the puppies play together for several minutes without human interference. Your best bet is a puppy in the middle of the pecking order — neither the bully nor the scaredy-cat.

- **Eye the eyes.** They should be bright, alert, and clear of mucus. (Don't mistake clear tears for mucus, though.)

- **Check the coat.** A healthy coat is smooth to the touch and glossy, with no bald patches. No puppy should have skin showing through on its back or sides.

- **Know the nose.** Breathing should be quiet and rhythmic and the nostrils should be free of mucous.

- **Note how puppies move when they play.** Despite a bit of baby clumsiness, they should appear quick, bouncy, and agile, standing straight on legs that look strong enough to carry their bodies.

Shopping for Puppy Gear

If you're introducing a Chihuahua to the household, here's your shopping list (see Chapter 5 for more details):

- Two dishes — one for water and one for food
- Puppy (or dog) food
- Collar
- Leash
- Natural-bristle brush (plus a hard rubber comb and a mat splitter if you have a long-coated Chi)
- Nail clippers
- Toothbrush and doggie toothpaste

- Shampoo (long-coated Chihuahuas also need coat conditioner)
- Three or four toys
- Dog crate
- Dog bed (optional)
- Warm sweater (if it's chilly outdoors)
- Pooper-scooper
- Identification
- An excellent veterinarian

Chihuahuas For Dummies, 2nd Edition

Finding a Good Veterinarian

Sharpen your search for a good vet with one or more of these tactics (also see Chapter 13):

- ✔ Ask your Chihuahua's breeder. Even if the breeder lives far away, he or she may have sold pups to people in your area who can recommend a vet.
- ✔ When you see people walking Toy dogs in your neighborhood, ask them what vets they use and if they're satisfied with the quality of care.
- ✔ Call the nearest major veterinary hospital for recommendations.

Visiting the Vet

Use this checklist to prepare for your Chihuahua's first checkup:

- ✔ To reduce the probability of carsickness, feed your dog a couple of biscuits an hour or more before driving to the clinic.
- ✔ Take along a roll of paper towels and a container of wet wipes in case a quick cleanup is necessary.
- ✔ Take a copy of your dog's health record.
- ✔ Transport your dog in a crate. Secure the crate so it won't tumble if you have to swerve or make a quick stop.
- ✔ Make a list of your dog care questions and bring it along. Vets are glad to answer appropriate questions about feeding, grooming, toenail trimming, and anything else related to your Chihuahua's health.
- ✔ Take notes when the veterinarian gives instructions.
- ✔ Follow the instructions exactly. Medications must be given at the right time and in the correct dosage or they won't work.

For Dummies: Bestselling Book Series for Beginners

Chihuahuas
FOR
DUMMIES®
2ND EDITION

by Jacqueline O'Neil

BICENTENNIAL
1807
WILEY
2007
BICENTENNIAL

Wiley Publishing, Inc.

Chihuahuas For Dummies®, 2nd Edition

Published by
Wiley Publishing, Inc.
111 River St.
Hoboken, NJ 07030-5774
www.wiley.com

Copyright © 2008 by Wiley Publishing, Inc., Indianapolis, Indiana

Published by Wiley Publishing, Inc., Indianapolis, Indiana

Published simultaneously in Canada

For general information on our other products and services, please contact our Customer Care Department within the U.S. at 800-762-2974, outside the U.S. at 317-572-3993, or fax 317-572-4002.

For technical support, please visit www.wiley.com/techsupport.

Wiley also publishes its books in a variety of electronic formats. Some content that appears in print may not be available in electronic books.

Library of Congress Control Number: 2007939647

ISBN: 978-0-470-22967-5

Manufactured in the United States of America

10 9 8 7 6 5 4 3 2 1

WILEY

About the Author

Jacqueline O'Neil is an award-winning author of more than a dozen books and a couple hundred magazine articles on animal care and training. She and her husband, Tom, a wildlife photographer, follow the sun around North America in a motor home. Favorite stops include the Florida Keys, Montana, Alaska, and the Yukon.

Before morphing into a Gypsy, Jackie was a successful dog breeder and trainer, handling her own dogs to top awards in the show and obedience rings.

A graduate of the University of Florida, Jackie is a member of the Outdoor Writers Association of America, the National League of American Pen Women, and the Dog Writers Association of America, where she also served two terms as a director. In addition to dogs, she's into horses, birds, fishing, scuba diving, and fiddling.

Jackie has two grown daughters, Peggy and Sunny Fraser, who have recently started their own menageries. The whole family is proud to be owned by a Chihuahua named Manchita.

Dedication

To my daughters, Peggy and Sunny Fraser, who served as mommies to a munchkin named Manchita, including their college and early career years.

Author's Acknowledgments

My husband, Tom O'Neil, took some of the photos for this book and proofread the manuscript before I sent it to my editors.

My mother, Dori Freedman, taught me that anything worth doing is worth doing right, and that once started, projects must be finished. Perhaps that's why I've been able to make writing my career.

My stepdad, Needham Parrish, contributed to the research in a big way by sending me books, articles, and videos on Chihuahuas. He also took the photos of the Chihuahua named Chiquita.

My daughter, Peggy Fraser, who hates posing for pictures, did it anyway. Thanks, honey.

Taco Bell Corp. provided information about Gidget, the world's most recognizable Chihuahua, and included photos of its superstar.

Publisher's Acknowledgments

We're proud of this book; please send us your comments through our Dummies online registration form located at www.dummies.com/register/.

Some of the people who helped bring this book to market include the following:

Acquisitions, Editorial, and Media Development

Project Editor (previous edition): Tim Gallan

Acquisitions Editor: Tracy Boggier

Copy Editor: Josh Dials

Technical Editor: Dr. Carey Wasem

Editorial Manager: Jennifer Ehrlich

Editorial Supervisor & Reprint Editor: Carmen Krikorian

Editorial Assistants: Erin Calligan Mooney, Joe Niesen, Leeann Harney, David Lutton

Cover Photo: © Gerard Lacz/Animals Animals

Cartoons: Rich Tennant (www.the5thwave.com)

Composition Services

Project Coordinator: Erin Smith

Layout and Graphics: Carl Byers, Reuben W. Davis, Alissa D. Ellet, Melissa K. Jester, Stephanie D. Jumper, Barbara Moore, Christine Williams

Anniversary Logo Design: Richard Pacifico

Proofreader: Bonnie Mikkelson

Indexer: Sherry Massey

Special Help: Natalie Faye Harris

Publishing and Editorial for Consumer Dummies

    Diane Graves Steele, Vice President and Publisher, Consumer Dummies

    Joyce Pepple, Acquisitions Director, Consumer Dummies

    Kristin A. Cocks, Product Development Director, Consumer Dummies

    Michael Spring, Vice President and Publisher, Travel

    Kelly Regan, Editorial Director, Travel

Publishing for Technology Dummies

    Andy Cummings, Vice President and Publisher, Dummies Technology/General User

Composition Services

    Gerry Fahey, Vice President of Production Services

    Debbie Stailey, Director of Composition Services

Contents at a Glance

Table of Contents

Introduction

Years ago, the then editor of the *AKC Gazette* asked me to cover the Chihuahua National Specialty, the breed's most prestigious annual dog show. The article I wrote was entitled, "Chihuahuas Charm Chicago," but the truth is, those Chihuahuas charmed me. Although I bred and exhibited American Staffordshire Terriers and was a veteran writer — in other words, I was used to studying a breed, attending national specialty shows, and submitting articles — I was smitten with Chihuahuas. I fell as surely as a young girl whose first date brings her flowers. From that day on, I had to have a Chihuahua.

From singles on the fast track to business success to seniors out seeing the world, many of my friends and acquaintances share their lives with Chihuahuas. And do you know what? Every single one of us had our first Chihuahua years before television commercials boosted the breed's popularity.

Today you can't turn on the TV or browse in a gift shop without seeing Chihuahuas. From fashion centers to flea markets, they've become one of the nation's most popular pets. But just because these critters attract attention with their incredible cuteness isn't enough reason to run out and get one. You wouldn't ask the prettiest cheerleader or the best football player to marry you when you don't even know her or his name, would you? Instead, let me introduce you to the Chihuahua with this book.

A little guidance — that's what I'm here for. So, turn to Chapter 1, or anywhere in the book for that matter, and let me do my job! Whether you're a potential new owner or have enjoyed the companionship of Chihuahuas for years, this book can help you and your dog make the most of your relationship.

About This Book

Chihuahuas For Dummies, 2nd Edition, is designed to be a complete reference guide. I tell you everything you need to know about selecting, raising, and training a healthy, well-mannered Chihuahua. And although I promote prevention — not only in health matters but also by proposing positive training methods right from the start — I explain how to correct the bad habits your dog may have already picked up.

But wait. Maybe you don't have a dog yet and you're reading this book because you wonder if a Chihuahua is the breed for you. Well, you've come to the right place! This book covers the unique Chihuahua personality and gives honest answers about both the pleasures and problems of living with a Chihuahua. Ohmygosh! What if you read those sections and then decide a Chihuahua isn't your dream dog after all? In that case, I just saved you a bundle of money and years of enduring a match that wasn't made in heaven. It's important to think about how *your* personality will blend with the unique disposition of this diminutive breed.

I wrote this book to make living with a Chihuahua easy and fun. Whether you have one Chi or half a dozen, this book simplifies daily care, tells you how to train your dog, and even helps you organize a nonviolent coup to take leadership away from a tiny tyrant!

Conventions Used in This Book

To make this book even easier to understand, I included a few conventions:

- ✔ *Italic* text indicates new words or terms that I define. I also use it for emphasis (I get excited!).

- ✔ **Boldfaced** type helps you remember the most important points when reading bulleted lists or numbered steps.

- ✔ I use `monofont` to set apart Web sites and e-mail addresses.

- ✔ Occasionally, I write "Chi" instead of spelling out "Chihuahua." I do this to make for faster reading, not because it's a nickname for the breed. It isn't.

Because my degree is in English, I know that the proper way to refer to an animal is "it," but I can't stand "it" when talking about a member of a family. So, I get around this by using gender references. In some chapters I discuss all Chis as if they're males, and in some chapters it's ladies' night. And occasionally, I'll name the Chihuahuas I talk about for fun. In some of the chapters, the Chihuahua is named Pepe, and in the others, the Chi is named Manchita.

What You're Not to Read

Although this book is brimming with essential info, it also contains some Chihuahua trivia, a few just-for-fun dog facts, and some technical stuff you don't really need to know but that may make for good conversation. In case you're in a hurry to find out what you do need to know, feel free to skip the following:

✔ **Text in sidebars:** The shaded boxes are sidebars, and although they're good reads, the info in them isn't essential.

✔ **Paragraphs highlighted with a Technical Stuff icon:** Yes, these icons precede good info, but you don't need to know it to be an ideal Chihuahua owner. The icon also points out really short true stories and Chihuahua trivia.

Foolish Assumptions

Before writing this book, I had to think about who I was writing it for, so I made some assumptions about you, my dear reader, and the type of book you need. Here they are; am I close?

✔ You like dogs in general, and the Chihuahua is one of the breeds you like in particular. You're thinking about making one a part of your family. But first you want to know more about the breed, the pros and cons of living with a Chihuahua, and how to select your ideal dog.

✔ You've already taken the plunge. Your Chihuahua puppy is coming home soon and you want to know what he needs right away and how to take care of him.

✔ Your Chihuahua puppy is home, but doggonit she wakes you up during the night and can't seem to get the hang of housetraining.

✔ Your Chihuahua is an adult. You want to read this book in your comfy recliner, but that darn dog claimed it. Lately, he growls and nips whenever anyone tries to sit in it. And don't even think about touching his food dish! Perhaps you want to know how to handle a stubborn Chi in his senior years!

✔ Your Chihuahua is well behaved and super smart. Everyone agrees that he's special, and now you want him to try obedience, agility, or maybe a dog show. Or perhaps you're considering training him to be a therapy dog.

✔ You don't have and don't want a Chihuahua, but your cousin just got one and her birthday is coming up!

How This Book Is Organized

Chihuahuas For Dummies, 2nd Edition, is divided into five sections, and each one covers an essential topic. If you're looking for a Chihuahua, you may want to begin in the early chapters. If you already have a Chi, you can skip around, going quickly in and out of chapters that address your curiosity or urgent needs. Either way, here's what you find.

Part I: Is a Chihuahua Your Canine Compadre?

Adopting a dog has a lot in common with adopting a soul mate of the human species: You know you're in for a lot of give and take! But don't let that scare you — bringing a Chihuahua into your life is both a serious commitment and one of life's huge pleasures. This section helps you make good decisions and shows you what's in store.

Part II: Fitting a Compact Canine into Your Life

What do you look for in a healthy Chihuahua? How do you prepare your home for your little amigo? What do Chihuahuas eat? How much exercise do they need? Part II provides the information you need to welcome a Chi into your household and have a good beginning to a special new relationship.

Part III: Positive Training for Your Petite Pal

Part III is your ready reference guide and everyday problem solver. Here I tell you how to raise a mannerly puppy and instill good habits in an adult dog. Housebreaking? Barking? Shyness? Dominance? I cover all the typical Chihuahua problems and their solutions here. I discuss plenty of fun, too. I include tricks Chihuahuas love to learn and a lot of info on dog shows and other activities you and your dog can enjoy together.

Part IV: Chihuahua Care and Concerns

Finding the right veterinarian for your dog — at a convenient location — is job one of the health plan. Part IV shows you how to find a good vet and make the most of your visits to the clinic. You also find out how to care for a senior Chihuahua and how to handle emergency illnesses and injuries. Basically, you use this section as a reference for identifying and dealing with common health needs of Chihuahuas.

Part V: The Part of Tens

So much to tell you about Chihuahuas, so little time! Part V is packed with more useful data. You find a handy list of questions to ask the breeder when you're thinking of buying a dog, along with Web sites where you can find a huge variety of additional information. Finally, I raise the curtain on a stageful of celebrity Chihuahuas, including Tinkerbell, Bruiser, and Gidget.

Icons Used in This Book

The pages of this book are peppered with icons in the margins. Besides adding a little salsa, they also give you a quick bite of Chihuahua information. Here's what's on the menu:

You'll see this icon quite often. It contains advice on Chihuahua care and training techniques and provides shortcuts to simplify life with a dog.

There are certain tidbits of information I'd like you to keep in your memory bank for the duration of your time as a Chihuahua owner. This icon highlights this information.

Whoa! This Chihuahua is on full alert. This information helps you to keep from skidding into common but potentially serious mistakes.

Every species has its own language and characteristics. These icons define the terms dog owners in general, and Chihuahua owners in particular, need to know. You also find some interesting dog lore and some fun trivia.

Where to Go from Here

Don't you just hate it when you pick up a book that you're sure has the information you need but it doesn't give you a clue where to find it? Well, I promise I won't do that to you. This book is organized for your convenience — whether you want to "read all about it" or simply find a trick you can teach your Chihuahua to do so that she can show off when Great Aunt Amelia visits.

You can start wherever you want to and easily find the information you need. Do you want to know how to raise an outgoing, social Chihuahua? Turn to Chapter 9. Are you concerned about housebreaking? Chapter 10 will help you handle that. Are you Chihuahua shopping? Chapter 4 will help you find a good breeder.

If you're still wondering if a Chihuahua (or any dog) is right for you, read Chapters 1 and 3. They tell you what you need to know about dog ownership in general and living with a Chihuahua in particular.

There's no need to read this book from cover to cover unless you want to. Flip through it at will. Let the table of contents and the index guide you quickly to the info you need. Happy reading!

Part I

Is a Chihuahua Your Canine Compadre?

The 5th Wave   By Rich Tennant

"I think the Chihuahua's been up on the counter again. There are several paw prints in the butter tub."

In this part . . .

In this part, you find out all you ever wanted to know about the Chihuahua's distinctive personality and body structure. I help you ponder the ups and downs of dog ownership and what you can and can't expect from your pet. In short, Part I is the key to deciding whether the Chihuahua's unique disposition fits your lifestyle.

Chapter 1

Sharing Your Digs with a Dog: A Big Decision

Can money ever buy you love? Sure. Just use it to buy a Chihuahua. Your Chihuahua won't waffle about making a permanent commitment to you. In fact, expect your Chi to envelop you in affection, do his best to protect you, and maybe even improve your health. No kidding! Scientific studies show that a pet's companionship alleviates stress and helps people relax. In many cases, dogs (and other pets) get credit for lowering their owners' blood pressure. However, although most Chihuahua owners are crazy about their pets, a few wish they had never brought a dog (or *that* dog) home.

I don't want Chihuahua ownership to disappoint you, so in this chapter, I talk about the ups and downs of living with dogs in general, and Chis in particular. Is this portable pet with the king-sized heart the right breed for you? In this chapter, you find the answer.

Deciding if and Why You Want a Dog

If you are *dog-deprived,* you know it. You greet all your friends' dogs by name, eye every dog that goes by on the street, and sometimes even ask strangers if you can pet their pups. Maybe you surf through your favorite breeds on the Internet or browse through the dog magazines at the bookstore. Do you have a list of possible puppy names in your head? You're already a *dog-goner*. It won't be long before other dog-deprived people are asking to pet your new puppy.

Ideally, you're drawn to dogs, and playing with them makes you feel good. But your reason for buying a dog may be less than ideal. For example, maybe you're lonely or bored, and you hope a dog can fill the void. The truth is, a little fur wrapped around a pleasant personality (like Manchita in Figure 1-1) spices up a bland life if you let it. Being loved by a dog is fulfilling in itself, and you can take it a step further and become involved in dog activities (see Chapter 12) that can bring you excitement, new friends, and a sense of purpose. So what's the problem? The glitch is that dogs purchased to relieve monotony often are ignored when the novelty wears off.

Before buying a Chihuahua, you must decide if you'll always appreciate your pet or if you just crave some instant entertainment. Still not sure? Ask yourself this: "Am I ready to love a dog for the duration (possibly 15 years for a Chihuahua), or will a cruise to the Caribbean be just as effective for banishing my boredom?"

Getting a dog is a big decision. After all, dogs are dependent, make demands on your time, cost money, and inhibit your freedom. Is your pet worth it? Absolutely. That's why there are more than 60 million pet dogs in the United States. But just because dogs and people have been best buddies through the ages doesn't necessarily mean you need to run out and get a puppy right away. Maybe Chihuahua ownership isn't right for you; maybe it is right for you, but not right now. Hopefully you'll find out by taking a look at the ownership requirements, the breed overview, and matchmaking tips in the following sections.

Chihuahuas are either smooth or long coated. Smooths have short hair that's soft and shiny (see Figure 1-1). Long coats have (you guessed it) long hair that may be straight or wavy (see Chapter 3 for more).

Figure 1-1: Manchita is a smooth-coated Chihuahua.

Doggy Dependents Aren't Tax Deductible: Chi-Care Duties

Like a child, a Chihuahua relies on you for food, housing, education, affection, toys, and medical care — and the IRS won't even let you declare him. Unlike a child, your puppy won't ever become independent. Your Chi won't fix his own dinner, brush his own hair, or pay his own medical bills. Instead, he'll depend on you for his health and happiness all his life.

Fortunately, most dog owners enjoy the small chores that make up daily dog care. For some, interacting with their dogs is a restful transition from a too-busy day. Others say that their dogs keep the nest from feeling empty and add laughter to their lives. And when you have a doggy dependent, you're always the most important thing in his life. He needs you from puppyhood through old age. He doesn't graduate, get a job, marry, or move halfway across the country.

You should discuss division of labor with your family before getting a dog, but don't expect even the most logical schedule to be carved in stone. In the end, someone — one person — must take responsibility, making sure your dog is fed, watered, groomed, trained, exercised, and taken outdoors when he indicates a need to eliminate. Because you're the one reading this book, I bet that someone is you. Will you relish or resent the responsibility?

Considering the long-term cost

Can you afford a dog? I'm talking not only about the price of the dog (which will probably be $300 to well over $1,000 for a Chihuahua puppy), but also the price of upkeep.

Some breeds — Chihuahuas for example — don't eat much, but they still need the following:

✔ Quality food (see Chapter 6)

✔ Puppy shots, an annual checkup complete with vaccinations, and regular worming (see Part IV)

✔ Minor surgery to spay or neuter (see Chapter 13)

✔ Medication to prevent heartworm

✔ A crate, grooming equipment, a collar and leash, dog dishes, and a variety of toys and treats (see Chapter 5)

And although Chis tend to be healthy, yours may rack up a big bill if he's ever in an accident and requires emergency surgery.

You want my take? Darn right you can afford a dog! As hard as you work, you probably can swing that cruise to the Caribbean — if only you had time to take a vacation. Truth is, people seldom make time for a social life. At least you deserve the pleasure of an adoring dog when you finally get home from work at night.

Placing your Chi in your daily schedule

So you're doing fine financially, but maybe you're working crazy hours to reach the next rung up the corporate ladder. In that case, your Chihuahua's excited antics when you come through the door can be just the ticket to turn your mood from office mania to bemused tranquility. Forget fuming over a frustrating meeting. Your dog needs to be walked and fed, and both of you will look forward to snuggling through a sitcom or two. Just keep in mind that no matter how frazzled you are, and no matter how late it is, your dog still needs your attention and affection. If you and he live alone, especially, you're his entire world.

Chapter 5 and the chapters of Part III deal with setting up a schedule for your Chi and socializing and training your little guy.

Some offices allow employees to bring well-behaved pets to work. My Chihuahua spent many hours in the office when I worked for the American Kennel Club (AKC) in New York City. Sure, that's a special case, but while we walked to work, we saw plenty of other pooches accompanying people carrying briefcases.

Fitting your Chi into your family's future

Your spouse's feelings about having a dog, your kids' ages, your activity level, and your travel plans are important considerations when deciding whether to make a Chihuahua part of your family. Bringing home a dog when your spouse doesn't want one is unfair to everyone. So is buying a breed your other half hates. Sure, a reluctant spouse, in some cases, comes to love the dog, but often one partner never quite comes around. Having to defend your dog on a daily basis gets old real fast, and you don't need that. Furthermore, no dog deserves to be dumped at the pound because everyone got tired of the hassles at home.

Are you hoping to settle down and start a family in the near (or distant) future? Some breeds (Chihuahuas are one of them) are long lived, so with luck, you can plan on your dog being with you for your wedding and the births of your babies. But as sweet as that sounds, it may not be a good thing. Will your spouse also love your dog, or will he or she consider your Chi excess baggage?

Another potential problem is that some breeds (Chihuahuas included) don't thrive around toddlers. It's a no-fault, lose-lose situation. Tiny dogs are too delicate for young children, and kids under the ages of 6 or 7 still are geared toward stuffed animals. Imagine how long poor Pepe would last if a toddler tripped over him or swung him by one leg like a stuffed teddy.

Picking up after your Chi

What kind of housekeeper are you? Is your home casual and relaxed — the kind of place where friends gather to munch popcorn and watch videos? Or is your house so immaculate that family members remove their shoes before stepping on the cream-colored carpet?

Puppies aren't perfect. Chances are you'll have to clean up some accidents while housetraining your Chihuahua. Not only that, he'll shed at intervals (or constantly) all his life (see Chapter 7). Long after he's reliably housebroken — maybe years after you've moved into your dream home — he can get sick and upchuck on the new sofa. When that happens, will you view the mess as a minor annoyance or a major tragedy? (The chapters of Part III deal with socializing and training your little guy.)

Even though a Chi's poops are small, they can make a big mess on the bottom of someone's shoe. Don't forget to clean up after your dog every time you walk him (see Chapter 8). In many places, it's the law!

Viewing the Chihuahua as a Toy Breed

Say that after reading about the ups and downs of dog ownership, you decide that you want a canine companion. Right on! You're going to love living with a dog — that is, if your dog lives up to your expectations. Humans breed dogs capable of doing an extraordinary number of things, but dogs are specialists in a sense, and no one breed does it all. A wrong match between dog and owner usually brings misery, like a bad marriage, while a good match means years of satisfaction and fun.

Some Toy dogs, such as the Toy Poodle, are downsized versions of their larger cousins. Others, like the Miniature Pinscher, have been around longer than the larger dogs that resemble them. The Chihuahua isn't a scaled-down version of anything. It's a true Toy breed: a breed created for the sole purpose of being companions to people. The following sections give you more details on this breed (for more, head to Chapters 2 and 3).

What's terrific about Toys

What do all the Toy breeds have in common? They're living proof that great things really do come in small packages. Here's the upside of a Toy dog:

- **Toy dogs are small.** They fit anywhere — sometimes even in your pocket — and can get enough exercise in a small apartment.

- **Toy dogs are cuddly and love human attention.** They form extremely strong bonds with their people, and many are content to warm a lap for hours.

Toy breeds on parade

The American Kennel Club (AKC) recognizes more than 150 dog breeds and divides them into 7 groups, depending on the function each breed originally performed. The Chihuahua is a member of the Toy Group — a companion breed to us people. The AKC recognizes the following Toy breeds:

- Affenpinscher
- Brussels Griffon
- Cavalier King Charles Spaniel
- Chihuahua (smooth or long coat)
- Chinese Crested (hairless or powderpuff)
- English Toy Spaniel
- Fox Terrier (Toy)
- Havanese
- Italian Greyhound
- Japanese Chin
- Maltese
- Manchester Terrier (Toy)
- Miniature Pinscher
- Papillon
- Pekingese
- Pomeranian
- Poodle (Toy)
- Pug
- Shih Tzu
- Silky Terrier
- Yorkshire Terrier

According to AKC statistics, the top three most popular Toy breeds in 2006 were the Yorkshire Terrier, the Shih Tzu, and the Chihuahua. Toy Poodles also are popular, but knowing where they rank is impossible because all three varieties (Standard, Miniature, and Toy) are counted as one.

✔ **Toy dogs are portable.** They're ideal for people who travel a lot and like to take their dogs along with them.

✔ **Toy dogs love to show off.** Most of them enjoy learning new things from upbeat trainers.

✔ **Toy dogs often are welcome where larger breeds are not.** For example, some condo associations limit the size of pets.

✔ **Toys are real dogs.** They're intelligent and affectionate, with bold, fun-loving temperaments. Many of them make alert watchdogs.

In the lingo of the dog fancier, the Chihuahua is considered a *natural dog*. That means his coat isn't trimmed, shaved, stripped, or plucked, and his ears and tail are left the way nature made them — not trimmed or docked (in the style of the Miniature Pinscher, among others). In dog-fancier slang, that makes the Chihuahua a *wash-and-wear breed*.

Potential problems with portable pets

Toy dogs need careful owners. Depending on your nature, that's one potential downside of owning a Chihuahua. Although most Chis think they're tough, they're more vulnerable to injury (especially being stepped on or tripped over) than larger dogs. Here are some other concerns:

✔ When Toy dog owners overdo carrying and cuddling and skimp on the training, their pets become spoiled. And that turns them into tiny tyrants or nervous wimps.

✔ Toy breeds are social creatures. Developing that typical Toy spirit means they need plenty of social interactions with a variety of people from puppyhood on.

✔ Toy dogs that are neglected during puppyhood, or that come from inferior stock, may suffer myriad physical and/or mental problems at maturity.

✔ Some people dislike Toy dogs and may make rude remarks about your Chi when you walk him. If you answer at all, smile and say something like, "Shhh. He thinks he's a tiger."

✔ Toy dogs are real dogs. Like every other breed, they need training and guidance. In other words, if you don't train your Chi, your Chi will train you.

Digging up the Mexican connection

Chihuahuas are lap warmers, and their purpose is companionship. But in tougher times — before people owned pets for pure pleasure — every creature had to have a function. "Just for fun" didn't cut it. Historians are still uncertain about the precise origins and uses of the earliest Chihuahuas, but legends about their beginnings abound — a combination of fact and fantasy that makes the dog world's littlest breed one of its biggest mysteries.

Relics from ancient Mexico include sculptures of small dogs that archeologists discovered while studying the remains of the Mayan, Toltec, and Aztec cultures. Although some of the statues (you can see them at the National Museum in Mexico City) don't look much like modern Chihuahuas, and little is known about the Mayans, some relics from the Toltecs have aroused researchers' attention.

The Toltec Indians lived in Mexico during the ninth century, and possibly even earlier. They had a dog called the *Techichi,* which some historians believe is the ancestor of today's Chihuahua. Stone carvings of these dogs exist at the Monastery of Huejotzingo (on the highway between Mexico City and Puebla), and they look much more like the modern Chihuahua than the statues that are believed to be Mayan.

Making a Match with a Chihuahua

All the Toy breeds make exceptional companions, but they aren't interchangeable. The 21 breeds come in a variety of shapes, coat types, and colors, and their temperaments and activity levels vary from lazy and laid back to extremely active and irritable. (Oops! I don't know any breed that I'd characterize as "irritable." Some individual dogs of any breed may be irritable, but definitely not the entire breed.) Is the Chihuahua the right breed choice for you? Here's a synopsis of what a Chi can and can't bring to a relationship. (And for more on the Chihuahua look and disposition, see Chapters 2 and 3.)

> ✔ **Pepe is the perfect pet — for some people.** Because he thrives on togetherness, a Chihuahua is the ideal dog for someone who's home a lot and spends some time sitting. That's because Chis love to sit beside you, or better yet, on your lap. If you work from a home office, or if some of your favorite things are watching television, reading, or surfing the net, your dog will be in puppy paradise. He's also an excellent family dog, provided the children are gentle and older than 7. But if you're on the go all the time and can't make space in your schedule to accommodate an accomplished lap warmer, this isn't the breed for you.

✔ **Pepe tires easily.** He enjoys a brisk walk around the block when the weather is nice, but if you want a jogging or hiking companion, check out some of the larger breeds. No, a Chihuahua isn't wimpy when it comes to walking. He just gets tired because he takes several strides to keep up with just one of yours.

✔ **Pepe is an alert watchdog with a bark much bigger than he is.** But he isn't a guard dog or an attack dog, no matter what he thinks.

✔ **Pepe is loyal and loving.** He believes in family first and is vigilant and discriminating when you have visitors. Your friends *may* become his friends after he gets to know them.

✔ **Pepe is easy to groom whether he's a smooth or a long coat.** If you're looking forward to fussing with hair, many other Toys have thicker, longer coats.

✔ **Pepe is a housedog.** He can't tolerate cold or rainy weather, garages, or drafty basements.

✔ **Pepe is super short.** That means you, your family, and your guests must watch where you walk. Don't worry. It becomes second nature in a day or two. But when you or your children have friends over, you must remind them to be careful.

✔ **Pepe plays games with you (you can find some in Chapter 8).** He may learn to fetch a ball or chase a small Frisbee, but he won't be able to handle any rough stuff. If you want a tough dog that plays hard, get a larger pet.

✔ **Pepe probably is a good traveler.** Most Chihuahuas adapt well to the open road and love to watch the world go by from the passenger's seat (especially when a passenger is in the seat). Of course, a crate (see Chapter 5) is safer.

✔ **Pepe must be taught manners, the same as any other dog.** Little and cute loses its charm real fast when your Chi develops bad habits.

✔ **Pepe is a natural born showoff with a good memory.** After he learns a trick or two, he'll be proud to perform for your friends (if he's familiar with them).

✔ **Pepe is sensitive.** He tries to comfort you when you're sad and dances for joy when you're happy. He won't feel secure in a house full of friction.

✔ **Pepe is delicate.** He needs your protection from bigger dogs, even if he doesn't think so. And not just when he's on the ground. Big dogs have been known to snatch tiny ones right out of their owners' arms (yes, that's rare, but I thought I should warn you).

Do you tend to get physical when you're angry? If so, it's best not to have any pet, especially not a Chihuahua. The first hot-tempered blow a Chihuahua receives will probably be his last.

🖊 **Pepe is intelligent and highly trainable.** In fact, he's capable of becoming competitive in active events like agility and obedience (see Chapter 12). But don't expect miracles. He'll prefer indoor activities to performing on damp grass.

Loyal, intelligent, trainable, portable, and incredibly cute to boot! If all those endearing Chihuahua charms have you captivated, you have plenty of company. In 2006, 22,562 new Chihuahuas were registered with the American Kennel Club. That ranked the breed 11th among the 155 AKC breeds. And in 14 major cities, Chihuahuas placed in the top 10. The little guys are big on popularity!

Chapter 2

What's Behind That Unique Chihuahua Look?

• •

In This Chapter

▶ Picturing the perfect Chihuahua

▶ Examining heads, tails, and other body parts

▶ Keeping perspective — nobody's perfect!

• •

*P*lenty of little dogs have compact bodies and expressive eyes (like the Toy breeds; see Chapter 3), so what makes a Chihuahua unmistakably a Chihuahua? Details. A whole bunch of details combine to create a dog that looks and acts like a Chihuahua and nothing but a Chihuahua. This chapter focuses on appearances and gives you the official (honest!) description of Chihuahua perfection.

Look for Yourself: The Classic Chihuahua

You may already have a mental picture of a Chihuahua from watching the old television ads that show Gidget, the Taco Bell dog (see Figure 2-1), mouth his polite request for a little grub. Of course, I should have said *her* request because Gidget is, after all, a gal dog playing a guy, but that's neither here nor there.

Next to its diminutive size, the Chihuahua's most recognizable feature is its apple-domed head, which you can plainly see in Manchita in Figure 2-2. Attached to Manchita's signature head are big eyes, brimming with intelligence and an inquiring gaze (Gidget's gaze is intense), and erect ears, a bit bigger than you may expect, that add to her aspect of alertness. On top of many Chihuahua heads, practically invisible but easily discernable through touch, is the *molera* — a soft spot similar to the one found on newborn babies. The molera is also called the *fontanel*.

Photo courtesy of Taco Bell Corp.

Figure 2-1: The head of the best-known Chihuahua on television.

A Chihuahua's body is surprisingly sturdy. Although Manchita's feet are dainty, her legs are muscular and swift. Her back is level, she's a little longer than she is tall, and she carries her tail confidently — either in a semicircle or in a loop over her back.

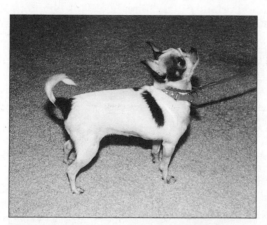

Figure 2-2: Manchita presents the classic Chihuahua look: apple-shaped head, prominent leg muscles, level back, and confident tail.

The apple-shaped head and a few other features pretty much describe a Chihuahua's distinctive appearance, but building a complete little superdog takes much more anatomy. Although knowing the details is important to successfully showing your Chihuahua (see Chapter 12), you don't need to know the finer points to love and enjoy your pet. So, if you want details, stick with me. But if anatomy isn't your thing, you can skip the following section.

Striving for the Picture-Perfect Chihuahua

Believe it or not, a blueprint exists for building a picture-perfect Chihuahua (and every other AKC registered breed). The blueprint is called the *Official Standard for the Chihuahua*. Of course, no dog is perfect (just as no person — not even a Miss America — is perfect), so no matter how charming a Chihuahua appears, the knowledgeable eyes of a good breeder or dog show judge always find room for improvement. Even the best breeders always have something to strive for.

Breed standards are serious stuff. Selecting breeding partners with the standard in mind is how breeders produce generation after generation of dogs that look and act like Chihuahuas. The best breeders try to produce dogs that come as close to matching the standard as possible, and dog-show judges select winners by comparing how closely each competitor matches its breed standard. (Head to Chapter 12 for more info on dog competitions.)

In Figure 2-3, you see dog lingo describing the external features of the Chihuahua. This is a handy diagram to refer to as you cruise through the details in the following sections. Pretty soon, you'll be able to speak the language of *dog people* — breeders, show exhibitors, and judges.

Just like schools, Chihuahuas have a parent group

Every breed of dog that the American Kennel Club recognizes is backed by a national organization known as a *parent club*. Parent clubs educate owners and breeders and create the standards of excellence for their breeds. Respected breeders within the parent club write standards that the club membership must approve. The standards are created for the long term, and they seldom change. The parent club for the Chihuahua is the Chihuahua Club of America (CCA).

What can reading the Chihuahua standard do for you? It helps you develop an eye for an excellent specimen and understand what makes the breed unique. The only problem: The standard is hard to follow because it was written as a guide for judges and breeders, who already understand dog lingo. Not to worry: Throughout the rest of this chapter, I translate the official talk into plain English.

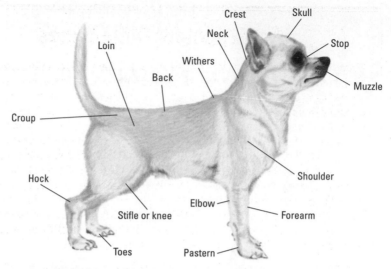

Crest Skull

Neck

Loin Stop

Withers

Back Muzzle

Croup

Shoulder

Hock

Elbow

Stifle or knee Forearm

Toes Pastern

Figure 2-3: All the parts of the Chihuahua.

General appearance and demeanor

The Chihuahua is a graceful, alert, swift-moving, and compact little dog with a saucy expression and terrier-like qualities of temperament.

A Chi is compact, feels solid in your hands, and appears well proportioned. She isn't long of body or lanky or too tall. Like a terrier, she's confident, animated, spirited, curious, and interested in everything happening around her.

Size and proportion

A Chihuahua is a well-balanced little dog, weighing not more than 6 pounds (to qualify for the show ring). Her body is *off-square,* to quote the official standard — she should be slightly longer when measured from point of shoulder to point of buttocks than she is tall at the *withers,* or the top of her shoulders. Somewhat shorter bodies (in length) are preferred in males. A Chi's height is the distance from the highest point of her withers to the floor; her length is the distance from the point of her shoulder to the point of her buttock. (Refer to Figure 2-3 to see all the technical terms applied to the dog.)

The reason a little more length is desired in females than it is in males is because females need the extra space to carry puppies.

A soft spot for Chihuahuas

Many historians contend that the Chihuahua is a native Mexican breed (see Chapter 1), but others argue that the breed originated in the Mediterranean — particularly on the island of Malta. According to proponents of the Malta theory, a tiny dog with a *molera* (a soft spot on its head — a trait unique to Chihuahuas) became established there and traveled on trading ships to European ports. To back up the theory, these historians point out that many paintings produced by European masters include small dogs resembling the Chihuahua. The most famous of these paintings is a fresco in the Sistine Chapel, created by Sondro Botticelli around 1482. Part of a series illustrating the life of Moses, *Sons of Moses* includes a little dog with a round head, big eyes, large erect ears, and other distinct Chihuahua characteristics. The painting was completed ten years before Columbus dropped anchor in the New World, so it's a sure bet that Botticelli never saw or heard of a Mexican dog, yet he painted something incredibly close to a Chihuahua.

Another theory contends that Chihuahuas originated in China and were brought to Mexico about 200 years ago. Supporters of this theory say that the Chinese were known for dwarfing plants and animals, and when wealthy Chinese merchants established homes in Mexico, they brought their little canine companions with them.

A Chihuahua needs a balanced appearance. That means every part of its body must be in proportion with its other parts. If her legs appear too long for her body or her head appears too small for her neck, she will look like she's made from spare parts.

In general, many breeds are considered *square,* meaning that their height is the same as their length. But the Chihuahua is supposed to be just a little longer than it is tall.

Head

To meet the standard, the shape of a Chihuahua's head should look sort of like an apple — rounded but not completely round. If she has a *molera,* you'll feel a slight indentation, like the soft spot on a baby's skull, when you gently stroke the top of her head. Breeders prefer eyes to be large, set well apart, radiant, and shiny — not close together, protruding, smallish, or dull. For perfect proportions, the middle of the eyes lines up with the lowest part of the ears. The following sections break down the rest of the head.

Ears

If a Chi has ideal ears, they'll be at a 45-degree angle to her head when she's resting, but they'll come to attention, held high, when she's alert. She may flatten them against her skull when she's moving fast or when something makes her uneasy.

How a dog holds its ears (for example, alertly erect or relaxed) is called its *ear carriage.*

Chihuahua ears must be left as nature made them. *Cropped ears* (surgically shaped or shortened ears) aren't permitted on Chihuahuas in the show ring. And broken ear cartilage, resulting in a droopy or lopsided ear, is grounds for disqualification from showing.

Muzzle (snout)

The standard calls for a muzzle, or *snout,* that's moderately short, but that doesn't mean shorter is better. A super-short muzzle is incorrect in the Chihuahua, because extremely short muzzles can cause breathing problems and crowd the teeth. Ideally, the muzzle should emerge from the skull at a right angle.

Teeth

If a Chi's upper-front teeth meet tightly outside her lower-front teeth, she has a *scissors bite;* if her upper and lower incisors (front teeth) meet flush with each other when her mouth is closed, her bite is *level.* The scissors bite is the strongest bite and is considered ideal. The teeth wear down faster when the bite is level.

Neck, topline, and body

An attractive neck from a side view flows smoothly and gracefully into your Chihuahua's withers without wrinkles or folds. Ideally, her neck is of medium length. Too short of a neck may be the result of improperly placed shoulder blades, which prevent her from moving well (see the section "Gait" later in this chapter). If her head appears to be attached directly to her shoulders, she'll look unbalanced and front-heavy.

On the other hand, an extremely long neck may be a sign that she lacks substance (appears weak). It may be accompanied by too-long legs and a lanky body. You should look for graceful lines. All the dog's parts should be well balanced in relation to one another.

A Chi's *topline* flows along the top of her back from the withers to the root of her tail (where the tail meets the body). Ideally, it should be level or straight, without a dip in the middle or a downward or upward slope. Her body should appear rounded rather than flat along the sides; she needs a roomy rib cage to house her heart and lungs.

A dog's *conformation* is the shape of her body from the top of her head to the tips of her toes and tail. It encompasses balanced body proportions and size, both of which need to be correct for the breed.

Tail

Figure 2-4 illustrates the Chihuahua's three correct tail positions and presents what a sorry tail tuck looks like. When a Chihuahua puts its tail between its legs, something is wrong. The dog may be timid, frightened, cold, or sick. *Note:* A cropped tail or bobtail disqualifies a dog from the show ring.

Forequarters

Well-laid-back shoulder blades are important in a Chihuahua. (Sloping shoulders can also be described as *well-laid-back*.) That means her shoulder blade, or *scapula,* connects her upper-arm bone with her vertebrae with an obvious backward slope from its bottom end (at the arm) to its top (just in front of the withers). Why are well-laid-back shoulder blades important? Because sloping shoulder blades allow a Chi's front legs to have a good range of motion. Shoulders that lack this slope are called *straight shoulders*. They're faulty because the upper end of the shoulder blade is too far forward — crammed right into the dog's neck. Besides making the neck look too short, straight shoulder blades shorten a dog's gait by limiting the forward reach of her front legs.

Here are some more forequarter considerations on the Chihuahua:

- ✔ Ideally, a Chihuahua's front legs should be straight while her toes point forward. Being bowlegged is a fault, as is an *east-west front* (toes pointing to either side) or *toeing in* (toes pointing toward each other).

- ✔ Feet that are elongated like a rabbit's foot or rounded like a cat's paw aren't desirable. Instead, her feet need to reach a happy medium between the two, with her toes separated but not *splayed* (flat and spread apart).

- ✔ The *pasterns* are the lowest points on a Chi's front legs, just above her feet. They need to be slender and straight.

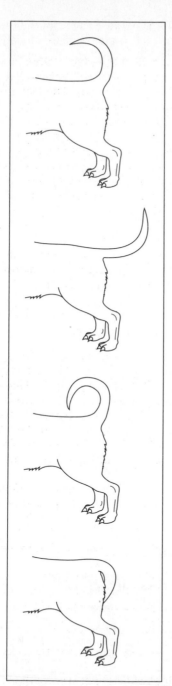

Figure 2-4: Three correct tail positions — and one sorry tail tuck.

Hindquarters

To give you a little taste of dog talk, the perfect Chihuahua's rear end is officially described as "Muscular, with hocks well apart, neither out nor in, well let down, firm and sturdy. The feet are as in front." Have you got that? Well the first word, "muscular," is obvious, and what the rest of it means is that a Chihuahua's hind leg has an upper and lower thigh, separated by the *stifle*, or knee joint, which is located on the frontal part of the dog's hind leg (don't forget Figure 2-3). The upper and lower thighs need to have sufficient muscle. Between the stifle joint and the foot is the *hock joint*. Hock joints that are much lower than the middle of the hind leg are better. *Well let down* means the hock joint is rather close to the ground.

Rear legs that are absolutely parallel when viewed from behind are ideal. Hocks turning toward each other, known as *cowhocks,* and hocks turned outward (bowed or spread) are faulty.

Coat

Chihuahuas come in two varieties — *smooth coat* and *long coat.* If a Chi has a smooth coat, her hair is short and close to her body, and she may or may not have an *undercoat* — a protective layer of shorter fur underneath the outer or top coat. A smooth Chihuahua that has an undercoat appears more thickly coated and usually has a furrier tail and a ruff of thicker hair around its neck. If a Chi has no undercoat, her hair is sparser. In fact, it may be so thin that she appears nearly bald on parts of her head, ears, chest, and belly.

If a Chi is long coated, she has an undercoat, and her outer coat is between 1 inch and 1 ½ inch long. She also has the following characteristics:

- ✔ Her ears are decorated with longish hair called *fringe* or *feathering.*
- ✔ She has an abundant ruff around her neck.
- ✔ She has long hair called a *plume* on her tail.
- ✔ She has wispy hair on the back of her legs.
- ✔ She sports *natural pants* — long hair on her buttocks.

Aside from that, she should look exactly like a smooth Chihuahua, because the two varieties have exactly the same conformation (body structure) underneath their coats. (For more on coats, jump to Chapter 3.)

A sparse coat disqualifies only long-coated Chihuahuas from the show ring. Short-coated dogs with thin hair are considered normal, although a thicker coat usually is more attractive.

Color

 Any color — solid, marked, or splashed, take your pick — and all combinations of colors and markings are acceptable in Chihuahuas. None are considered better or worse than others.

Gait

If you walk at a normal pace, a Chihuahua should easily be able to keep up with you by moving along at a smart trot. When she gaits properly, she wastes no motion — no high-stepping hackney or goose steps. Her feet don't turn in toward each other or wing out to the side. In fact, her movement is lively but effortless, and only her legs are involved. Her back (*topline* in dog lingo) should remain level and not roll from side to side, bob up and down, or appear concave (dip in the topline) or convex (roached back).

 One way to check your Chi's movement is to watch while someone else trots her squarely toward you and away from you on a leash. If her movements are ideal, you'll see only her front legs as she approaches you and only her rear legs as she moves away. While watching her from the side, her front legs should reach out but stay close to the ground, and her rear legs (which actually power the dog) should have good drive. None of her legs should interfere with each other. If you're not sure about rear drive, watch her trot away from you again. Can you see the pads of her back feet? If so, she probably has plenty of drive.

 When a Chihuahua stands relaxed, her front feet may turn ever so slightly away from each other, toward either side, and still be correct. In fact, if they point perfectly in front when the dog is in a casual stance, chances are they'll point toward each other (toe in) rather than straight ahead when the dog moves.

Temperament

A Chihuahua should be bright, bold, and saucy, but that's just the gist of it. Chihuahua temperament deserves a full chapter, not a paragraph. Read all about it in Chapter 3.

What if Manchita Doesn't Match the Standard?

To be honest with you, the real Manchita misses out on matching the breed standard in several places. (You can't see Manchita's faults in Figure 2-3. The picture was taken before she developed them.) Yet, she's happy, healthy, and pushing 12 years old, with the attitude and energy of a puppy. Her bite is wrong, but she chews just fine. She's *fiddle-fronted* (bowlegged with her toes turned out), but she's agile and likes going for brisk walks. If you've just read about the Chihuahua standard and discovered that your precious pet isn't perfect, don't worry. As long as her faults don't affect her health and mobility, only a top breeder or judge will know or care.

The truth is, no dog — not even an AKC Champion — matches every word of the standard. Show dogs just have to come pretty close, or their careers end early.

Naturally, it's most important that dogs used for breeding comply with the standard, because their quality is reflected in the next generation. Breeding to its own standard is what makes each breed of dog unique. If breeders ignore the details, soon Chihuahuas, Papillons, Miniature Pinschers, and other Toy dogs will resemble each other, and the individual breeds will gradually fade away. Chapter 4 covers the ins and outs of choosing a breeder, and Chapter 16 provides questions you can ask a breeder to make sure he or she has taken the proper steps to produce the best dogs.

Chapter 3

Perusing the Particulars of Chihuahua Charm

In This Chapter

▶ Examining Chihuahua traits and trademarks

▶ Exploring a Chihuahua's relationship with other people and dogs

▶ Comparing dogs with different coat lengths

▶ Focusing on male and female personalities

▶ Dealing with problem personalities

*W*hat makes the world's smallest dog one of our nation's most popular pets? The Chihuahua's perky personality, of course. Yes, this unique breed has more going for it than a serious case of the cutes. Chihuahuas are protective despite their size and react appropriately to their owners' moods. They love lovin', travel well, and adore creature comforts. In this chapter, I talk about the traits of a typical Chihuahua — complete with all its characteristics and quirks.

I discuss how Chihuahuas usually react to other animals; the personality differences between Chihuahuas with short and long coats; and what must go right so your Chi can mature with the personality traits typical of the breed.

This Bit of a Dog Is Big on Character

The breed standard for the Chihuahua describes its temperament as "terrier-like," so I'll start by talking about typical terrier personality. Most small terriers (think Fox Terriers and Scottish Terriers) originally were bred to go to ground after prey. They helped keep wily foxes out of henhouses and rats from fouling the feed in barns, and they didn't hesitate to take on badgers, snakes, or anything else that intruded near their people or property. Although few terriers do their traditional work today, most retain their feistiness and are brave to a fault. Terriers are alert to their surroundings, quick to defend home and family, and positive that they're tougher than the biggest dog on the block, making them alert watchdogs and energetic, playful companions.

The following sections break down the individual characteristics of the Chihuahua.

Petite protectors

Although few Chihuahuas care to go rat hunting (aren't you glad!), they do have several terrier traits. Bravado is one example. When your Chi trots down the street with you, he appears animated and confident — a bantam rooster with a proud posture.

Most Chihuahuas don't realize that they're small. Given the opportunity, they may approach big dogs in play, and occasionally — especially if the large dogs are invading their territory — they may act aggressively.

Although a tiny terror, barking and running full force, sends some gigantic dogs packing, this situation isn't safe. Toy breed owners need to exercise caution around strange dogs, because even the friendliest medium-sized dog can seriously injure a small one during rough play.

The Chihuahuas' bravado makes them good watchdogs. Like terriers, they're alert and have amazingly keen hearing, and they possess a bark that's loud and shrill for their size. To top it off, they can tell the difference between a family member's footsteps or a stranger's stride nearing the door, and they know when a vehicle other than the family car pulls up to the house.

Chihuahuas have an unjust reputation for excessive barking. Most bark an alarm when a stranger approaches, but when properly trained (see Part III), they won't be any noisier than most other breeds.

Close companions

A Chi is an affectionate animal that dogs your footsteps from room to room, because awake or asleep, he wants to be near you. Some breeds always seem in search of mischief, but the typical adult Chihuahua is content with its owner's company (see Figure 3-1 for an example). After your Chi grows out of his busy puppy stages, he's happiest when you and he are close — preferably touching. An accomplished cuddler, the Chihuahua lies on your lap for as long as you'll let him, helping you relax as you read the paper or watch television. He adores being stroked when you have a free hand, and a gentle massage transports him to puppy paradise. Don't be surprised if he rolls over to beg for a belly rub!

Figure 3-1: Chihuahuas need affection and thrive on togetherness.

After all that togetherness, your Chi may not want you to leave him, even at bedtime. Many Chihuahuas sleep in their owners' bedrooms, but not necessarily in their beds. You can train him to snooze in his own soft bed or crate, which is where he'll curl up when the lights go out (see Chapter 10). It's safer than sharing space with him in your bed. Sure, he'd rather snuggle up with you, but he can easily get hurt if you roll over onto him during the night.

Comfort-loving creatures

Chihuahuas are heat seekers and masters of the art of relaxation. Indoors, your Chi will play bathing beauty, stretching out on the carpet right where a sunbeam shines through the window. On gray days, he'll seek out another source of warmth, napping near a heating vent or in his own bed — that is, if your lap isn't available.

You'll know that your Chihuahua is a little chilly when he curls up into a ball with his nose under one leg. Dogs do that because it allows them to breathe in air that got preheated by the warmth of their bodies. Inhaling the warm air helps keep them cozy.

The ultimate house dog

If you pick up a leash and say, "Wanna go for a walk?" most breeds beat you to the door while dancing in ecstatic circles. Nevertheless, don't be surprised if your Chi plants his feet and gives you a long-suffering look that translates into, "Do I have to?"

Most Chihuahuas (some exceptions live in semitropical climates) prefer their homes to the great outdoors. Lovers of warmth and softness, they consider cold concrete and dewy grass hardships to be endured, not enjoyed. (If your Chi is a smooth coat, he chills easily, sometimes shivering from ear tips to toes. See the later section "Decisions, Decisions: Comparing Long/Smooth Coats.") He also hates rain, and it's no wonder. Imagine being so low to the ground that every step you take splashes cold water onto your bare belly! Of course, you must take your pet outside no matter what the weather so he can eliminate on schedule (see Chapter 10). (Chapter 5 covers accessories you can purchase that help keep him comfortable.)

On cold days, it's amusing to see how fast some Chihuahuas get their business over with so they can rush back to their warm homes. When I lived in New York, I carried Manchita to the curb during winter; otherwise, she squatted the second her toes touched the sidewalk!

Cautious compadres

Typical adult Chihuahuas are sassy with strangers and discriminating about making new friends. Few Chihuahuas, no matter how well socialized they are, run up to a houseguest and vie for his or her attention. Instead, Pepe makes sure you know a stranger is in the house by barking at the intruder until you tell him "Enough!" (see Chapter 10). After that, he'll probably take a position with a view of your visitor from across the room for several minutes until deciding that the person deserves canine company. Then his likely approach will be a slow and gradual offering of his furry friendship — provided that your guest lets him make the first move and resists the temptation to grab at him.

Environment trumps heredity

Although caution in choosing friends is a Chihuahua trait, not every adult Chihuahua is persnickety about meeting new people. Three-pound Manchita, for example (see Chapter 2), makes a merry dash into the arms of anyone who shows interest in her. When she was a puppy, my daughters were teenagers who had friends coming and going daily. All the kids fussed over Manchita during her formative months, so she grew up believing that every human is a potential petting machine. Manchita is almost 12 years old now, and she still falls for friendly people at first sight.

To speed up the buddy-making process between your friends and your dog, tell your guests to ignore your Chi until he approaches them. Then they can reciprocate by tickling him on the chest or under the chin. These actions are less threatening than reaching over him to pet his head. Chihuahuas don't like it when strangers swoop down on them from above like hungry hawks. If your friends squat down and let your Chi check them out, they'll soon become best buddies.

A Chihuahua probably will make friends much faster on neutral ground (such as a park) than in his own home, because he doesn't feel the need to defend neutral territory.

Spirited, but not hyper

Although they're playful pets, Chihuahuas aren't hyper little dogs. In fact, most of them don't have an especially high activity level.

Rather than racing around the living room, your Chi prefers spending part of his day on your lap or burrowed beneath a blanket. His attitude about exercise is easygoing — ready to play when you are but content to relax when you aren't in an active mood.

As Chihuahuas mature, they tend to take on the same activity level as their people. The same dog that acts frisky when he's around his active family will turn into a contented cuddler when grandma and grandpa dog-sit.

Even though Chihuahuas prefer human company, properly trained adult dogs can occupy themselves for hours without looking for trouble or demanding attention. The Chapters of Part III cover training exercises, including making your dog feel comfortable when alone.

Unusually adaptable

Chihuahuas thrive in living quarters ranging from country estates to studio apartments. Don't worry about stairs or elevators; after you introduce your Pepe to them (see Chapter 9), he will handle them just fine.

Because Chihuahuas are so small, they don't need fenced yards or kennel runs to get their exercise. You can give yours a few toys (see Chapter 5) and he'll play active games right in the living room. Or better yet, you can join in the fun, and both of you will get some exercise. I suggest some games you can play together in Chapter 8.

Chihuahuas are good travelers and adjust to moving better than many breeds. They feel at home wherever their owners are. That attitude, plus their small size, makes Chihuahuas an ideal dog for people who have to move frequently and for retired couples who crisscross the country in RVs.

If you move often, a Chihuahua won't mind — but you should think twice before buying one anyway. Finding rental housing that allows dogs often is difficult. My daughters faced that problem when they took Manchita to college, but they finally solved it by taking her along to meet potential landlords. When one landlord saw how petite and polite Manchita was, he made an exception. And the girls did their part by keeping her in a well-equipped playpen (the type meant for an infant) when they weren't home to supervise (see Chapter 5).

Sensitive supporters

Chihuahuas can sense their owners' moods and will react accordingly. When you arrive home after receiving a promotion, your Chi will recognize right away that something wonderful happened and dances around you with glee. But he'll also sense when you're sick or sad, and he'll try to be consoling. Stories abound about Chihuahuas that stopped playing and had to be reminded to eat and even eliminate when family members were bedridden with serious illnesses. These companions tried to spend all their time with the sick persons.

Quick studies when trained with TLC

Although housetraining any dog (see Chapters 10 and 11) is a chore, most of the other training you give your Chi should be pure pleasure for both of you. Chihuahuas love being center stage and are eager to learn — provided that the training is gentle, upbeat, and complete with plenty of positive reinforcement (read: praise and treats). Because they're so people oriented, Chihuahuas have longer attention spans (when they're past the puppy stage) than many other breeds. If you make training fun, your pup will focus his big eyes on you and pirouette happily every time you praise him.

After he learns a new trick, your Chi will never forget it. He may, however, try to improvise. Some Chis are so clever that as soon as they perfect a trick, they invent a new way to ham it up. Many Chihuahuas are successful in competitive sports such as obedience and agility. You can read all about those activities in Chapter 12.

Long-term friend

If your Chi is a healthy, well-bred Chihuahua (see Chapter 2) and you take good care of him, chances are he'll live well into his teens. Chihuahuas are one of the longest-lived breeds. And that's great news for the humans who love them!

Friend to (most) other critters

Your Chihuahua may sass strange dogs when he's out for a walk (basic obedience training cures that; see Chapters 9 and 10), but he should get along with the other pets in your home. After you make the introductions (see Chapter 5) and the pets get used to each other, your Pepe likely will curl up with your cat, ignore your caged birds, and become buddies with your bigger dog.

Don't be surprised if he shows a jealous streak over who gets the most attention, though. Dogs usually work these things out for themselves (with the Chihuahua often becoming the dominant dog). Just be sure to supervise the animals closely until they get used to each other and obviously get along.

Have you read about the terrier traits I talked about earlier in this chapter? You should keep little critters like hamsters, gerbils, iguanas, and small birds out of your Chi's reach, or pouncing on them may be just too tempting.

One unique Chihuahuaism is that the breed recognizes, and almost always welcomes, its own. Even though your Chi may seem sassy or even scared around strange dogs, in most cases he'll become ecstatic at the sight of another Chihuahua, and the two will quickly make friends.

Decisions, Decisions: Comparing Long/Smooth Coats

When deciding whether you want a long-coated or a smooth-coated Chihuahua (see Chapter 2), you should consider more than just the length of coat you want to cuddle. That's because the differences are more than skin deep. In general (with some exceptions), slight personality differences exist between the two coat types. Here are the more obvious differences:

- ✔ **Long coats can handle the cold better.** Although no Chihuahua can stand the cold for long, many long coats enjoy a short walk in brisk weather and may even play in the snow (provided it's only a couple inches deep). Not the case with smooth coats. Chihuahuas with short hair are miserable in cold weather and should wear a sweater outdoors on chilly days, even when going for a short walk (see Chapter 5).

- ✔ **Smooth coats cuddle closer.** A short-coated Chi will enjoy feeling the warmth of your body on his nearly bald belly as he lies on your lap while you read or watch television. His long-coated counterpart wants your company, too, but he's more likely to sit beside you rather than on you. Differences also are noticeable if you decide to bed down with him. A smooth coat curls up under the covers, and a long coat usually lies on top of the blankets.

- ✔ **Long coats shed less.** No, that isn't a misprint. Long-coated Chihuahuas shed seasonally — usually twice a year. During those periods, they lose a lot of hair quite quickly. But a few good brushings, plus vacuuming the carpets and furniture, put an end to the problem for several months (see Chapter 7). Smooth coats, on the other hand, shed old hair and replace it with new hair all the time. Consequently, a few tiny hairs always will work their way into your clothes, furniture, and carpets.

- ✔ **Long coats are a bit more reserved.** Smooth coats often are more outgoing and accept new friends faster than long coats. Although long coats like attention, too, they tend to be a little more reserved and need more time to warm up to friendly strangers.

Long coats and smooth coats often are *littermates,* which means they're brothers and sisters born in the same litter. According to an old wives' tale, at least one long-coated Chihuahua appears in every litter of smooth coats — a gift from Mother Nature to keep its short-coated littermates warm. Although this is a sweet story, it doesn't always happen that way. Besides, smooth-coated pups don't need the help. They do just fine by cuddling up to their mom and to each other.

Battle of the Sexes: Observing Male and Female Traits

You can find plenty of Chihuahua lore concerning which sex makes the better pet. Some people favor males while others extol the virtues of females. The truth is, the personality of a puppy's parents is a much better indicator of potential temperament than which sex the pup happens to be. Even so, you should be aware of a few characteristic differences between the sexes before you decide on the dog you want:

- ✔ Unspayed females have heat cycles (usually twice a year), and these can make a mess on your clothing and furniture. And even if your female is indoors almost all the time, neighborhood males still can smell her enticing scent and serenade her. You can't let her out of your sight when she's in season, or it could result in an unwanted pregnancy — or worse if her suitor is big enough to injure her.

- ✔ An unneutered male has a sex drive that makes him follow a female's sexy scent until he finds the female — no matter how big she is or how many larger dogs also are competing for her favor. Consequently, he can become quite the escape artist and put himself in life-threatening situations. He also may take out his frustrations by becoming affectionate with a throw pillow or someone's shin (see Chapter 11). Some unneutered males tend to be aggressive with other dogs, and a Chihuahua in a fighting mood believes that he's the biggest bruiser on the block — a dangerous situation.

- ✔ Male and female Chihuahuas are equally affectionate and appealing, and initially take about the same amount of time to housebreak. But many males (if they haven't been neutered) disregard their training when they get old enough to lift their legs and mark their property (a sign of sexual maturity) and may regress to urinating in the house You can correct the problem by catching it early and returning the male to his crate-training puppy schedule (see Chapter 10) for a few weeks. If that doesn't do the trick, you can find help for hard cases in Chapter 11.

The good news is that spaying or neutering nullifies much of the behavior in the previous list, making males and females equally excellent as pets. Chapter 13 discusses the altering procedure and its importance for your pet.

Checking a Chi Pup's Résumé

Several things must go right before a Chihuahua puppy grows up to be typical of his breed. A puppy will mature with characteristics that people admire if it is

- ✔ Well bred (comes from good stock; see Chapters 1 and 2)
- ✔ Adequately cared for on a daily basis (a clean habitat and quality food, for instance)
- ✔ Socialized by a caring breeder
- ✔ Further socialized by its owner (see Chapter 9)
- ✔ Raised with attention and affection
- ✔ Taught basic house manners (see Chapter 10)
- ✔ Never abused or neglected

If any of these necessities are missing during the dog's upbringing, or if it gets neglected or abused, chances are it won't behave like a typical Chihuahua. Unfortunately, Chihuahuas often get a bad rap from people who meet sorry excuses for dogs and decide that the entire breed behaves badly.

The following undesirable traits are the ones that frequently plague poorly bred, undernourished, unsocialized, untrained, or unloved members of this breed. These traits are, in a sense, typical of the atypical:

- ✔ Timid, shy, or extremely nervous
- ✔ Frail and sickly
- ✔ Temperamental
- ✔ Refuses to accept friendly strangers
- ✔ Yappy
- ✔ Vicious (snaps at people without warning and for no reason)
- ✔ Possessive (defends his food dish, toys, or favorite chair, even from his owners)

Oh my! That's a scary list, isn't it? I bet it doesn't sound like anything you want in a dog. Don't panic. In Chapter 4, I tell you how to avoid the unhappy traits and find a Chihuahua with the potential to grow up with all the breed's best characteristics.

Part II
Fitting a Compact Canine into Your Life

The 5th Wave   By Rich Tennant

"Okay, before I let the new puppy out, let's remember to be real still so we don't startle him."

In this part . . .

*I*f you've decided that a Chihuahua is the pet for you, your most important task is to choose a healthy Chihuahua with a great disposition. This part helps you with that task. And when you get home, this part has a chapter dedicated to helping you welcome your new pet into your lifestyle. You also find out how to keep your pet glowing with good health from puppyhood to old age and discover what your Chi needs and doesn't need in the way of food, toys, grooming, housing, and exercise.

Chapter 4

Choosing Your Ideal Chihuahua

· ·

In This Chapter

▶ Shopping for a Chihuahua breeder

▶ Checking out pet shops and classified ads

▶ Selecting a mature dog

▶ Exploring the meaning of pedigree

· ·

*W*hew! You've made the really big decisions (if you haven't, head back to Chapters 1–3). You're sure you want a dog, and you think a Chihuahua is the breed for you. But you aren't finished yet. Now you have to make the most important decision of all — picking the one special Chihuahua to share your life.

Easy now. Don't rush. Picking your pet may be your only opportunity, outside of marriage, to actually choose a member of your family! All Chihuahuas and Chihuahua distributors aren't created equal, so in this chapter, we go shopping together. I can help you find a good breeder and a healthy dog with that charming Chihuahua character. And I help you understand all the paperwork involved in the process — such as AKC registration applications and pedigrees.

There's no such thing as a teacup Chihuahua. Contrary to false advertisements, Chihuahuas aren't classified by size. Typical Chihuahuas weigh between 3 and 6 pounds. Dogs a little larger than 6 pounds make excellent pets — especially when children are in the family — but you should think twice before buying an especially tiny Chihuahua. Pups wrongly advertised as *miniature* or *teacup* often are too delicate for the average home and may have health problems.

Buying from a Breeder

The first step toward finding a fabulous four-legged family member is locating a respected breeder. The best Chi breeders usually specialize in Chihuahuas, devoting years to preserving the breed's finest traits (see Chapter 2). Good breeders often are members of the Chihuahua Club of America (CCA; www.chihuahuaclubofamerica.com), and perhaps local dog clubs as well. Whether they have just a few adult dogs or a large kennel, their breeding stock is excellent, they give their puppies plenty of affection, and they probably exhibit at dog shows (see Chapter 12).

Here are several general suggestions to help you find a good kennel in your area: After you find one, the following sections take you all the way through the process, from visiting a breeder to picking out your puppy:

- ✔ **Go to the American Kennel Club's Web site (www.akc.org) and click on its Breeder Referral link.** Or you can call AKC Customer Care at 919-233-9767 for suggestions.

- ✔ **Ask the Chihuahua Club of America (www.chihuahuaclub ofamerica.com) for literature on the breed and for the address of the regional Chihuahua club closest to you.** Contact that club for a list of member-breeders. You can do it all on the Net (see Chapter 17 for more resources).

- ✔ **Talk to local veterinarians (see Chapter 13).** They know which breeders have healthy dogs with terrific temperaments.

- ✔ **Find the all-breed kennel club nearest you.** Almost every sizable city has an all-breed kennel club. Ask around at a veterinary clinic, or call the library. Contact the all-breed club to find out if any of its members are Chihuahua breeders.

- ✔ **Look at the breeder ads in dog magazines.** You can check out *AKC Gazette, Dog World,* and *Dog Fancy,* for instance. Besides being available by subscription, the magazines are sold in many bookstores and at newsstands.

- ✔ **Go to a dog show.** Good breeders travel many miles to show their dogs, and they'll be glad to talk to you after they finish competing. (Don't bother them during the heat of competition!)

Dog shows are fun and educational even if you have no interest in showing your dog. With luck, you'll see several Chihuahuas in the show ring. Watching them may help you decide what traits appeal to you. If several of your favorites come from the same breeder, you know where to look first. Find out from your local all-breed kennel club or the American Kennel Club (AKC) when shows are scheduled in your area (see Chapter 12 for more).

Visiting the breeder

Most reputable breeders cherish their Chihuahuas as a hobby, not a business. They're proud to show you their facilities and tell you about their dogs. Just be sure to contact them ahead of time to set up appointments. Breeders don't keep regular business hours like pet shops do, and their facilities are almost always attached to their homes. So meeting a breeder and seeing his or her stock is a lot like visiting someone socially.

Making a list of what you want in a Chihuahua and letting the breeders know your criteria before you visit simplifies things. For example, tell the breeder if you're set on a male or a female, a smooth or a long coat, a certain color, and whether you plan to show your dog (see Chapter 12). That way, a breeder can save you a trip if he or she doesn't have what you want, and he or she may be able to send you to another kennel where your dream dog awaits. Try visiting a few breeders and seeing several puppies before making a decision.

Evaluating the breeder

Locating a Chihuahua breeder and setting up an appointment is only the first step. Just because you locate a breeder doesn't mean he or she is reputable or right for you. Here's how to make sure you've found a good breeder (see Chapter 16 for more evaluation advice):

- ✔ If you see brood stock of several different breeds on the premises, or notice that the puppies are treated like merchandise, don't purchase a puppy from that kennel. The best breeders specialize in one or two breeds, enjoying their dogs as a hobby rather than a business. They may even exhibit their stock at dog shows.

- ✔ Healthy puppies come from clean kennels. Check out the floor or grass the puppies are playing on. Has it been washed or pooper-scooped recently, or is it covered with miniature messes? Sneak a peek at the food and water dishes. Is the food dish clean, or is ancient goop stuck to the sides? Is the water clear or has yellow slime invaded the bottom of the dish? Use your nose. Sure, you'll catch a whiff of fresh puppy poop, but if the stench is stale or overwhelming, try another kennel.

- ✔ The puppy play area shouldn't be bare; the puppies should have a few toys to play with. Toys serve a purpose. They stimulate puppies physically and mentally, motivating them to exercise, play together, and learn.

Even the healthiest pups become limp as dishrags when they're sleepy. If the pups you're visiting can't seem to stay awake, ask the breeder to schedule another visit at a different time of day.

✔ A good breeder knows the puppies' personalities inside out and should gladly discuss them with you. In fact, he or she may talk nonstop and tell you even more than you want to know about the puppies, their parents, and extended family. Yes, good breeders may brag about their dogs, but that's a good sign. It proves that they're proud of their breeding and spend enough time with their dogs to know them well.

✔ A good breeder should give you a grilling (see the following section). That means he or she wants to be sure that a Chi is the right breed for your family and that you'll give the puppy a good home. Steer clear of money-hungry puppy vendors who pretend Chihuahuas are ideal pets for everyone. It simply isn't so.

✔ Chihuahua puppies need to stay with their dam and littermates until they're at least 8 weeks old. Beware of any breeder who's willing to let a pup leave for its new home any sooner than that.

✔ A good breeder will tell you that if you ever have to give up your Chihuahua, he or she will take her back and find her a new home.

✔ A good breeder may feed you endless data about how to raise and care for a Chihuahua. You may get annoyed by all the *you shoulds,* but cut the overprotective mommy or daddy some slack. You're talking to a caring person who willingly shares information and who someday, when you need advice, will be willing to help.

✔ Don't be surprised if the breeder displays the puppies' pedigree with pride. That's a good sign that the litter came from well-planned breeding.

Do you like the breeder? Okay, maybe not for a best friend, but well enough to call on if you need advice about health or training? Or do you hope you never need to talk to the breeder again? If you have a bad feeling about the breeder, the facility, or any of the dogs, trust your intuition and look elsewhere for your puppy.

Oh gee, why the third degree?

All responsible breeders should grill you about your intentions and your situation, so don't be surprised or insulted when you're asked about your lifestyle. Instead, be glad you found a breeder who truly cares about the puppies' welfare. It all evens out in the end. After all, you should be evaluating the breeder while he or she assesses you.

Here are some of the questions many breeders are likely to ask you, and why they want to know:

- **What made you decide on a Chihuahua?** The breeder is making sure you chose the breed because you truly like Toy dogs and especially Chihuahuas — not just because they're "stylish" or you think a little dog costs less to feed or is easier for your 2-year-old to tote around.

- **Have you had dogs before? What happened to them?** Good breeders want their puppies to have loving, permanent homes. If you've never had a dog before, the breeder probably wants to fill you in on the facts of dog ownership just to make sure you know what you're getting into. If you had a beloved dog that eventually died of old age, the breeder will be happy to sell you a puppy. But if your previous dog ran loose and got killed by a car or died of a disease that you could've prevented, a responsible breeder won't sell you a dog. Truthfully, you don't deserve one — unless you've learned from the sorry saga and won't let it happen again.

- **What are your hours? How much time do you spend at home?** The breeder wants to be sure that the puppy will get enough attention. Puppies must be fed and walked on a regular schedule to become housebroken (see Chapters 8 and 10).

- **How old are your children? Are they gentle with animals?** Tots and Chihuahuas aren't a good match. Toddlers are too young and uncoordinated to safely handle small dogs, and Chihuahuas are too tiny for rough handling. Teasing by youngsters also turns nice dogs into holy terrors.

- **Do you have a fenced yard?** The breeder wants to make sure your dog won't be turned loose to be flattened by a car, mauled by a bigger dog, or poisoned by eating something spoiled. Although fenced-in yards make dog ownership easier, many Chihuahua owners live in apartments or condos and exercise their dogs by walking them on the leash (see Chapter 9).

- **Is everyone in your family looking forward to getting a Chihuahua?** It isn't fair to the Chihuahua if someone in the family despises little dogs but was out-voted. A dog can sense the disdain immediately; the person may go so far as to sabotage the socialization or training.

- **What do you expect from your Chihuahua?** Tell the breeder if you want a dog solely as a companion or if you also want to show your dog. Will your Chihuahua live only with adults, or do you have kids in the family? Will your dog live at home or travel in your RV? Will you have your pet spayed or neutered, or are you considering using the dog for breeding?

Small size doesn't mean small price tag

Just because Chihuahuas are little, don't expect the purchase price to be less than what you'd pay for a larger dog. Chihuahuas have small litters, and the cost of breeding them (including stud service and possibly a Caesarean section) is high. Raising healthy, outgoing Toy dogs takes a lot of time and energy. You should expect a good breeder to be happy with breaking even, though. They do it for love, not money.

When tempted to buy a bargain puppy, remember that the purchase price is only a small part of what you'll spend on your dog during her lifetime. It's smarter to pay more and get a dog that makes your heart sing. (For more on pricing and other basics, refer to Chapter 1.)

The more the breeder knows about your plans for the pup, the better he or she can help you make a selection. After all, the breeder has observed the litter since birth and knows each puppy's personality.

Pick of the litter

Gotta have the pick of the litter! But which one is it? Everyone wants the pick of the litter, but it's a different puppy for different people:

> To the show exhibitor, the pick is the puppy that comes closest to the description of the ideal Chihuahua in the breed standard (see Chapter 2).

> To the woman who lives alone in the city, the pick is the puppy that alerts instantly to strange sounds.

> To the young couple with kids in elementary school, the pick is the largest and liveliest puppy.

> To the retired couple in the condo, the pick is the quiet puppy that loves to cuddle.

The truth is, the pick is the puppy that appeals to you — provided that it's healthy and has the right temperament to share your lifestyle (see Figure 4-1). If you're dealing with a show breeder but have no intention of showing, you don't need the puppy the breeder considers the pick of the litter. Chances are, the breeder won't sell it to you anyway! It's destined to become a show dog and possibly be the *sire* (father) or dam of the breeder's next generation of champions. But one of its brothers or sisters may make you the perfect pet.

Figure 4-1: Pick a puppy that appeals to you on first sight, but check its health and disposition before making a purchase.

At the best kennels, show puppies and pet puppies come from the same litters. In fact, the last choice in a top breeder's litter may be of higher quality than the first choice in a mediocre litter.

If you want to buy a show potential puppy, don't be surprised if the breeder insists on keeping it until it's 6 months old. That's perfectly normal. Why? Because it takes that long to be positive (well, almost positive, anyway) that a puppy has what it takes to become an AKC champion.

Whether you decide to pick out your own puppy or ask the breeder for input, the following sections offer helpful suggestions to guide you on the big day: puppy picking day!

Bring on all the puppies

You better have a plan when meeting the puppies, or canine Cupid will sting you with an arrow. The following suggestions help you choose a puppy with your head as well as your heart:

> ✔ **Trust your instincts.** Did one puppy catch your eye immediately? Do you keep going back to her even though you want to give them all equal time? Are you already naming her in your mind? First impressions are important when picking a puppy, and love at first sight can last a lifetime. Just take the time to make sure your furry favorite is healthy and has a pleasing personality.

✔ **Be observant.** Watch the puppies play together for several minutes without human interference. (Chihuahua litters are small, so you can probably observe two to four littermates interacting with each other.) Your best bet is a puppy in the middle of the pecking order — neither the bully nor the scaredy-cat.

One sign of superior character is a puppy that stands up to the bully and then goes on about her business peacefully.

✔ **Eye the eyes.** The puppy's eyes need to be bright, alert, and clear of mucous. Don't mistake clear tears for mucous. Many Chihuahuas (and other Toy breeds) have too-small tear ducts, so tears occasionally fall from their eyes. A telltale sign is a small water stain at the inner corner of each eye. This isn't a sign of sickness, but you shouldn't convince yourself that the stains will fade away as the puppy matures. More than likely, the dog will always sport the tear stains, but they won't affect her health or happiness.

✔ **Check the coat.** Bald may be beautiful on my husband, but it's a bad sign on a puppy. A healthy coat is smooth to the touch and glossy, with no bald patches. Smooth coats without an undercoat may have thin hair on their temples and practically bald bellies, but no puppy should have skin showing through on its back or sides.

✔ **Know the nose.** The puppy's breathing must be quiet and rhythmic, and the nostrils should be free of mucous.

✔ **Watch the puppies move when they play.** Despite a bit of baby clumsiness, puppies should appear quick, bouncy, and agile. Puppies standing up straight on legs that look strong enough to carry their bodies is a good sign.

✔ **Check the teeth and running gear.** If a show career is in your puppy's future, don't forget to check her teeth for a *scissors bite* (the upper-front teeth meet tightly outside the lower-front teeth). And although it isn't easy to do with a tiny puppy, try to evaluate her *gait* (the way she moves at a trot) by watching her move both straight toward you and directly away from you. Front legs moving parallel with each other as she trots toward you and rear legs moving parallel with each other as she trots away are good signs. Study the breed standard (see Chapter 2) before selecting a potential show dog.

If you want a show puppy but don't have a clue how to select one, take along someone who's knowledgeable about show dogs when you meet the puppies. Another option is making absolutely sure that you're dealing with a successful show breeder and then letting him or her choose a puppy for you.

When choosing your Chihuahua, avoid orphan puppies or litters of only one, because hand-raised orphans and solo pups get everything they want instantly. Consequently, they don't learn how to handle frustration or get along with other dogs. In general, puppies that are raised by their *dams* (their mothers), along with at least one littermate, make better companions.

One on one

After watching the litter play together, it's time to meet your favorites up close and personal. But first you need to know how to hold a puppy. Novices often hold puppies high, with their back legs dangling, but dogs hate being held that way. Instead, when lifting a puppy (or an adult Chihuahua, for that matter), use both hands. Place one hand under her chest and brace her bottom in your other hand, and then cradle the puppy close to your body. Little puppies are wiggly and a fall can be fatal, so keep your grip gentle but firm. And don't let your fingers push the pup's elbows outward or squeeze her front legs together, because either error could damage the dog.

Never lift a puppy by its front legs. Not only is it painful, but it also can cause permanent injury to the puppy's shoulders.

Sit on the floor to play with the puppies during this first meeting. You'll enjoy it more because you won't have to worry about dropping a pup, and the breeder's blood pressure will normalize.

Now you're ready to see how well each puppy relates to people — especially you. Follow these steps to meet your potential pups:

1. **Ask if you can take your favorite puppy or puppies out of sight (one puppy at a time) of the breeder, their dam, and their littermates so you can test their temperaments.**

   Begin by giving each puppy at least two full minutes to survey her surroundings (time it or you won't wait long enough). Watch her attitude while she explores. Is she curious or fearful? Lively or laid back?

2. **Sit down and try coaxing the pup into coming to you.**

   When she does, praise her. Then get up, move away from her slowly, and try talking her into following you. If she does, that's a good sign that she enjoys human company and likes you just fine.

3. **Show the puppy a small ball or other dog toy just the right size for her, and roll it about 3 feet away from (never toward) her.**

Does she seem interested? If she doesn't respond right away, that's okay. It may take three or four tries before she understands the game. Does she eventually chase or follow the rolling toy and examine it when it stops moving? That's a good sign that she learns quickly, isn't afraid to try new things, and is willing to play on your team. If she picks up the toy in her mouth and carries it part of the way back to you, that's even better.

4. **Pick up the puppy and cradle her securely against your body.**

   She should feel strong (for her size) and solid in your hand. The puppy may struggle briefly, but she should soon relax and enjoy the attention. After she loosens up, does she sniff your hands, maybe even lick you? These are signs that she has a good temperament and was well socialized by the breeder.

5. **Try a little TLC before giving up.**

   When you pick up the puppy and cradle her, does she stiffen with fear or struggle nonstop? Neither reaction is good, but don't give up too soon. The puppy may just need a little more time. Talk to her while stroking her soothingly. Does that tight little body relax? Good. If not, she may have missed out on early socialization. Pick another puppy.

No matter how super a puppy looks and tests, make sure some chemistry exists between you. During your first couple months together, both of you go through a period of adjustment. But a Chihuahua that charms a smile out of you makes all the adjustments seem minor.

Potential problem pups

Not every puppy will ace your tests from the previous sections. Here are some signs that may warn you away from a pup:

- **Don't buy an unhealthy puppy.** This could include a skinny puppy or one with pimples or raw patches on its skin, excessive dander, mucous seeping from the nostrils or the corner of the eyes, or diarrhea.

- **Please don't purchase a puppy out of pity.** When an active litter of puppies vies for your attention but one hangs back or hides in a corner, she isn't an abused baby in need of comfort. If the breeder neglected or mistreated the pups, every one of them would shy away from people. The truth is, that puppy has a temperament problem. Yes, she may improve a little with time and a lot of socialization (see Chapter 9), but her apprehensive attitude is probably a permanent problem.

✔ **Go for impy, not wimpy.** Don't pick a puppy that shies away from its littermates' games. I know it's tempting to take home a little underdog, but resist as hard as you can. Pups that allow themselves to be terrorized by their littermates seldom become confident pets.

✔ **Avoid anxious Annie.** Don't buy a puppy that runs away or crouches fearfully in one spot when you take her out of sight of her breeder and four-legged family. It's okay if it takes her a couple minutes to get her bearings, but after a few moments, expect her to show some interest in her surroundings and be curious about you.

A puppy that tests well probably will make someone a wonderful pet, but that someone may not be you. How do you feel when you play with the pup? Is she the tiny soul mate you've been searching for? Or are you thinking of buying her only because she tested well and you're tired of Chihuahua shopping? When tempted to think that way, remember that you're choosing family. Keep looking until you know you've found your canine counterpart.

Meeting the extended family

When looking at a litter of puppies, ask to see their dam and any other close relatives that live with the breeder. With luck, you may get to meet the puppies' grand-dam, a couple of aunts or uncles, or even an older brother or sister from a previous litter. You may also see the sire but don't be disappointed if he lives far away from the breeder. Good breeders find the best possible matches for their brood bitches. No matter where the sire lives, a breeder will take (or ship) his or her bitch to him and pay a fee (or possibly a puppy) for his *service*. If the sire isn't on the premises, the breeder should be able to show you his pedigree and probably his picture.

A mature female dog is a *bitch,* no matter how sweet she is! And when used for breeding, she's a *brood bitch.* The mother of a litter of puppies is the *dam* and the father is the *sire.*

The more of your potential puppy's close relatives you meet, the better. Why? Because their attitudes and appearances give you a good indication of how the puppy may turn out. For example, does the pup come from a friendly family? Or do its relatives aggressively attack your ankles or cringe behind a couch in terror? Do you find the family attractive? Or do most of the dogs have a trait that you'd rather avoid?

Breeder contracts

Many good breeders will provide a breeder contract to buyers. The contract spells out the conditions of the sale. The contract, and/or a separate agreement, may include items such as the following:

- Whether the puppy is to be spayed or neutered

- Whether the puppy's AKC registration will be full or limited (see the final section of this chapter)

- How soon you should have the pup checked out by your veterinarian to rule out genetic problems

- An explanation of the breeder's responsibility if a genetic problem turns up

- Whether you're expected to exhibit the pup to her championship should she grow up show quality (if you buy a pup with show potential)

- An explanation of the breeder's responsibility if you plan on showing your pup but she doesn't become show quality at maturity

Surveying Additional Places to Purchase a Puppy

Chihuahua puppies are frequently sold in pet shops and advertised in the classifieds and online. In this section, I tell you why you should proceed with extreme caution when you see a cute puppy in a pet shop, and I discuss the possibilities you may encounter in the classified ads.

As for online ads, they span every extreme. Top show kennels have Web sites (see Chapter 17), but poorly bred specimens are also offered on the Internet. If you make contact with a breeder through an online ad, use the info I present earlier in this chapter to figure out if you've found a good one.

What about pet shops?

Be wary about buying a puppy from pet shop. The darling "Doggie in the Window" can cost you a small fortune if you run into hereditary health problems, for instance.

The pet shop itself usually isn't the problem. The puppies in most pet shops are clean and well nourished, have toys to keep them occupied, and are petted often by the employees. The problem is where they came from before arriving at the pet shop. You see, good breeders plan matings carefully, breed to the standard, socialize their puppies, and, after all that, want to check out every potential puppy owner. But the people who sell puppies to pet shops breed only to make money. They choose breeding partners out of convenience rather than quality and willingly sell entire litters to middlemen without caring who ends up with the pups. Sometimes their facilities are dirty, and they usually have far too many dogs to give any of them individual attention. And that's a serious problem.

Lack of human attention early in life results in puppies that are nervous and shy, and a dirty habitat during the formative weeks can make the puppies hard to housebreak. Sure, time and affection help, but the bottom line is this: No matter how hard you try, you can't cure bad breeding.

Dog lovers have a name for the over-crowded, filthy facilities that breed litter after litter and sell hundreds of poorly bred puppies every year. We call them *puppy mills*.

Classified canines

Should you check out the ads for Chihuahua puppies in your local newspaper? That depends on what's on your Chihuahua wish list. With the right knowledge, you may find a nice pet through the classifieds, but don't look there if you want a show dog.

Although both parents you see through a classified ad visit may be healthy Chihuahuas with excellent dispositions, it's better to have plenty of knowledge about picking puppies before trying to select a pet from the litter. See the section "Pick of the litter" for plenty of advice on picking out the right puppy.

If you dream of owning a show champion, buying from an established breeder is your best shot at success. Why? Because puppy sellers who advertise only in the paper or online, and not through the dog journals, probably bred their pets to their friends' pooches without studying the standard (see Chapter 2) or comparing pedigrees.

The Ups and Downs of Choosing a Mature Chihuahua

After a brief period of adjustment, an adult Chihuahua bonds to a new owner just as strongly as a puppy does. But why would you want an adult dog? Maybe because even though puppies are precious, they're also babies. And like infants, they're sloppy eaters, go potty often, and sleep a lot — but not always on your schedule. They need constant supervision for several weeks, or else they may teethe on the table legs and leave puddles (or worse) on the carpet.

A mature dog may be easier on your schedule. And although not every mature Chihuahua is housebroken, and unsupervised young adults may still exercise their choppers on the chair legs, grown dogs have bigger bladders and longer attention spans than puppies, so they tend to learn the house rules rather quickly.

But isn't acquiring an adult dog kind of like buying a used car? Isn't the adult just someone else's problem looking for a new place to happen? Maybe, but certainly not always.

Practically perfect adult dogs often find themselves homeless because of factors out of their control — a divorce or death in their families, family members' allergic reactions to dog hair, or owners moving and being unable to find proper housing, for instance. Many breeders also won't breed their bitches past a certain age and are happy to place them in loving homes. (And lost or abandoned dogs often are available for adoption through a rescue or humane organization. See Chapter 17 for more on Chihuahua rescue organizations.)

You must beware of baggage, though. All adult dogs have a past, so every member of the family should meet an adult Chihuahua before a decision is made to buy or adopt it. That's because something in its past may have caused it to love men but hate women (or vice versa) or become defensive around children.

Selecting an adult Chihuahua is a lot like choosing a puppy but without some of the guesswork, because her personality and habits are already formed. Here are some tips to help you sift through the problem pets and single out your future best friend:

> ✔ When meeting a mature Chihuahua, remember that you're a stranger and adult dogs are more discriminating than puppies. Don't force your attention on the dog. Instead, sit down and talk to the owner for a few minutes until the dog warms up to you.

✔ Check for general good health by looking at the dog's eyes, nose, coat, skin, and movement. The eyes should be clear and bright (not cloudy). The nose free of mucus. The coat should cover the body with a healthy shine. The skin smooth and supple, without bumps, lumps, or pimples. And movement should be easy and animated — not stiff or labored.

✔ You and the dog need to appeal to each other. Give her time to accept you and then pet her if she allows it. Does she relax and enjoy your company, or is she fearful or aggressive? Ask the owner to place her on your lap. Is she content to cuddle? Or is she scared stiff or frantic to escape?

✔ Ask if you may put a leash on the dog and take her for a walk. Encourage her to walk beside you with soft, happy talk. Does she trot down the street with you willingly, or does she freeze in place, cry, balk, or try to make a break for home?

✔ Perform the smile test. Does looking at this dog make you smile? That's good chemistry, but it should work both ways. After the dog knows you, does she wag her tail and dance a few happy steps when you talk to her? Liking each other is the most important criteria of all.

Many dogs are protective of their homes but warm up to friendly strangers easily on neutral ground. Moving to a neutral site is worth a try if you like everything about an adult Chihuahua but she doesn't seem to like you.

Understanding Pedigree

The word *pedigree* is often used incorrectly — especially in classified ads, where the term "pedigreed puppies" almost always means purebred puppies. The truth is, every dog has a pedigree, whether it's purebred or not. Honest. A *pedigree* is nothing more than a list of ancestors, just like a family tree. For example, one of your grandparents may be Hungarian, another Russian, another Irish, and so on, but each one of them appears on your family tree. By the same token, a mutt's grandparents may be a Miniature Pinscher, a Chihuahua, a Yorkshire Terrier, and a Toy Poodle, and that's the dog's family tree. The dog has a pedigree, but it isn't a purebred.

What is a *purebred?* It's a dog that descended from dogs that were all the same breed. A purebred Chihuahua has two Chihuahuas for parents, four Chihuahuas for grandparents, eight Chihuahuas for great-grandparents, and so on, as far back as records can be traced.

Crossbreed fables abound

One fable about Chihuahua origins contends that the Chihuahua came from a cross between a dog and a rodent in the desert surrounding Chihuahua, Mexico. Another theory claims the Chihuahua evolved from a cross between the Techichi and a small wild dog called the *Perro Chihuahueno,* which lived in the area now known as the state of Chihuahua. And if that isn't enough, a few historians think the Techichi may have been crossed with a small hairless dog that was brought across the Bering Strait from China to Alaska.

Through studying pedigrees, you discover a lot more than just the names of a dog's ancestors. For example, if any of its ancestors won a title, that shows up on the pedigree document. A good breeder will provide you with a copy of your pup's pedigree and will be proud to decipher the titles for you — and with good reason. The dog's pedigree illustrates the beauty, trainability, and temperament of the dog's ancestors.

The following sections dig deeper into the topics of registration and pedigree.

Deciphering full or limited registration

The American Kennel Club (AKC) gives breeders the option of selling a puppy with either full or limited registration. A Chihuahua with full registration, if bred to another Chihuahua with full registration, will have puppies that are eligible for AKC registration (full or limited, depending on the breeder's wishes). Dogs with limited registration may be lovely to look at and delightful to live with (and they usually are), but they should be spayed or neutered, not bred. And if they are bred, their puppies aren't eligible for AKC registration. *Note:* Dogs with limited registration may compete in AKC (and other dog clubs') obedience and agility events, but they're not eligible to compete in conformation (see Chapter 12).

If the puppy you fall for has been selected by the breeder for limited registration, ask why. Usually it's because of some small fault that won't matter to you anyway unless you're planning to show and/or breed your dog. In fact, a puppy with limited registration from an excellent breeder usually is far superior to a puppy with full registration from a strictly commercial breeder.

Registering your new dog

When you purchase a dog that's AKC registrable, you should receive a registration application that has been filled out and signed by the seller. The form includes a section for the new owner (congratulations, that's you!) to complete. Do it ASAP (because the price goes up if you wait too long) and send the application to the American Kennel Club (the address is on the form), along with the required fee. As soon as your dog's paperwork is processed and recorded, you'll receive a registration certificate. Finally, you own an AKC registered dog!

Thousands of eligible dogs aren't registered even though their owners think they are. That's because their owners put the registration applications in a safe place but never read them. That official-looking piece of paper is only an application. It means your dog is *eligible* to be AKC registered. For the dog to actually *be* registered, you must fill out the form and send it in.

One of the more important things you write on the registration application is your dog's name. Decide carefully, because after your dog is AKC registered, the name stays the same forever!

Don't be surprised if the breeder/kennel where you purchase your Chihuahua wants to either name your puppy or include its kennel name as part of your dog's registered name. That isn't an unusual request. Breeding superior dogs is an art form, and putting a kennel name on a top-quality dog is the same as an artist signing his or her work. Most of the time, you and the breeder can get what you want. For example, if you buy your dog from Talko Chi Town Kennels and want to name her Susie, her registered name may be Talko Chi Town Susie. In dog-show lingo, Susie is her *call name*.

If a seller doesn't have a registration application for your puppy but assures you that one is coming, proceed with caution. Maybe the seller didn't apply to the AKC soon enough and expects the paperwork in a week or two. If you trust the seller enough to buy on that basis, ask for a bill of sale signed by the seller that includes your dog's breed, date of birth, sex, color, the registered names and AKC numbers of the pup's sire and dam, and the full name and address of the breeder. That way, if you don't receive official paperwork in a week or so, you can write to the AKC and fully identify your dog.

Don't be shy about demanding the previous info. According to American Kennel Club rules, anyone who sells dogs eligible for AKC registration must provide complete identification in writing. If you want a registered dog and the seller can't give you the registration application or every bit of the necessary information, pass up the puppy.

Chihuahuas without credentials

If you adopt your Chihuahua from a rescue or humane organization, she'll probably come to you without papers. Does this matter? Only if you want to compete in AKC events, such as obedience or agility (see Chapter 12).

The American Kennel Club allows purebred dogs with no papers to compete in obedience and agility if they have _Indefinite Listing Privilege_ (ILP) numbers. A form for you to fill out is available at www.akc.org, or you can call AKC Customer Care at 919-233-9767 and ask a representative to send you an ILP form.

Chapter 5

Welcome Home, Little Amigo

*I*t's almost dog day! You can feel the excitement in the air. I bet you can hardly wait to bring your puppy home, but first, you need to do a little organizing. This chapter helps you decide when to bring your Chihuahua home and tells you how to keep his curious tongue out of toxic things. It also helps you decide what your new dog needs and doesn't need so you won't be tempted to buy every toy and food option in the pet shop!

Are you wondering how to handle your Chihuahua when he's the new dog on the block? How to guide your children or grandkids into a good relationship with their new pal? How to introduce your Pepe to your other pets? What you'll do during those uncertain first couple days? How you'll keep your Chi safe and free from escape temptation? Don't worry. That's all here, too.

Timing the Homecoming Just Right

The best time to bring home a new dog is when nothing new is happening at your place. Wait until the repair people are finished, the relatives have gone home, and the holiday season is over; this gives your Chi quiet time to get to know you and adjust to his new home.

If your Chihuahua is a holiday gift from your spouse to you or vice versa, settle for a photo of him under the Christmas tree or beside the Hanukah candles. If you have kids at home, gift-wrap a collar and leash, a food and water dish, and dog toys to go with the photo (see the later section "Shop till You Drop: Gathering the Chi Goods"). Bring the dog home only after the parties are over and the decorations have been boxed. A normal home has enough gizmos to tempt a puppy into trouble. Halls decked out for the holidays can be downright dangerous.

Don't ever give a dog as a present unless you're absolutely sure the recipient wants one and that the breed you picked is his or her favorite. Better yet, before you pay for the pup, invite the potential owner to meet him and check out the chemistry between them.

Dogs are social animals, so being alone in a strange place makes a Chihuahua feel lonely and insecure. It's better if you can bring him home when you have a vacation or a long weekend so you can be around to help him settle in. Is a regular weekend the best you can do? Bring him home as early as possible on Saturday morning. Don't opt for Friday night, because bedtime without his dam (mother) and littermates is the hardest time for a puppy, and he'll feel better if he has a whole day to acclimate first.

Puppy-Proofing Your Chi's Room

Until he's housebroken (see Chapter 10), the right place for your Chihuahua (when no one can supervise) is in one easily cleaned room of your home. Most people find the kitchen ideal, unless yours is exceptionally large. In that case, a bathroom may be suitable.

Your Chi's room must be puppy-proofed for his safety. Puppies are curious, and because they don't have fingers to feel things, they try to taste everything (no matter how yucky the things may smell to you). Keep all cleaning agents, pesticides, antifreeze, and other household and garden chemicals out of your puppy's reach. Do the same with electrical wires. If it isn't possible to eliminate every electrical cord your Chi can reach, coat them with a bitter spray (found at pet stores). The spray is a safe, evil-tasting liquid, formulated to prevent chewing.

Place a wire mesh baby gate across the doorway; this works better than a solid door, which isolates the puppy, adding to his loneliness and frustration, and leads to incessant barking, temper tantrums, and tiny tooth prints in the door. Make sure the mesh is strong enough to withstand sharp teeth and that the mesh pattern is too small for him to chew through or get caught in.

If you can't give your Chi the run of a whole puppy-proofed room, a baby's playpen with mesh sides is a good (and portable) alternative.

A rock in a hard place

When my Chi Manchita was a puppy, she earned the nickname Hoover because she behaved like a vacuum cleaner, inhaling everything in her path. One day while we were out walking, she snatched up a small rock and swallowed it before I could get it out of her mouth. The next day, she strained to eliminate, couldn't pass the rock, and became sick. Luckily, the veterinarian was able to dislodge it by medicating her at both ends. Otherwise, our 2 ½ pound puppy faced emergency surgery!

Do you have houseplants? Identify every one (not just the ones in the puppy-proofed room) and look them up to find out if they're poisonous (or take a leaf to a nursery and ask). Many popular houseplants are deadly when ingested, including poinsettia leaves and those merry mistletoe berries. Placing all plants, even the safe ones, out of your dog's reach is a good idea, because no puppy can resist playing with a plant. But extra precautions are necessary with the poisonous plants. They shed leaves and berries even though they may be hanging high, and your Chi is bound to pick them up. Your best course of action? Get rid of them.

If you like your nonpoisonous houseplants right where they are, and you want your Chihuahua to know that he needs to leave them alone, spray them with Bitter Apple leaf protector.

When young and unsupervised, your Chi will try to teethe on everything he can reach, from your bedroom slippers to your shower curtain . . . even a box of dishwasher detergent, if you leave the cupboard door ajar. But keeping his curious mouth out of mischief isn't as hard as it sounds. You can secure closet and cupboard doors and flip the shower curtain up over the rod, for instance. After you have your dog for some time, these actions will become second nature.

Shop till You Drop: Gathering the Chi Goods

You've puppy-proofed your Chi's special room and your home, and you have a long weekend coming up to welcome your new pet (see the previous sections). You'll be ready for Chihuahua life as soon as you go shopping. Your Chi needs a few things right away.

Wait until you see the colorful display of dog toys, collars, leashes, food and water dishes, and even canine clothing in the pet store. It's tempting to buy twice what you need. How will you know what's necessary and what isn't? By using a shopping list. In this section I explain each item so you can get the perfect one for your Chi.

Essentials for your new Chihuahua

The following shopping list contains the essentials you need for your new Chihuahua:

- ✔ Two dishes — one for water and one for food
- ✔ Puppy (or dog) food
- ✔ Collar and leash
- ✔ Grooming equipment
- ✔ Three or four toys
- ✔ Dog crate
- ✔ Dog bed (optional)
- ✔ Warm sweater (if you live in a chilly climate)
- ✔ Pooper-scooper
- ✔ Identification
- ✔ An excellent veterinarian

Practical dishes

What's a practical dog dish? One that's easy to clean and hard to tip over. Some of the nicer dishes are made of stainless steel, although acrylic, heavy-duty plastic, stoneware, and porcelain are good choices. Some dishes are wider at the bottom than at the top and others are weighted; these are good features because it makes them impossible to tip over, even if your Chi likes to play with his bowl.

If you buy ceramic dishes for your Chihuahua, make sure they were made in the United States. Some foreign glazes still contain toxic stuff, including lead. Look for ceramics that are well glazed (read: glossy).

Place your Chi's dishes where they won't slide around the floor while he eats and drinks. A corner usually works well.

Eating meals indoors is best for your Chihuahua, but if you decide to give him an outdoor picnic on a pretty day, pick up his dish as soon as he finishes. Otherwise, every bug in the neighborhood will be attracted to your yard and the bowl.

So many choices: What should your Chi eat?

Kibble? Soft-moist? Biscuit? Pellets? Canned? Chopped or chunky? Are you confused yet? Don't be. Feeding your dog a good diet is easy and mighty important . . . so important that it has its own chapter in this book. So instead of giving Chihuahua chow your best guess, turn to Chapter 6. It tells you what food to buy to meet your Chi's nutritional needs during every stage of his life.

A collar and leash

 Wait until you bring your puppy home before buying a collar so you can get one that fits his neck perfectly. Your Chihuahua's collar should apply no pressure as it encircles his neck, but it shouldn't be so loose that it slips over his adorable apple head. Don't buy a collar that's too large so your puppy can grow into it, either. Collars that are too loose are a choking hazard if they become caught on something.

Shop for a flat collar, made of nylon webbing or leather, that closes via a buckle and has a D ring for attaching a leash. Some of the newer nylon collars have a plastic clasp similar to those used on camera bags and fanny packs (but in miniature form), and they come in a variety of attractive designs.

Check the fit of your Chi's collar weekly. Although he won't grow much, puppies do grow fast, and you must replace his collar right away if it feels tight. It isn't unusual for puppies to go through two or three collars before they mature, so keep that in mind when pricing puppy collars.

What's a collar without a lead? Simply an accessory! The length of your Chi's lead should be between 5 and 6 feet. Leather, nylon, or other flexible fabric leads are preferred. Expandable leads that allow a dog to get several feet away from its owner also are available. They give dogs a feeling of freedom while still allowing owners to maintain control, but they should be considered optional. The traditional lead is still the safest choice in crowded places. (To find out how to lead break your puppy, see Chapter 9.)

Don't buy a leash or collar made of chain. Chain is too cumbersome and can hurt your Chihuahua's legs if he gets tangled in it. And don't buy any type of training collar (they also come in nylon and webbing) with a ring at both ends that tightens up when you or your dog pulls away. Commonly called *choke collars,* these training devices should be used during obedience training only (never for everyday wear), and Toy dogs (like your Chi) don't need them at all.

Grooming gizmos

Smooth Chis have easy-care, wash-and-wear coats, so for their grooming, you can get by with purchasing the following:

- ✔ A quality shampoo that's pH-balanced for dogs
- ✔ A natural bristle brush
- ✔ A toothpaste formulated for dogs
- ✔ A soft toothbrush made for small dogs or human babies
- ✔ A doggie nail clipper

Other items like cotton ear swabs also are useful in grooming your Chi, but you probably have most of them in your medicine cabinet already.

Long-coated Chis are also easy to maintain, but they require a few more things (in addition to the previous tools):

- ✔ Both you and your Chi will appreciate a coat conditioner formulated for dogs. Besides making his coat a cinch to comb after his shampoo, it will keep it soft and silky.
- ✔ A hard rubber comb is a must for keeping mats out of a Chi's coat — especially behind the ears.
- ✔ If you don't use the comb often enough (don't worry, it takes only a minute or two), you'll probably need a mat splitter to put your Chi's coat back in good condition.

Chapter 7 tells you how to use your grooming gizmos to keep your dog's skin and coat healthy.

Don't buy a nylon or metal comb or a brush made with anything but natural bristles. Natural products do the least damage to a dog's coat. If you comb your dog during the winter with a nylon or metal implement, you'll probably zap him with static electricity. He'll hate it and won't want to be groomed anymore.

Toys for Toys (Dogs, that is)

Think of your Chihuahua's toys as essentials, not extras. He needs something safe to gnaw on while he's teething and a couple of toys available to play with the rest of the time. Although your Chihuahua continues chewing after he grows up, he won't wrap his fangs around everything he can reach the way teething puppies do. Be glad your mature Chi still likes to chew (for example, see Figure 5-1). Besides keeping him content, chewing promotes healthy gums and teeth.

Toy dogs need chews and playthings that are small enough for them to manipulate but big enough that they can't swallow them. Rawhide chew toys are a traditional favorite, but on rare occasions, dogs have accidentally choked to death when pieces of rawhide got caught in their throats. You don't have to boycott rawhide altogether; instead, let your dog enjoy it when you're with him and replace it with something safer when you leave him unsupervised.

Figure 5-1: She may be pushing 12, but Manchita is still serious about her chew toys.

Chew toys made of hard nylon are safe in a Toy dog's mouth even when no one is home. Chihuahua puppies, and many adult dogs, prefer the softer and equally safe gummy-nylon chews. Solid, hard-rubber toys also are safe and fun.

On the other hand, squeaky toys (featherweight rubber or plastic critters with squeakers inside) are popular with pups but are safe only when you're supervising — or better yet, when you join in the fun. Squeaky toys are easily chewed open (yes, even by a Chihuahua), and the squeaker inside is mighty dangerous when swallowed. Like rawhide, you don't have to deprive your Chi of a squeaky toy. Instead, buy him one but keep it out of his reach. Get it out once every few days as a special treat, and watch the fun when he play-kills it.

 Don't use old leather shoes, purses, or wallets as dog toys. Sure, your dog likes sinking his teeth into the well-worn leather, but this teaches him that leather objects with your scent on them are chew toys. That won't do any of your new accessories any good.

Flat, fleecy toys (shaped like gingerbread people or other animals, for instance) are popular, and dogs like cuddling up to them. They're machine washable and safe as long as your Chi doesn't shred the edges and swallow some of the material. Just keep an eye on fleecy toys and throw them away if they ever become worn enough to worry about.

 Tug-of-war toys — such as ropes or thick bands of rubber with loops at both ends — look like fun, but resist the temptation and don't buy them. Playing tug games with your dog teaches him that fighting you for objects is a cool game. After he gets that in his head, it won't be long before he initiates a tug game by grabbing and shaking the hem of your pants. Also, playing tug-of-war games is known to cause aggression with dogs. Many behavioral issues can be tracked back to these types of games. For plenty of safe and fun games you can play with your Chihuahua, head to Chapter 8.

 Don't let your Chi have all his toys at once. Instead, put a few away and rotate them every couple days. That way your dog won't become bored with his belongings. Keeping at least three toys (but no more than five) in service at one time is a good rule of thumb. Put one in his crate, one or two in his playroom (if he has one), and one or two in the room where the family gathers. Although indulging an older dog is okay, an overabundance of toys scattered throughout the house may lead a puppy to believe that whatever he can reach is his to chew.

A cozy crate

Dogs descend from denning animals that spent much of their time in the relative security of their lairs, so it won't take long before your Chihuahua feels comfortable and protected in a dog crate. Some new dog owners imagine that crate confinement is cruel, but crates have saved dogs' lives and owners' tempers for decades.

If you can't give your Chi his own puppy-proofed room, a crate becomes even more essential. It keeps him from stalking snakes (that's electrical cords to you) while you're away. Because they're so curious, many dogs are bound to get into mischief (or danger) when left at home alone. Besides, coming home to a safely crated puppy is much nicer than coming home to teeth marks on table legs and a soiled carpet. Because dogs don't like to soil their beds, a crate is a big help during housetraining. It also keeps your dog out of trouble while you're asleep. (For more info on introducing your Chi to his crate and using it to housetrain, see Chapter 10.)

Buy your Chi a crate that's only big enough for a full-grown Chihuahua to stand up and turn around in comfortably. Bigger isn't better for two reasons:

- ✔ Chihuahuas enjoy the cozy comfort of a just-the-right-size den.
- ✔ A too-large crate loses its potty-training potential.

Most crates are made of wire or plastic (with a wire door). Both types have their benefits, but I'd advise that plastic is the best choice for smooth-coated Chihuahuas. The solid sides (except for ventilation holes) keep a Chi draft free.

The inside of your Chihuahua's crate is his private place within your home, as well as his home away from home, so you should create a comfortable den. Include bedding that's easy to wash or change and not dangerous if chewed or swallowed. An old twin-bed sheet works nicely. If you don't have one, you can use several thicknesses of newspaper (black and white, not color or glossy like the comics or ads). For extra coziness, rip one section into long, thin streamers and place them in the crate on top of the whole sections (Chis love having something to burrow under). When you're sure that your Chi can keep his crate clean (which doesn't take long if you follow the schedule in Chapter 10), you can give him a nicer "mattress." A fleecy crate pad or soft rug sample are two possibilities.

The best place to put your Chi's crate is in his puppy-proofed room (if you have one). When it comes to crate placement, caring for your puppy works on the same principle as caring for a human baby. Just visualize his puppy-proofed room as his nursery and his crate as a combination crib, playpen, and car seat. Of course, you may opt to use a real playpen or a made-for-dogs exercise pen in addition to his crate.

For the ultimate crate toy, buy the smallest sterilized bone you can find (available at many pet supply stores) and stuff it with cheese. This concoction will keep your Chi occupied for hours.

For safety's sake, always crate your Chihuahua when taking him for a drive, and secure his crate so that it won't slide or roll over during turns or quick stops. A crated dog has a better chance of surviving a car accident. Not only that, but you drive better without your Chihuahua vying for your attention.

A snug bed

If a crate doesn't satisfy your concept of interior design, you can let your Chihuahua graduate into an attractive doggie bed after he's housebroken (see Chapters 9 and 10). Most beds are made of wicker and come with a nice mattress. Be sure to place the bed in a draft-free area and top it with a snugly blanket.

A useful sweater

Some canine couture is created just to look cute; fortunately, other clothing actually serves a purpose. Because Chihuahuas chill easily, your Chi may need a jacket or sweater that actually helps him stay warm — some even need a sweater in an air-conditioned room. Look for one that covers his chest, part of his neck, and as much of his belly as possible (see Figure 5-2). If your Chi is a female, the more of her bald belly the sweater covers, the better. When fitting your male, remember that he'll wear his sweater outdoors when he goes potty, and you won't want him to wet the material. Most canine clothes are machine washable, but read the labels just in case.

Figure 5-2: Manchita's coat is functional and stylish, as she shows with her pose.

Pooper-scooper

Poop-scoops are available in a variety of styles at pet supply stores. A scoop is convenient for cleaning up your yard and for cleaning up after your Chi when you take him on walks. Most scoopers have long handles so you don't have to bend down to clean.

If you don't mind bending down, you can get by without a pooper-scooper. Instead, stock up on plastic sandwich bags. Put a couple in your purse or pocket before walking your dog. Turn one inside out for a quick pick-up, pull the mess back through to the proper side, close the bag, and toss it in the nearest garbage can (not someone's recycle bin!).

A trusted veterinarian

Your Chihuahua's veterinarian is his other best friend, so you need to choose one before bringing him home. How will you know which dog doc is best for your puppy? Check out Chapter 13, which covers the details of the pet/vet relationship.

ID for dogs

You new dog should "carry" identification on him all the time. The puppy ID can take the form of a tattoo, a microchip, or a collar tag. The best ID is a collar tag plus either a tattoo or a microchip. Chapter 13 tells you all you need to know about identification and its importance.

Surviving the First Two Days

Time to go! You have everything you need, and now it's time to pick up your Chihuahua! Get off to a smart start by taking your crate along so your puppy can ride in it on the way home. The crate is his safest sanctuary in a moving vehicle.

When you arrive home, give your Chi an opportunity to relieve himself outdoors before going in (see Chapter 10). Then take him to his puppy-proofed room, give him fresh water in his dish, and let him explore *his room* to his heart's content (see the earlier section "Puppy-Proofing Your Chi's Room"). You're not depriving him by keeping him from investigating your whole home right away. Too much new territory is confusing, and besides, if he's teething and isn't housebroken yet, more space simply means more trouble. If you don't have a puppy-proofed room, keep a close eye on him as he inspects his new digs. And use a crate when no one is supervising.

Make sure extra warmth is available whenever your Chihuahua needs it. Whether you use a crate, playpen, a dog bed, or all these options, his space needs to be equipped with a sheet or blanket that he can burrow under.

After your Chi has a drink (and some food if it's feeding time), take him outdoors again. Then put him back in his puppy-proofed room, give him a toy, and play with him quietly. No matter how excited you are, this isn't a good time to overstimulate your puppy. Chances are, he's tired from the trip home and seeing so many new places and faces. When he gives out (some puppies go from playing to sleeping so quickly that they appear to have passed out), crate him or put him in his bed and let him take a nap. He'll love sleeping on your lap, of course, and it helps both of you bond, but don't put him on your lap for every nap. Your Chi has to learn to sleep alone, too.

For the first couple days, try to keep household activity normal . . . even low key. This isn't the time for Junior to jam with his band or for Julie to invite her friends over to practice for cheerleading tryouts. Don't start your spring-cleaning, either. And remind enthusiastic family members and friends not to rush at your Chi. Unfamiliar surroundings and strange voices are enough for a puppy to get used to during the first 48 hours. After that, household activity can gradually return to normal.

Because consistency is the key when training a puppy, and because your Chihuahua arrives full of curiosity with a brain like a sponge, the ideal time to start housetraining is day one. See Chapter 10 to find out how.

How to pick up your puppy

Sure, puppy Pepe fits into your palm; but you need to use two hands to pick him up anyway, right from the get-go. One hand goes under his chest and the other cups his rear. Check your hands the first few times to make sure your fingers don't apply pressure to his front legs — either spreading them too far apart or squeezing them together. Habitual spreading can cause permanent damage to your puppy's elbows, and repeated squeezing can harm the legs and shoulders. Best bet? Place your thumb on one side of your dog and your little finger on the other, supporting his chest with the middle three fingers. After you try this method once or twice, it should become automatic. Hold him gently but firmly (puppies wiggle) against your body with both hands so no part of him dangles.

Never leave your puppy alone in a place where he could fall. For example, if you and your Chihuahua are watching television in the recliner and you get up to check out the fridge, place your pup on the floor until you return. When he matures, he becomes able to jump on and off the furniture by himself, but that's a dangerous leap for a puppy.

Blending dogs and kids

Please don't skip this section just because you don't have any kids at home. You may have grandchildren or friends with children, and what you discover here will ensure that visiting kids and your Chi will have pleasant (and safe) visits.

Chis and young children typically aren't a good combination. Sometimes kids and dogs scare each other without wanting to. Tiny dogs fear shrill sounds and fast movements (especially swooping down on them), and youngsters come well equipped with high-pitched voices and jerky movements. When dogs feel threatened or cornered, they usually growl, warning the offenders away. But many young children don't recognize the warning or simply ignore it, and that's how bites happen. On the other hand, children fear shrill noises, too, and a Chihuahua's piercing puppy bark may make them cringe.

The truth is, kids and dogs can hurt each other. But many people have surmounted the obstacles and succeeded in raising children and Chihuahuas at the same time. How? By being vigilant and never leaving little children and Chihuahuas alone together. Using careful and calm supervision every time a child and puppy are together keeps the child and the pup from fearing each other.

From about the age of 3 or 4, children — depending on their individual self-control and emotional maturity — *can* help you care for a Chi. Provided that you have patience and won't freak out over spilled food or water, kids can do many things, such as picking up your Chi's dirty dishes and bringing them to you and giving your Chi his water or food after you fill the dishes. Kids also get a kick out of giving dogs an occasional treat.

When children are young, helping to take care of a pet should be fun — a privilege, not a responsibility. Do it yourself when you're in a hurry. Chubby little fingers sometimes spill stuff.

Children who are ready to help care for a puppy also are ready to follow some simple rules. Here are a few rules that work on your own kids and visitors, too; you may have to create others to fit your situation:

- ✔ Always sit on the floor to play with the dog.

- ✔ Don't put your face close to him.

- ✔ You may pet him, but don't close your hand when doing so. This keeps children from squeezing or grabbing a leg, ear, or tail.

- ✔ Don't tease or poke the dog. You may have to explain what teasing is.

- ✔ Never give him anything to eat or play with without permission.

- ✔ When he wants to leave, let him go. Don't hang on and try to stop him.

Matching older children and Chihuahuas

By the time they're third- or fourth-graders, some kids become attuned to animals. In fact, older children often have better relationships with their pets than grownups do because they take the time to discover the animals' body language. Responsible older kids can share in your Chihuahua's care by feeding, grooming, and walking him. And they may surprise you by teaching him a few tricks!

Kids learn the most valuable lessons about pet care when it's a family affair. Don't expect a child (or teenager) to take full responsibility for your Chi, even if she promised she would when she begged you to buy him. Instead, give kids an excellent example (yes, that's you) to follow. Most important of all, never make threatening remarks — "If you don't do those dishes right now, I'm giving that dog away!" A dog isn't a disposable object like outgrown skates or a broken barrette. Yours deserves affection, care, and a permanent home, and threatening to give him anything less sends your child a sorry message.

No matter how good your children are with the family Chihuahua, keep an eye on the situation when their friends visit. Other children with little or no experience with tiny pets may want to experiment ("What would happen if we fed him this?") or may even harbor a mean streak. And the best of kids (like yours) may find themselves helpless in the face of peer pressure.

Introducing dog to dog

The best way to introduce Rover to your new Chihuahua is on neutral ground so Rover doesn't feel the need to defend his territory from an intruder. Just half a block down the street does fine if both dogs know how to walk on a leash. Your Chi must stand on the ground (not in your arms) to participate in a proper doggie intro-duction, so if he isn't leash broken, borrow a fenced-in yard for the opening ceremony.

The easiest way to accomplish a successful meeting is to ask a helper to take your Chihuahua to the designated place. Then you take Rover for a walk, on leash, and meet them there. Follow these steps as you approach the meeting place:

1. **As the dogs near each other, start a conversation with your helper, but watch while the dogs go through the motions of meeting.**

2. **Give Rover just enough slack in the lead so he can sniff your Chi all over, but maintain complete control of the situation.**

   Act nonchalant so the dogs don't sense any anxiety in you, and don't pet either dog.

3. **As soon as Rover displays gentleness toward your Chi, praise him verbally.**

   In most cases, dogs will be civil — even friendly — to each other. However, if Rover appears threatening or overly excited, give an immediate jerk on the lead and walk away with him. Try again when he simmers down.

4. **When the dogs seem comfortable with each other, walk them home together if both dogs walk on leash.**

   Otherwise, let your friend carry your Chi while you walk Rover, praising him occasionally along the way.

5. **When you get home, try to make Rover think that invit-ing his little friend in was his idea by praising him by name for being gentle ("Gooood Rover!") and giving him more than his share of attention.**

6. **Inside, put your Chi on the floor in the same room with Rover and supervise closely.**

   Most dogs treat little puppies gently as long as they don't suddenly feel unloved. Give Rover at least as much atten-tion as you ever did. Ignoring Rover creates the canine equivalent of sibling rivalry. And if ol' Rov is a big boy, the situation may be dangerous. Just imagine how a 3-year-old child would react to her new brother if she's suddenly shoved aside while the baby gets all the attention.

Don't leave the dogs alone together until you're sure that they get along. Use their crates, or keep them in different rooms, when no one is home.

If you have more than one dog, introduce them to your new dog or puppy one at a time. Start with your calmest canine and work up to your most excitable.

Why cats get the last meow

Dogs and cats in the same household usually get along, and some even become best buddies. At first introduction, if your Chi isn't especially agitated at the sight of Tabby, he may become curious and try to sniff noses with her. If she sniffs back, that's a good sign. Chances are they'll be friends in no time (see Figure 5-3). While waiting for that to happen, keep a watchful eye on them when they're together. Some dogs, even little ones, have an undeniable urge to chase cats. And although some cats run from Chihuahuas, others may take swipes at the tiny tormentors, which can damage your Chi's eyes and nose.

When a dog and cat live together, the cat always has the advantage. Why? Because Kitty can leave an area whenever she wants to. All she has to do is jump on the bed or chair out of your Chi's reach, and he can't annoy her or cuddle her until she decides to come near him again. This may not seem fair to you, but don't interfere. When your cat has had enough of your Chi (even if that happens in less than a second), let her go. You can't force friendship; it will probably occur on its own after Kitty gets used to the interloper and they learn each other's limits.

Living with furry, feathered, and scaled critters

Furry, feathered, and scaled caged pets — such as hamsters, birds, rabbits, lizards, turtles, and mice — may appear to be prey to your Chihuahua. Dogs (yes, even little ones) instinctively catch and kill prey. The best solution is to keep these critters out of his reach and correct everything from too much interest to a menacing growl with a firm "No!" Your Chi doesn't have to make friends with these animals. You can rest easy when he learns to ignore them. Most dogs lose interest in caged pets after they get used to seeing and smelling them on a daily basis. But until then, supervise your Chi every time he's in the same room with your caged critters.

Figure 5-3: If you're wondering why Boudreux the cat's bowl is up on a stool, it's because cat food isn't good for dogs.

Suppressing That Dangerous Fantasy of Freedom

Some dog owners think their dogs somehow miss out on a facet of life if they never experience absolute freedom. In fact, millions of dogs die every year from accidents encountered while roaming free. A loose dog can be crushed by cars or picked up by animal control officers, or he can lick poisonous substances like antifreeze (it's sweet) or lawn herbicides.

Besides being a menace to your neighbor's flowerbed, a loose Chihuahua also faces dangers like being stolen, attacked by a bigger dog, or even snatched by an owl or hawk (it happens). He may also be handled roughly by a small child. And if the child frightens or hurts your Chi, your dog may bite during his efforts to escape. Now you're in danger of a lawsuit.

Putting your Chihuahua in a position to become a statistic isn't doing him a favor. A Chihuahua is more than a domestic animal — he's the ultimate house dog. Rather than freedom, give him what he really wants: your companionship.

Chapter 6

What's on the Chi Menu?

*J*ust look at the pet-food aisle at any major supermarket. It's stacked high with an array of kibble, meal, biscuit, semi-moist, and canned canine cuisines — some for puppies, some for adult dogs, and some for seniors. And they all claim to offer optimum nutrition. That's only the half of it. Pet supply stores stock several high-priced but more-concentrated brands, and each proclaims its advantages. Are you confused yet? You don't have to be. Selecting a healthy diet for your Chihuahua can be easy. In this chapter, I help you choose the right meals for your Chi to feed her through every stage of her life.

How Nutrients Work

If you understand human nutrition, you can skip this section. Nutrients serve practically the same function in dogs as they do in people, so you already know how your dog utilizes them. For those of you who were daydreaming when your teachers talked about the body's building blocks, the following sections detail what some of the more important nutrients do for your dog.

Building a healthy Chihuahua

Chihuahuas, and people, need a variety of nutrients to stay healthy:

✔ Carbohydrates are starches, sugars, and fiber. They aid in digestion and elimination and provide energy and the proper assimilation of fats. Excess carbohydrates are stored in the body for future use.

✔ Protein can come from meat or vegetable sources. It isn't stored in the body, so your dog needs to eat it every single day. The body uses protein for bone growth, tissue healing, and the daily replacement of body tissues burned up by normal activity.

✔ Fats are necessary as an energy source. They also add suppleness to your dog's skin and luster to her coat. However, excess fat is stored under the skin and can lead to an overweight dog.

Fat balance is important. Too much fat leads to the same obesity problems that humans suffer, and too little robs your Chihuahua of necessary protection from changes in temperature and can make her overly sensitive to cold (as if she isn't sensitive enough to cold already!).

Vitamins and minerals

Humans need vitamins and minerals in their diet, and so do their dogs. Here are some of the essentials and their roles in keeping your Chihuahua healthy:

✔ The body uses vitamin A for fat absorption; it's also necessary for a healthy, shiny coat, for normal growth rate, good eyesight, and reproduction.

✔ The B vitamins protect the nervous system and are necessary for normal coat, skin, appetite, growth, and vision.

✔ Dogs synthesize vitamin C in the liver, so this vitamin isn't often mentioned in an analysis of commercial dog food or vitamin supplements. Some breeders add it to the diet anyway.

✔ Healthy bones and teeth and good muscle tone are dependent on vitamin D, but the vitamin must be ingested in the correct ratio with calcium and phosphorus.

✔ Vitamin E is associated with the proper functioning of the muscles and the internal and reproductive organs.

✔ Most dogs can synthesize vitamin K in their digestive tracts, and this vitamin is essential to normal clotting of the blood. If your Chi seems to bleed too long from minor cuts, mention it to your veterinarian. This could indicate a deficiency of vitamin K.

✔ A puppy's body must receive calcium and phosphorus in the correct ratio to provide protection from rickets, bowed legs, and other bone deformities. They also aid in muscle development and maintenance.

✔ Potassium is necessary for normal growth and healthy nerves and muscles.

✔ Sodium and chlorine boost your Chihuahua's appetite and enable her to enjoy a normal activity level.

✔ Magnesium is necessary to prevent convulsions and nervous-system disorders.

✔ Iron is needed for healthy blood and prevents fatigue from anemia.

✔ Iodine prevents goiter in dogs the same way it does in people.

✔ Copper is necessary for growing and maintaining strong bones. It also helps prevent anemia.

✔ Cobalt aids normal growth and keeps the reproductive tract healthy.

✔ Manganese also aids growth and is necessary for healthy reproduction.

✔ Zinc promotes normal growth and healthy skin.

Feeding for the First Few Days

The only right food to feed your Chihuahua for the first few days after you bring her home is the one she was eating before you got her. Even if your new Chihuahua is an adult, make only gradual changes in her diet. She's experiencing enough newness in her life right now. Many breeders give new owners a small amount of puppy or dog food and a written schedule to get them started, but if your breeder offers you nothing, ask the following three questions about your new dog's eating habits:

✔ What brand of food has she been eating?

✔ What's her feeding schedule (how frequently is she fed and at what hours)?

✔ How much does she eat at each feeding?

Besides using the same food, sticking to the feeding schedule your Chi is used to is best, at least for the first three days. After that, you can gradually change food and chow time until her schedule blends into your household routine.

Assuming you feed your Chihuahua in the kitchen, you may want to put a carpet sample under her bowl. Many Chihuahuas (and other dogs, too) like to eat on the rug. They accomplish this by putting a few morsels in their mouths, trotting off to the closest carpeted area, and then munching them there. If your Chi is determined to eat dinner on a comfy carpet, an area rug may (notice I'm not promising anything) keep her in the kitchen.

Dogs are omnivores, which means they eat both meat and plant matter.

How to change dog foods

What if you've decided on a dog food and it isn't the one your new Chi was raised on? No problem. After a few days of feeding her the brand she's used to, introduce the food you've selected by adding just a little bit of it to her usual diet. Watch to make sure she eats it and check her bowel movements. As long as everything is fine (no constipation or diarrhea), add a little more of the new food and take away a little more of her old food every day. You can complete the transition by the end of a week as long as nothing appears wrong.

If your dog becomes constipated (has to strain to eliminate) or gets diarrhea, add more of the food your Chi was raised on and less of the new food. When she normalizes, try gradually changing her diet again by substituting a very small amount of the new food daily. If problems persist, consult your vet. The problem may be caused by something other than a change of food, and persistent diarrhea is dangerous.

When to change dog foods (if you must)

Now that you know *how* to change dog foods, are you sure you want to? Look at your Chi. Is her weight right for her height? Does she have enough energy? Does her coat have a healthy glow? Gee, her breeder must have done something right. As the old saying goes, "If it ain't broke, don't fix it." If she eats most of her meals and has regular bowel movements, an upbeat attitude, and a healthy coat, the best dog food for her (at least until she reaches another stage in her life) may be exactly the one she's eating. See Figure 6-1 for an example of a healthy-looking, properly fed Chihuahua.

Figure 6-1: A glossy coat, bright eyes, and an alert attitude are signs that your Chi is eating a healthy diet.

However, if your Chi is too thin or too fat, lacks energy, has a dull or dry-looking coat, or suffers from constipation or diarrhea, see your veterinarian. If he rules out parasites or an illness, consider changing her dog food. You may also want to change her diet if the one her breeder recommends is too time consuming to concoct. Some breeders create their own formulas, and many of these formulas are way too complicated for working pet owners. Besides, quality commercial food is probably better for your dog in the long run — provided that you opt for an excellent brand. The following section helps you understand the countless choices you see on the store shelves.

What You Need to Know about Commercial Dog Food

Good nutrition is essential to prevent dietary deficiency diseases. The right diet helps your Chihuahua fight off infections and reduces her susceptibility to organic ailments. The best (and easiest) way to feed your dog a balanced diet — giving her the nutrition she needs — is to choose an excellent commercial brand and stick with it. (Always make sure fresh water is available, too.) The following sections compare the many options available and help you choose the right one for your situation. I also give you the lowdown on treats and other foods you can give your pup.

Beware of bargain brands

How about I start this section with the don'ts. As in, don't buy a bottom-of-the-line dog food for your Chihuahua. Bargain dog food is seldom a bargain. The nutritional info on the package may say it has the same percentages of protein (or other nutrients) as the better-known brands, but the amount of usable (digestible) nutrients is what's important. For example, an old leather purse is protein but it has no nutritive value at all.

The truth is, generic and economy brands are made of the cheapest ingredients available, and tests have found that many of them don't contain what their labels proclaim. In fact, many are downright dangerous for Toy breeds. Why? Because smaller dogs have higher energy requirements per pound than large dogs, but because of their size, they eat only a little at a time. Consequently, they need high-quality, easily digestible dinners . . . not cheap, empty calories.

So many nutritional deficiencies have shown up in dogs fed a diet of economy or generic foods that the Veterinary Medical Teaching Hospital at the University of California, Davis, has labeled the syndrome *generic dog food-associated disease.* The common evidence of the syndrome is abnormally slow growth, coat and skin problems, and skeletal abnormalities.

Regular brands versus premium brands

I tell you in the previous section not to go bargain hunting, but you still must consider two other qualities of dog food — the regular brands and the premium brands:

- **The regular brands** are the well-known names you've seen on supermarket shelves for years. Their ingredients are more digestible and made from higher quality ingredients than the economy foods. Costwise, they're the middle-of-the-road brands — neither the cheapest nor the most expensive.

- **The premium brands** are the highest-priced dog foods, and seldom are they seen in supermarkets. Instead, they're sold at pet supply stores, pet shops, and some veterinarians' offices. What sets them apart from the regular brands? Regular brands usually use wheat, corn, or soybeans as their primary ingredient, but many premium foods use a meat source as their main ingredient. Likewise, because premium foods contain only top-quality, highly digestible ingredients, they're considered *concentrated.* That means dogs eat less of them and still get optimum nutrition.

> So even though they cost more, premium brands go further than regular brands. Another advantage is that concentrated food makes for smaller, more compact stools, giving you easier cleanups. Of course, that's more important to a St. Bernard owner than it is to you, but I thought I should mention it anyway.

I bet you think I'm going to tell you to run right out and buy a premium brand. But the choice isn't that simple . . . at least not with Toy dogs. Yes, I know you want the best for your Chihuahua, and yes, premium food is the way to go if it agrees with her. But it may not. If you try a premium brand for a few weeks and she starts to show signs of constipation (straining to eliminate), gradually change back to a grain-based brand. Some small dogs do best on less-concentrated food and stay more regular when eating food that contains corn. If your Chi is one of them, find a reputable brand that keeps her bowels regular and stick with it. (For more on foods formulated for different stages of a dog's life, see the section "Foods for Special Reasons.")

The ingredients on a container of dog food are listed in descending order, by weight. But just because chicken is the first ingredient doesn't mean the food is mostly chicken. The next four ingredients may be wheat flour, corn meal, barley flour, and wheat germ. When combined, the plant-based ingredients probably weigh a lot more than the chicken.

Dry dog food

Dry dog food, sold in bags or boxes, is the most popular commercial-style feed. Here are the pluses of dry food:

- ✔ It's easy to feed and store.
- ✔ It has a decent shelf life (three to six months).
- ✔ It has little odor.
- ✔ It's good for your dog's teeth (when fed dry).

Now consider the minus side: Chihuahua puppies may not consume enough dry dog food to meet their energy needs. They eat larger servings when the nuggets are soaked and softened, but that removes the teeth-cleaning benefit. Read the labels on dry food carefully, because some are meant to be consumed dry, others form gravy when moistened and are meant to be eaten slightly wet, and still others may be consumed dry or moistened.

When choosing a dry food for your Chihuahua, check the size and texture of the pieces before buying. A Chi prefers small pieces she can easily chew as opposed to large, extra-hard chunks that make it hard for her to close her little mouth.

Also, consider that the freshest food is the best food. After you choose a brand of dry dog food, buy it in the smallest bag or box you can find. As you get down toward the bottom of the bag, check to make sure it still smells fresh, like biscuits, rather than stale or moldy.

Canned dog food

The best canned foods are made mostly of meat products, have a high moisture content, and usually contain some vegetable products, too. If you want to use canned food exclusively, read the label on each candidate carefully. Some canned foods provide total nutrition, but others are formulated to be mixed with dry food. If the canned food alone provides every nutrient a dog needs, the label says something like, "100 percent complete" or "Complete dinner."

Personally, I choose cans with complete nutrition even though I mix the canned food with dry. Some brands provide a choice of either chopped or chunky. The nutritional values are the same, but Chihuahua puppies, and most adult Chis, prefer the chopped version.

The best thing about high-quality canned foods (those made mostly of meat) is that dogs like them. In addition, they're easily stored, have long shelf lives, and some of the top brands for Toy dogs are conveniently available in the supermarket.

The downside of canned dog food is that the best brands (the only ones you want for your Chi) are expensive when compared to dry food. They also have an unpleasant smell (to some people) and won't help scrape tartar from your dog's teeth like dry foods do. In addition, you have to cover and store them in the refrigerator after opening.

Semi-moist or soft-moist foods

As their name implies, the moisture content of semi-moist foods is higher than that of dry food but less than canned. The result is dog food with a chewy texture. The best thing about semi-moist food is its convenience. It usually comes packaged in individual servings; however, that helps owners of average-sized dogs more than it helps you. Because the serving size is probably more than a Chihuahua eats at one time, you still must put the leftovers in an airtight bag so that they don't dry out before her next meal.

Semi-moist foods are usually priced higher than dry food but lower than quality canned dinners. Many dogs like semi-moist food, but the reason they eat them so eagerly makes them a minus rather than a plus in the nutrition department. The truth is, semi-moist foods contain more sugar (or sweeteners such as corn syrup) than your dog should eat. They often contain too much salt, as well, and a variety of artificial colors and preservatives. In short, I don't recommend semi-moist foods.

What's the solution?

After you know a little about the popular types of dog food (see the previous sections), which one should you choose for your Chi? Many long-time Chihuahua owners say their dogs do best when they're fed a diet of dry and canned food mixed together. A popular ratio is ¼th canned to ¾ths dry, mixing well before serving.

A good-quality commercial food likely contains all the nutrition a Chihuahua needs to glow with good health. The better brands of commercial food are balanced, providing your dog with the best canine nutrition known to modern science. That's why they're healthier than anything you can create at home for twice the price. The right balances of protein and carbohydrates, fats and fiber, and vitamins and minerals are too important (and complicated) for our guesstimates and are best left to the test kitchens of the major dog food companies. Feeding a quality commercial food also protects puppies from the dangerous but all-too-human tendency to believe that if a little of something is good, a lot is even better. Nutrition doesn't work that way; more of some substances actually can be toxic.

For more advice on what to choose based on your Chihuahua's place in life, see the section "Foods for Special Reasons."

Do you remember a Hill's Pet Products commercial from back in the early 1980s? It showed a *guaranteed analysis* just like the ones displayed on dog food cans. Protein was listed at 10 percent, fat at 6.5 percent, fiber at 2.4 percent, and moisture at 68 percent — all typical numbers for those nutrients. Finally, the ad displayed the actual ingredients: eight worn-out, leather work shoes, a gallon of used crankcase oil, a bucket of coal (crushed), and 68 pounds of water. When analyzed, the items equaled the guaranteed analysis, but imagine how much nutrition your Chihuahua receives from such a concoction!

Loaves of frozen dog food are available in some locales. The best ones have a high percentage of meat. Dogs like them, and they're stored in the freezer so they seldom spoil. Check the date on the package before purchasing, and thaw your dog's portion thoroughly before serving. You can use them alone or mix them with dry food.

What about treats and table food?

The problem with giving your Chihuahua table scraps is that tiny tummies can't hold much food at a time, and no matter how nutritious your dinner is for humans, chances are your dog's food is much better for her. Also, dogs that eat table scraps usually lose their taste for dog food completely.

Don't give your Chihuahua food directly from the table or she'll become an accomplished beggar. If you have healthy leftovers like chicken or pot roast (not scraps like the fat you trimmed off your steak), you can serve them mixed with your Chi's dinner. First chop or mash them well and then mix them in with her regular ration. If you get lazy and leave them chunky, she'll inhale them first and walk away from the rest of her meal.

High-quality biscuits are good treats because they help scrape tartar from a dog's teeth. Just don't give her too many. Most of your dog's calories should come from her regular meals. Many companies make miniature dog biscuits just the right size for Toy dogs. One company near me even offers dog cookies shaped like tiny postmen!

Some dogs even enjoy an occasional cooked vegetable cut into Chihuahua bite-sized pieces, such as carrots, yams, green beans, or peas. Tiny digestive systems don't do well with raw veggies, so offer them only when they're well cooked and have cooled to room temperature. An occasional bit of hardboiled egg is good, too, but raw eggs are a no-no. Treats that are good for training include tiny pieces of cheese (provided that your dog isn't lactose intolerant) or chicken.

Many dogs love a bit of cheese for a treat, but some of them can't handle dairy products because of lactose intolerance. They suffer from diarrhea and gas cramps (yep, you'll suffer, too) when they dine on dairy. The only way to find out if your dog can handle cheese is to try it, so offer just a tiny tidbit at a time until you're sure that she can digest it without problems.

Foods for Special Reasons

Many of the major dog food companies offer special formulas (dry or canned) for every stage of a dog's life. And that's a good thing. Dogs have different nutritional requirements at different times, just like people. The following sections break down the different stages or options and their nutritional requirements.

Grub to grow on

Whether you choose dry food, canned food, or a combination of the two, your Chihuahua needs to eat a diet formulated for puppies (often called a *growth formula*) until she's 1 year old. Growth formulas contain more protein and fat than adult diets. Puppies need extra protein for growth and extra fat to keep up with their energy levels.

Maintenance meals

After your Chi celebrates her 1st birthday, you can switch gradually to a commercial adult (*maintenance*) food (clearly labeled as such). You can use it until she's an oldster, provided that it keeps her healthy inside and out. A poor coat usually is the first sign that your dog's diet is letting her down. And depending on her activity level, you may want to adjust amounts a little bit over the years to keep her from gaining or losing weight.

Provisions for performers

If you decide to enter your Chihuahua in dog shows or train her for high-energy events such as obedience or agility competitions (see Chapter 12), consider feeding her a performance (sometimes called *stress*) formula. Most performance foods have higher protein and fat percentages than maintenance foods, making them similar to puppy food. In fact, some exhibitors simply keep their dogs on top-quality puppy food as long as they're competing.

Low-calorie lunches

When it comes to weight issues, prevention is the best policy. Make sure your Chihuahua exercises enough, eats a regular diet of dog food (not table scraps), and doesn't get a treat each and every time she begs. If she starts getting pudgy anyway, a variety of reduced-calorie dog foods are available to help her slim down. Most of them contain lower percentages of protein and fat and higher amounts of fiber than normal maintenance formulas.

Although the fiber helps your dog feel full on less food and a lower fat content helps her lose weight, other weight-loss options usually are healthier. The best option is increased exercise. If that doesn't do it, try feeding her a little less of her regular food at each feeding. Start by giving her 90 percent of her normal ration for a month. After that, if you don't see any improvement, talk it over with your veterinarian and consider a low-calorie cuisine.

Senior cuisine

Diets for geriatric dogs contain less protein than maintenance foods, which may or may not be a good thing. If your Chi is a healthy oldster, changing chow may not be necessary. But if she suffers from an ailment such as kidney disease, your veterinarian may recommend a senior formula because less protein puts less stress on her kidneys. See the section "Supper for seniors" later in this chapter for more on this topic.

Prescription dog food

If your Chihuahua has a specific health problem — such as diabetes, heart disease, renal failure, pancreatitis, or certain skin ailments — your veterinarian may prescribe a diet formulated especially for dogs with that issue. Prescription diets are available only through veterinarians, because the formulas are so different that they aren't good for healthy dogs. If your veterinarian puts your Chi on a prescription diet, he or she wants to monitor her progress — at least during the first few months.

Setting Puppy Feeding Schedules

Depending on your Chihuahua's age at the time, her breeder probably fed her between three and five times a day. The younger and tinier the puppy, the less she can eat at a time and the more often she needs nutrition. As she grows older, she'll chow down on larger amounts at a time and therefore will need less frequent meals.

Most Chihuahua puppies need four meals a day when they move into their permanent homes, but they won't have to eat that often forever. How do you know when to cut back to three feedings? Easy: Your Chi will tell you. She'll simply start ignoring all or most of the food at one of her meals (usually when she's around 3 months old). After she leaves most of one meal several days in a row, cut out that feeding. Give her slightly larger portions than before, but offer food only three times a day.

At around 6 months old, your Chi will lose interest in another meal (usually the middle one). Now it's time to increase the portions again and feed her only two meals a day, between 10 and 12 hours apart. Many large dogs wolf down a big dinner once a day and do just fine, but that doesn't work with a little dog. A Chihuahua's energy requirements are big and her belly is small, and too much elapsed time between meals can cause a dangerous drop in blood sugar.

 As a starting point, offer your puppy a minimum of half a cup of food at every meal. If she finishes it quickly, licks her bowl, and looks for more, you can increase the amount. No tried-and-true rule exists for how much a puppy needs to eat, and appetites vary. Your eyes are your best gauge. They tell you if your pup is gaining or losing weight or staying just right.

Don't let your Chi keep her food dish for longer than 15 minutes. If she hasn't finished her meal by then, remove it until the next feeding. This will help her learn to eat when she's fed.

 Don't try to teach your Chihuahua to clean her plate by giving her the same stale meal at every feeding until she finishes it. That won't teach her to eat and may make her sick. A dog needs fresh food in a clean bowl at every meal.

Filling a Mature Chi's Belly

Adult Chihuahuas do best on twice-a-day feedings, but the meals don't have to be identical. After your dog is 1 year old, you may try giving her dry food served dry in the morning (good for her gums and teeth) and dry food slightly moistened and mixed with canned food in the evening (or vice versa).

If you feed a healthy, parasite-free Chihuahua properly, she will maintain the same weight month after month, along with bright eyes, a shiny coat, healthy skin, steady nerves, and enough energy. If something is missing from her diet, or if she consumes too many calories, you'll notice. Poor nutrition displays itself through coat and skin problems and sometimes a lack of energy, and excess calories lead to obesity.

 Most Chihuahuas are good eaters. In fact, some Chihuahua owners have to watch their pets' weights to prevent obesity. Please don't let your Chihuahua get fat. It's bad for her bones and organs. Obesity does as much damage to dogs as it does to people. It's a major health problem in American dogs. In fact, it's estimated that nearly 50 percent of the dogs in the United States are overweight.

After you find a high-quality dog food that your dog enjoys and obviously does well on, you have no reason to change. Your Chi won't get bored with the same food every day like you would and doesn't need to discover new shapes, colors, or sizes in her bowl at frequent intervals.

Supper for seniors

When your Chi becomes a golden oldie (around age 10 or 11), try feeding her so she maintains the same weight she carried in healthy middle age. You can adjust the amounts, or even how the food is presented, to keep your senior Chi in top condition.

If she has less of an appetite than she used to, try tempting her with a few easy options:

- For starters, warm up her food. That's often all it takes to stimulate an old dog's appetite.

- Another option is treating her as though she's in her second puppyhood by feeding her small meals at frequent intervals.

- If that doesn't help, try soaking her dry food until it softens, which makes a difference when sore teeth or gums are the problem.

- The final option is mashing tasty goodies, like boiled chicken, cooked ground beef, or cottage cheese, into her regular dinner.

   It's only fair to tell you that special foods spoil your pet and make her expect the same treatment at every meal! But then, that isn't so terrible. If your Chi is well into her teens, a little spoiling may make both of you feel better.

 Most breeds are considered seniors when they're older than 7, but because Chihuahuas are so long lived (usually well into their teens), they aren't oldsters until their ages reach double digits.

Supplements for adults

Supplementation may be a good idea at certain times in a Chihuahua's life. A dog may benefit from dietary supplements in the following situations:

- Show dogs stressed from constant travel
- Performance dogs competing in obedience or agility events
- Dogs recuperating from illness or injury
- Dogs used for breeding

If you think your Chi needs a little extra help nutrition wise, check with your veterinarian. He may recommend a prepared vitamin-mineral powder or tablet, or simply suggest the addition of cottage cheese, hard-boiled (never raw) eggs, or a little fat to her diet.

Over supplementation with vitamins and minerals can be dangerous — even toxic. Check with your veterinarian before adding supplements to a balanced dog food.

Warning: Don't Feed Your Dog Any of These Foods

The following list presents a rundown of forbidden foods for Chihuahuas; some items may surprise you:

- ✔ **Chocolate, onions, or any highly spiced, greasy, or salty foods:** Chocolate contains theobromine, a substance that's poisonous to dogs. Onions (raw or cooked) can also be toxic, and spicy sauces and junk food lead to upset stomachs.

  Children often want to share their treats with their pets; unfortunately, their favorites usually include chocolate chip cookies, brownies, and chocolate ice cream. You must let your kids know that chocolate, in all forms (even icing), is off limits to your Chihuahua.

- ✔ **Bones:** Chicken, turkey, and pork chop bones, for example, can shatter and slice open your dog's intestines. There is an exception, however. Bones cooked in a pressure cooker until they're soft (it takes a long time at a high temperature) are actually good for dogs.

- ✔ **Beer, wine, or any other alcoholic beverage:** Alcohol poisoning is deadly, and it doesn't take much to poison a little dog. Also, be careful not to leave leftover cocktails where your Chi can find them.

- ✔ **Grapes and raisins:** These have been known to cause kidney failure in dogs. The dogs become critically ill, and many die even with aggressive treatment programs.

- ✔ **Macadamia nuts:** Some dogs have had serious reactions from eating macadamia nuts.

- ✔ **Cat food:** Feed your cat out of your Chihuahua's reach. Dogs love cat food, but it contains more protein and fats than they can handle.

✔ **Spoiled or moldy stuff:** Don't even consider giving your dog the leftover piece of chicken that you ignored for several days in the fridge. And be careful that she doesn't snatch it out of the garbage. The bad food's "enticing" odor will attract her. If the food is too old for you to eat, it's just as dangerous for her.

Of course, you wouldn't even think of feeding your Chi any of the following dangerous items, but I mention them because it's important to always keep them out of her reach:

✔ **Baking power and baking soda:** If you spill some, clean up the mess before your Chi can lick it. These agents can cause myriad problems in dogs, including congestive heart failure.

✔ **Coffee grounds or coffee beans:** These items can cause caffeine toxicity.

✔ **Fruit seeds, pits, and stones:** Fruit seeds contain cyanide, which is poisonous to people and pets. Most people have the good sense not to eat them, but pets may consider them chew toys.

Chapter 7

Grooming the Body Beautiful

*Y*ou want some really good news? Less than five minutes of daily grooming keeps your Chihuahua squeaky clean! But the benefits of grooming go way beyond time considerations. Brushing, for instance, helps his skin and coat stay healthy by stimulating circulation and the secretion of natural oils. It also removes dirt, dead hair, loose skin particles, and dandruff.

Grooming also makes a Chi more lovable. After all, whether his coat is sporty smooth or luxuriously long, nice, clean hair is mighty inviting for petting and hugging. No one likes to snuggle with a smelly, matted dog that's frantically scratching itself. Smelly! Not your Pepe! Don't worry. In this chapter, I talk about how just a few minutes of your time can keep your Chihuahua's coat enticing to the touch. I also discuss how you can care for his ears, teeth, nails, and eyes, and I finish up with a section on bathing your little guy.

Keeping the Shine in Your Chihuahua's Coat

Grooming your Chi's coat daily is ideal, but if that isn't possible, make three times a week the bare minimum. Caring for his coat gives you a chance to look for lumps and bruises, scratches and skin infections, and for signs of external parasites like fleas and ticks (see Chapter 14). Everything is easier to treat when discovered early.

Although most ticks are easy to spot on a smooth's sleek coat, they're a little harder to find on a long coat. Favorite hiding places are in the ears, just behind the ears, between the toes, in the thick neck hair, or in the rump area just before the tail. To uncover fleas, rough your Chi's coat in the opposite direction from the way it grows. You may not see any of the minuscule pests move, but tiny black specks on the skin will tell you that fleas are having a free lunch courtesy of Pepe. If you see the telltale specks, ask your veterinarian to recommend a treatment program (see Chapter 14) and use the products exactly as recommended.

The following sections give you some general coat care advice, discuss grooming tables, and take you through the process of brushing your Chi's coat.

A Chihuahua's coat grows in cycles. As it grows, it should look glossy, but eventually it stops growing, dries out (doesn't look quite as shiny), and finally is shed. The cycle takes a little more than one-third of a year, or about 130 days, but it varies considerably between Chis. In fact, smooth coats shed some hair all the time. Dogs that spend a lot of time outdoors always shed their winter coats in the spring, but because Chis are house pets and don't always grow winter coats, they tend to shed on their own personal schedule.

Early starts are best

How soon do you start grooming your pretty puppy? As soon as he settles in — just a day or two after you get him (see Chapter 5). Condition your Chihuahua from puppyhood to accept grooming as a fact of life, and he'll soon learn to like it. Talk to him softly at first as you work on him (go on, tell him what a handsome fellow he is!). If he becomes fidgety about being handled on any part of his body, say "No!" sharply and firmly (but not loudly or in a threatening tone) and continue grooming gently. Soon the sessions will become routine.

If your pup is adamant about not wanting you to touch a certain part of his body — his feet, for example — don't force the issue. Instead, use the peaceful ploy I present at the beginning of Chapter 9.

Grooming tables

You can groom your Chihuahua on your lap or another surface with traction if he cooperates (see Figure 7-1), but some Chi owners prefer placing their dogs on grooming tables. Special tables just for grooming are available through pet supply stores, at booths at dog shows, or in animal supply catalogs. They even come in small sizes for Toy dogs.

You can also create your own grooming table. Any tabletop does well as long as it's the right height for you to work on and stands absolutely steady, without even a hint of a wobble. Provide traction by attaching rubber matting to the top of the table. And never turn your back when your dog is on the table — not even for an instant.

Brushing

Whether your Chi is a smooth or a long coat (see Chapter 2), you'll wear less of his hair and he'll stay cleaner and need fewer baths if you brush him regularly. Just before brushing, give him a full-body massage. He'll love it because it feels good, but it serves a functional purpose, too: You're actually stimulating his skin and examining him from head to toe at the same time. Figure 7-1 shows a Chi undergoing such an examination. Now you're ready to brush.

The general brushing process

Grab a natural bristle brush for your brushing duties and then follow these steps:

1. **Place your dog so he faces away from you on your lap or on a nonslip grooming table.**

2. **Start brushing his body against the lay of the hair, from just in front of his tail to the top of his neck.**

   Giving a few strokes in the opposite direction of hair growth is the quickest way to loosen his dead hair. Do the same along each side.

3. **Brush his back, sides, neck, and legs in the same direction as his hair grows.**

Figure 7-1: During grooming, examine your dog from head to toe.

4. **Gently turn him upside down in your lap or on the table and brush his chest, belly, and the underside of his neck.**

5. **Place him right-side up and, if he's a smooth coat, finish by brushing his tail.**

6. **Praise him for being such a cooperative boy and give him a treat!**

That's all there is to it unless today is teeth-cleaning or toenail-trimming day. I tell you how to handle those procedures later in this chapter.

Brushing a long coat

If your Chihuahua is a long coat, you need a rubber comb for the finishing touches after you complete the general steps (see the preceding section). With your Chi right-side up, comb his ear fringe and the long hair on his legs (see Figure 7-2 for an example of a groomer making her way to the legs). Be gentle, but make sure you get all the way to the skin. Next, brush his tail and then comb it. Simple as that — unless his coat is (horrors!) matted.

Figure 7-2: Cindi Zablocki grooms her long coats outdoors during nice weather.

Chihuahua long coats have their own lingo. The hair on their legs is called *furnishings;* the tail hair is *a plume;* and the fine hair falling from their ears is called *fringe.*

Mats (balls of hair you can't get a comb through) seldom occur on a dog that's groomed daily, but when they do, they usually show up just behind the ears. (Of course, leg hair and tail hair is also susceptible to matting.) You can loosen minor mats with your fingers by separating each hair patiently until the mat is gone. An implement called a *mat splitter* (available at pet supply stores) usually is necessary for major mats. The splitter loosens the mat while removing the worst of it. Use it gently or it can hurt your Chi's skin and make him wary of grooming.

If you have a long-coated Chi that has gone ungroomed for too long, your best bet is to take him to a professional groomer. The pro will bathe your pup, remove the mats, trim his toenails — basically, she'll put your Chi's coat back in shape so you can easily care for it yourself.

Do your clothes and furniture look furry? Don't blame poor Chi. All that dead hair would be on your grooming brush rather than your navy suit if you brushed him daily.

Ears Looking at You Chi!

Don't forget your Chihuahua's perky ears when giving him the grooming once-over. Healthy ears are pinkish on the inside, and their edges are smooth. They don't have nicks, splits, or places along the edge where the hair is stuck together as if smeared with dark glue. When something is wrong, your nose may be the first to know. That's because nasty odors or discharges are early signs that ear mites have set up camp. These pests live in the ear canal, irritating your Chihuahua's sensitive ears and producing a dry, rusty-brown or black discharge.

Even if no unusual odor or discharge is present, suspect something if your Chi paws at his ears, shakes his head, or stands with his head unnaturally cocked to the side. Ear mites are easily banished, and ear infections are quickly cured, when discovered early. As soon as you see any of these signs of trouble, visit your veterinarian.

Are your dog's ears driving you crazy because they're erect one day and flopped over the next? The ears may be all over the place because he's teething. A Chi's ears generally stay up by the time it's 6 months old, but if your Chi's ears are still hanging like a hound dawg's by the time he's 8 months old, you may as well learn to like it. They're going to stay that way!

Keeping Those Pearlies White

According to the American Veterinary Medical Association (AVMA), 80 percent of adult dogs develop gum disease by the time they're 3 years old. That is outrageous and unnecessary. If you brush your Chihuahua's teeth three or four times a week (no, I'm not kidding), you can keep plaque under control.

If you can, start when your Chi is a puppy so he can become accustomed to having his teeth brushed. For puppies and older Chis, follow these steps to start down the road to a healthy mouth:

1. **Begin by letting him get used to you lifting up his lips and gently touching his teeth and gums with your finger.**

   The more matter-of-fact you are about it, the sooner he'll learn to live with it.

2. **When he stops pulling away from your finger, introduce him to a soft toothbrush; either the smallest one made for dogs or one made for human babies.**

At first, just touch his teeth with it, but gradually apply a little more pressure.

3. **When he tolerates that, move the brush so it touches his back teeth and gradually add pressure.**

4. **Finally, use a gentle up-and-down brushing motion all around his mouth.**

It won't be long before you can clean all of his teeth with relative ease.

Pet supply stores sell toothpaste and toothbrushes for dogs in a variety of flavors; you may even find one that makes your pup look forward to his brushings. But don't count on it! If he hates all the varieties you try, using plain warm water is better than no brushing at all.

Never use a toothpaste meant for people on your Chihuahua. Adult toothpaste is bad for dogs and probably upsets their stomachs.

At least once a year (twice is better), ask your vet to check your Pepe for plaque or early signs of gum disease. A professional cleaning may be necessary if his teeth have been neglected for years.

The following sections dig a little deeper into a couple more oral issues you should consider.

Removing retained puppy teeth

Dogs, just like people, have two sets of teeth during their lifetimes. The puppy, or *deciduous,* teeth should all be gone by the time your Chi is 6 or 7 months old, replaced by permanent teeth. But that isn't always what happens. Toy dogs often have a problem with deciduous teeth refusing to fall out to make room for the emerging permanent teeth. This creates havoc in a dog's mouth. When permanent teeth can't slip into their slots because baby teeth are blocking them, they grow in whatever direction they can. The result is a mouthful of crowded teeth pointing every which way.

Now that you're aware of the possibility, don't let it happen to your dog. Just by looking into his mouth, you can tell if a new tooth is trying to emerge before a baby tooth falls out. Take him to your veterinarian so she can remove the retained baby tooth so that the permanent one can come in strong and straight.

Heeding the symptoms of gum disease

If your Chihuahua was an adult when you got him, he may already have gum disease. The symptoms of gum disease are

✔ Bad breath

✔ Swollen, bright red, or bleeding gums

✔ Tartar against the gum line

✔ Loose or infected teeth

Sometimes dogs that appear to be finicky eaters actually are hungry, but they have such sore mouths that they chew only enough to survive. If your pup has any symptoms of gum disease, see your veterinarian right away.

Most adult dogs have 42 permanent teeth, but Toy dogs, with their tiny mouths, often have fewer than that.

Puppy-cure: Trimming the Toenails

A Chihuahua's toenails are too long if they make clicking noises on the floor when he walks or touch the ground when he stands still. Dogs with long nails are forced to walk on the backs of their feet, leading to *splayed* (that's dog lingo for "spread") toes and an awkward gait. When untrimmed for months, toenails and *dewclaws* (the higher, useless extra toenail that your dog may or may not have) eventually curl under the foot, circling back to puncture the pads.

Are you wondering why wolves, coyotes, and even stray dogs trot along just fine even though no one trims their toenails? In their quest for food, these animals cover enough ground to wear down their nails to a practical length — something that won't occur during Pepe's stroll from the carpet to the tile.

Trim your dog's toenails a minimum of once a month; once every two weeks is better. My favorite type of toenail clipper for Chihuahuas is the small, guillotine-style implement, although others on the market work just fine.

Don't trim your Chi's toenails during the first week you have him. Instead, get him used to having his feet touched first (see Chapter 9).

Some people use a grooming table when trimming nails (see the section "Grooming tables" earlier in this chapter); others do the clipping when their Chihuahuas are on their backs in their laps. Pick the place and posture that works best for you and your dog, and then follow these steps:

1. **Start the job by lifting your Chi's foot up and forward.**

2. **Hold his foot firmly but gently in your left hand so your right hand can do the trimming (reverse this if you're left-handed).**

3. **Avoid cutting the quick by trimming the nail just outside of the vein.**

   You won't be able to see the quick in dark nails, so trim just the tip of the nail, at the point where it starts curling downward. If he has white or light nails, your job is easier because the blood vessel inside each nail is easily seen through a light-colored nail.

Trim his nails properly, and your Chi will feel nothing more than slight pressure — the same as you feel when trimming your own toenails. If you accidentally cut the quick, his nail hurts and bleeds. Stop the bleeding with a styptic pencil made for people, or you can use the styptic powder sold at pet supply stores. In an emergency, pressing the bleeding nail into a soft bar of soap for a minute or so also will stop the bleeding.

 Without a doubt, a dog prefers prevention. Work under good lighting so you can cut his nails without a mishap. Your dog may forgive a cut quick if it's a rare occurrence; but if you hurt his toes often, he'll struggle and scream when you try to work on his feet. Wouldn't you?

Chihuahuas that are terrified of having their toenails trimmed morph into monsters at the sight of a toenail clipper. If your Chi is scared, it may take two people to accomplish the nail clip — one to hold him and the other to wield the clipper. But remember, regardless of how frustrating the job becomes, no rough stuff. That tiny leg you're holding is breakable. If you can't do the job safely at home, don't hesitate to take your Chi to the veterinarian or a professional groomer for his trimmings.

Gazing into Your Chi's Eyes

Oh, those big, beautiful eyes — the mirrors of a Chihuahua's semi-sweet soul. To keep them sparkling, all you have to do (most of you, anyway) is occasionally wipe a bit of "sleep" out of the corners with a clean, damp cloth.

Does your Chi have stains under his eyes that make him look like a woman leaving a tearjerker movie with mascara traces on her cheeks? His stains are *tearstains;* but, trust me, your dog didn't cry when Leonardo died in *Titanic.* When a Chihuahua has tear ducts that are too small, the overflow trickles down his face. To combat the issue, wipe the area every morning with a soft cloth dipped into distilled water (it becomes a habit like washing your own face).

Although no treatment for tiny tear ducts exists, check with your veterinarian about the issue anyway. Some tearstains may be caused by an infection called *conjunctivitis;* by *entropian,* a genetic condition where the eyelashes turn in and rub the cornea; or by *ectropia,* a condition where the lower eyelid sags and lets in foreign matter. Your vet needs to check out the situation. The good news is that these problems aren't common in the Chihuahua.

If your Chi doesn't have tearstains, his eyes won't need any special care unless he develops a problem (see Chapter 15). Just use common sense in your day-to-day dealings. Don't get shampoo in his eyes (even the tear-free type); never spray insecticide near his head; and don't let him put his curious orbs out of the car window. If a small stone hits him in the face while you're driving, the consequences can be tragic.

Bathing Your Beauty

Your Chihuahua seldom needs a bath if you brush him regularly (see the section "Keeping the Shine in Your Chihuahua's Coat"). And that's a good thing. Shampooing washes away the natural oils that moisturize his coat and skin, so bathe your Chi only when necessary — no more than once a month, unless he rolls in something smelly. Actually, many experts say one bath every two months is best. The following sections let you know what to bring to bath time, how to execute the bath, and how to properly care for your long-coated Chi.

The well-equipped bath

Gather up all your Chihuahua's bathing equipment before you get started so you won't have to turn your eyes away from a soapy-slick dog after you begin. Here's what you need:

✔ Old clothes for you

When your pup shakes, you get wet, too!

✔ A tub, preferably with a drain, so your Chi won't have to stand in soapy water

Many Toy dog owners use the sink for baths, because it's much easier on the back (and you can use the spray tool). But if you put your dog in the sink, don't take your eyes or hands off him for even an instant. A leap to the floor could be fatal.

✔ A rubber bath mat for traction in the tub or part of a rubber mat to line the sink

✔ An unbreakable cup for dipping water or a spray hose attachment

✔ A pH-balanced dog shampoo, or insecticide shampoo or dip if necessary

✔ Coat conditioner for dogs (this is optional but nice — especially for long coats)

✔ Cotton balls

✔ A washcloth

✔ Mineral oil

✔ A nice fluffy, terry-cloth towel (100-percent cotton)

Let's get wet!

The following list presents the simple steps (or so I say) for bathing your slick little Chi.

Wait! Before putting your Chihuahua into the tub or sink, take him for a walk outside and give him time to relieve himself. Otherwise, the excitement of bath time may make him want to or have to rush outdoors immediately after his bath, which is a bad idea. He needs to stay inside until he's thoroughly dry, because Chis get chilled easily.

1. **Begin by placing a cotton ball inside each of your dog's ears (gently; don't push it too far down) to keep the water out.**

2. **Spray or pour warm water (temperature test it on the inside of your arm) over his whole body, with the exception of his face and head.**

   Massage him gently as you wet him, helping the water soak in to the skin.

3. **Put a few drops of shampoo on his back, spread it around, and massage the lather into his coat.**

   Add a drop or two as needed to soap his legs, underbelly, tail, and neck.

4. **Now you've reached the most important part of the procedure: the rinse.**

   Never rush this step. If shampoo dries in his coat, he'll itch like crazy and you'll rob his hair of its shine.

5. **After the rinse, use coat conditioner (optional), following the label directions and rinsing it out well.**

6. **After his body is rinsed, wet a washcloth in warm water, wring it out well, and wipe his face and head.**

7. **Remove the cotton balls from his ears and clean each ear gently (again, not too far down) with a fresh cotton ball dipped in a tiny bit of mineral oil.**

8. **Wrap him in a towel and dry him thoroughly — from his ear tips to his toes.**

   Pay special attention to his easily chilled chest and underbelly.

Finishing touches for your long coat

After towel drying your long coat, you need to finish the job with a hand-held blow dryer. Don't spend much time drying the same spot, and don't hold the dryer too close to his body, because the hot air can burn a Chi's coat and skin. Use the warm setting (if your dryer has one) and blow his coat in the direction it grows — starting at his neck and working toward his *plume* (yup, that's the tail).

When long-coated Pepe is dry, brush him with a natural-bristle brush. Then use a hard rubber comb on his ear fringe, *furnishings* (the long hair on his legs), and plume. Wow! I bet he's gorgeous. And he knows it! Just watch him strut when you put him down.

Is the thick hair around your Chi's anus often dirty? Use a pair of sharp scissors and trim away just a little bit of hair from each side of the anus and from just below it. That should keep it from becoming soiled during bowel movements. Trim carefully so you don't break the skin.

Chapter 8

Chirobics: For Fitness and Fun

. . . .

In This Chapter

▶ Exercising and bonding with your Chi

▶ Teaching your petite player new games

▶ Seniorcizing with your mature dog

. . . .

*A*lthough Chihuahuas are small enough critters to get a good workout in a one-room apartment, many become obese because their owners don't encourage them to be active. Poor owners (and Chis). They don't know how much fun they're missing! Sure, exercise is essential to your Chi's health, but it can also be a great bonding experience for you both — and tons of fun. Exercise doesn't have to feel like work. In this chapter, I tell you how to make your Chihuahua's bodybuilding breaks so much fun that you'll find yourself looking forward to them, too. I also include some advice for exercising senior Chis, because they need activity, too!

Make Exercise a Happy Habit

Make exercise a habit for your Chi, even if its form changes from day to day. Otherwise, your puppy may become the pudgy and pooped type. If Chihuahuas were people, you'd find them in the hammock on sunny summer days instead of hiking, canoeing, or swimming. Many Chis become lazy while still young in life.

If your Chi leads a moderately active life, instead of becoming a couch puppy, she'll look much better *and* live longer. The muscles rippling beneath her coat aren't the only ones that exercise strengthens and tones. Her heart is almost entirely muscle, and even her intestine contains muscle tissue. Regular exercise keeps a healthy supply of blood circulating through these vital muscles. Chances are, if your Chi gets enough exercise, she'll behave better, too. Simply giving a problem puppy more exercise cures countless behavior problems!

What's the best way to exercise a Chi? A brisk walk, an indoor game, or playing with another Chihuahua all help keep her fit. *Note:* Although your Chihuahua may play with a variety of small dogs, most Chis prefer their own kind.

When it comes to exercise, though, variety is best. I know a professional trainer whose motto is, "Never let your body know what you are going to make it do next." According to her, if you get on an exercise schedule and stick with it day after boring day, your body gets so used to it that the workout stops being as beneficial as it should be. Vary your regimen so your Chi's body has to stay fit to handle an assortment of activities. Now doesn't that make exercising your Chi easy? You may try a walk around the block one day (see Figure 8-1) and an indoor game the next. You can even exercise her from your recliner (or lawn chair if you have a fenced yard)! Organized activities like obedience and agility (see Chapter 12) also provide exercise for dogs (and their owners).

Figure 8-1: When it comes to exercise, nothing beats a brisk walk.

Any form of exercise you and your Chi feel like doing is fine, as long as it keeps her moving and isn't too much for her. Too much? Yes, you can overdo exercise with a tiny dog. Compare a Chihuahua's stride to the stride of a Labrador Retriever or other big dog. See the difference? It isn't that tiny dogs don't need as much exercise as big dogs — they do — but they can satisfy their exercise needs in much less time, using much less space.

The next time you take your pup for a walk, notice how many strides she takes to keep up with just one of yours. Sure, she can do it, and it's good for her, too, but within reason. If you stroll too far, or the day is hot and humid, give her a rest in the shade and a drink of water at the halfway point, or simply carry her home.

Although the type of exercise you give a Chihuahua isn't important, consistency is. She needs exercise in some form all her life. When she's young, your Manchita may help you invent games that provide excellent exercise. When she's a senior, you may have to initiate play. The following sections in this chapter dig deeper into these topics.

Games You and Your Chihuahua Can Play

The time has come to introduce your sweet Chi to some fun games. Some Chihuahua games are so much fun, you forget that their main purpose is your Chi's health! Most healthy, well-adjusted puppies learn physical games in a jiffy, but adult dogs that have never played take a lot longer to adjust. If your mature Chihuahua isn't interested in playing games after a week or two of opportunities, don't give up. First, check your attitude. Perhaps you're trying too hard and making it look like work rather than fun. Next, check your timing. Was your Chi full from dinner or even sleeping when you tried to excite her? A change of attitude or timing may be all it takes to turn her into an avid game player (see Figure 8-2).

When playing games with your pup, treat her like the healthy animal she is, but don't overwhelm her with your physical superiority. Because food is a reward in many games, play before her mealtime so she wants to earn a tasty tidbit. Is she a little chunky? Give her a smaller supper if she eats several treats during playtime.

The games I describe in the following sections are fun for Toy dogs of all ages. Show your Chi how to play these games when you're in a good mood, and always stop playing *before* she wants to. No matter how much fun a game is, it will feel like work if you keep at it until she's bored or tired. But if you quit while your Chihuahua is still having fun, she'll always be eager for the next round.

Figure 8-2: Cricket's owners encourage her to exercise by playing games with her and providing her with soft toys to play-kill.

Tile and other hard, slippery floor surfaces make maneuvering difficult for dogs. Exercise your Chi on flooring with good traction, on the rug, or in the grass. And participate with her. Even if you have a Chihuahua-safe fenced-in yard, putting your dog outside for an hour or so during nice weather doesn't guarantee her a good workout. Chihuahuas don't like to exercise alone any more than most people do. Indoors or out, a Chi won't get active without a companion. And that companion is you, unless you have more than one dog!

Hide 'n seek

Some physical games are also educational for your Chi. Hide 'n seek is one that may enhance your Chi's memory and scenting ability. Start playing hide-and-seek by following these steps:

1. **Put your pup in another room and close the door.**

2. **Hide a treat in a different room, perhaps beside a table leg or under a chair (the type she can easily walk under).**

3. **Open the door, and when she comes into the room, tell her to "Find It" in an excited voice.**

   Of course, she won't know what you mean at first, so keep repeating the words while encouraging her toward the treat.

4. **Help her locate the goodie, but let her make the actual find.**

   In other words, she must pick up the treat from the floor, not your hand. When she does, tell her "Goood Dooog" (dogs love words with stretched out sounds) while she eats it — a double reward!

5. **Put her back in the other room and place another treat exactly where the first one was.**

6. **Open the door, say "Find It," and watch what she does.**

   You'll probably have to help her find the treat a few times before she goes straight to it on her own.

7. **When she succeeds by herself, repeat the game one more time and then quit for the day. (No, that wasn't enough action to count as exercise, but later on this game gets lively!)**

8. **Use the same hiding place for the next few days; soon, she'll race to the treat all by herself on the first try, with you cheering her on, of course.**

9. **When she does, throw her a curve. Put the treat in a new hiding place, farther from the starting point, and start over by helping her find it.**

   Don't tell her "No!" when she goes back to the original spot. She's finding out how to use her memory, and that's good. Instead, have a treat waiting in the old hiding place every so often (once every five to ten times). Eventually, your Chi will remember several rewarding locations (from one end of the house to the other) and will sprint from room to room until she finds her treats.

10. **Continue adding new hiding places (after she's familiar with all the old ones) as long as she enjoys the game.**

    Chances are, she may start exercising her sense of smell as well as her body and her memory.

Variations of hide 'n seek are easy to create. Adding a second person, perhaps your spouse or child, is one way. Have the person hide behind the drapes or in a closet with the door slightly ajar. Instead of saying "Find It," ask her "Where's Tom?" Meanwhile, Tom's waiting to reward her with a treat.

Catch 'n release

Make yourself a Chihuahua fishing rod and bait it to catch your Chi! Use a piece of string about 5 or 6 feet long and tie one end of it to a stick. Bait the other end by tying on a small stuffed animal or a squeaky toy. Now sit down and start fishing. Puppies usually can't resist little twitches, but try a variety of "casts" to see what movements attract your dog.

Read your dog and make adjustments for her temperament when teaching and playing games. Some Chihuahuas love to hear you clap and cheer and will play all the harder to keep excitement in the air. Others tend to be more timid, and owners who double as pro cheerleaders may spook them under their couches.

Munchkin in the middle

Munchkin in the middle takes two people and a rubber ball that's small enough for your Chihuahua to hold in her mouth but too big for her to swallow. Use the ball only for playing games together, and put it away when fun time is over.

To play the game, the partners sit on the floor facing each other, with about 8 feet separating them. From this position, they roll the ball back and forth. You may want to put on a show to entice your Chi to join in at first, so laugh and act like scooping up the ball is a really big deal. If your partner is a child, remind the youngster to roll the ball gently so your Chi doesn't shy away from it.

Manchita should get curious about all the fun on the floor and try to intercept the ball. When she captures it, clap and cheer her on for a few seconds while she parades her prize (many dogs strut with pride when they capture a ball). Then say "Out," take the ball from her by trading it for a treat, and start the game over. Gradually increase the distance between the partners so your Chi must run farther when chasing the ball. Be sure to keep her interested by letting her win sometimes (but not all the time!).

Fetching fun

Fetching (retrieving) games are favorites with some Chihuahuas, but others have no interest in them at all. Any number of objects — from sticks, to small balls, to miniature flying discs — are suitable for fetching games, as long as their diameters and weights are compatible with a Chihuahua's size.

Tiny dogs running free in Aztec palaces!

During the 500 years that the Aztecs ruled Mexico, they had tiny dogs that were pampered by the rich but ignored and sometimes even eaten (according to some historians) by the poor. *Montezuma II,* last emperor of the Aztec nation, supposedly kept hundreds of Chihuahuas' ancestors running free in his palace to assure him of a smooth journey after death. Another legend describes an Aztec princess who kept more than a thousand tiny dogs, and each one had its own servant. When a dog died, its servant was slain so he or she could take care of the dog in the next world.

The Techichi's fortunes fell when the Conquistadors, led by Hernando Cortez, conquered the Aztec nation early in the 16th century. It's said that the Spanish conquerors used the Indians' pets and holy dogs for meat. In fact, some historians believe the Conquistadors ate so many Techichis that the tiny dogs nearly became extinct. And for the next 300 years, nothing much is known about Chihuahua history.

When rolling or tossing something to play fetch with your pup, seeing it leave your hand is important for her — especially if she's a rookie. If she chases the object and brings it all the way back to you, give her a treat and rejoice — she's a natural! But if the more likely scenario occurs — your Chi chases the object, picks it up, and parades it triumphantly without bringing it back — attach a long leash to her collar before the game begins (see Chapter 5 for more on this equipment). After she chases and picks up the object, you can gently reel her in while encouraging her in a happy tone. When she brings the object all the way back to you, trade it for a treat. If she drops it long before she reaches you, don't give her anything, but don't be upset, either. Many Chihuahuas don't have a strong retrieving instinct — but that doesn't mean you should give up. Keep trying occasionally, even if she shows no desire to retrieve. Chis have been known to change their minds a time or two!

 If your Chihuahua loves chasing the object but won't retrieve it, play ball with three or four balls at a time. Roll one in a straight line. Roll the next one sideways so it rebounds off the wall. Toss the next one so it bounces gently. You get the picture. Soon your Chi will run in all directions.

 Always roll the object away from (never toward) your Chi. You want to awaken her chasing instinct, not spook her into thinking that a strange object is heading for her. Make your tosses short at first, and increase the distance gradually as she catches on.

If retrieving excites your Chi, keep her in that state of mind by limiting the number of times you play to four or five in a row, which is plenty. After that, play something else. If she becomes a fetching fanatic, add variations to the game by rolling the ball a little faster and a lot farther; rolling it so it rebounds off a wall; or throwing it (not hard) so it bounces (instead of rolls) away from her.

Note: If your Chi learns to fetch well — bringing her ball all the way back to you every time — you'll be able to exercise her the lazy way: right from your recliner!

The word retriever is part of some dogs' breed names. The Labrador Retriever, the Golden Retriever, the Chesapeake Bay Retriever, and the Flat-Coated Retriever are just some of the breeds that are born with the inclination to retrieve. And even they need training to hone their natural talents!

Play-killing a critter

Play-killing a squeaky toy is good exercise, and most Chihuahuas love this sport. If your Chi starts playing this game as a pup, she'll always get excited when you bring out her mousie, hedgehog, or whatever critter she loves to "kill." But if you acquired her as an adult and she never learned to play, she may be clueless about what to do with her new critter.

First, give your Chihuahua time to settle into her new home and actively seek out your attention. When she begins to trust you, it's time to uncover her sense of humor. To do it, you need to set an example by acting silly first (try it, you'll like it!) and encouraging her to follow suit.

Choose an exciting squeaky toy with plenty of appendages so her small mouth can easily grip it. Play with the toy yourself while she watches. Throw it, catch it, drop it, and chase it, amid plenty of laughter. That should get her attention.

As she watches you enjoy the toy, occasionally, and only briefly, tease her with it, but don't give it to her. If another family member joins in, you can roll the toy to each other, squeak it, and shake it — but don't get wild enough to frighten an insecure dog. After two or three minutes of fun, "accidentally" drop the toy near her to see if she shows interest in it. If she ignores it, pick it up and continue playing for another minute. Then put the toy away until another day.

The first time your Chi takes the toy, allow her to play with it without interference for about 20 seconds. At that point, trade it for a treat, play with it yourself for a few seconds, and then put it away.

Soon, she'll want a longer turn, so she'll probably amuse you by tossing and pouncing on the toy and shaking it as hard as she can. Let her play huntress for awhile and then trade the toy for a treat and put it away. Bring the toy out only for this special game, because toys with squeakers aren't suitable for everyday use.

It isn't a good idea to play tug of war with your dog because it teaches her to compete with you for ownership of objects. Not cool when the object happens to be the cuff of your pants! And dogs just don't understand the difference between safe tug objects and off-limits tug objects.

Exercising Your Super Senior

One of the wonderful things about dogs is that deep down inside, they'll always be puppies. They don't outgrow their toys or become too serious to act silly. Your dog needs exercise all her life. An old dog may amble rather than trot, and that's just fine. But most senior Chihuahuas retain their sense of humor and their desire to participate in activities.

The same games puppies play appeal to Chihuahuas of all ages — especially when a treat is involved. Many sassy seniors still play-kill their mousies, and hide 'n seek is a perennial favorite. Watch your golden oldie's weight, though, and reduce the size of her dinner if she already downed several treats.

Keep your mature Chi interested by varying the routine — a nice, slightly-longer-than-usual walk one day and an indoor game the next. Daily physical activity — even a mild activity such as walking — will help keep your senior's muscles strong and her weight down.

If your old dog suddenly ignores her favorite toy, refuses to play the games she's always loved, or doesn't get excited about going for a walk, see your veterinarian (see Chapter 13). Something may be very wrong.

Part III
Positive Training for Your Petite Pal

The 5th Wave   By Rich Tennant

"Oh, we've got to nip this little trick in the bud right away."

In this part . . .

*E*veryone loves a confident, well-mannered dog.
Therefore, everyone will love your dog if you heed
the advice of Part III! Here you find out how to give your
Chihuahua a solid base for a happy life. I discuss socialization
methods to begin your training. I cover everything from
housetraining to commands you can teach your puppy. I
help you get back on track if your Chi claims ownership of
the household. Finally, for those pups that master training
and obedience, I explore the world of dog shows and other
obedience and athletic events that owners and dogs can
participate in together.

Even if you've never trained a dog before, just follow my
time-tested methods and your precocious pet can mature
into a mannerly, responsive member of the household.
Good dog!

Chapter 9

Socializing Your Chihuahua

You can raise a puppy only once, so if you're lucky enough to have the opportunity, make the most of it. Socialization is a very important aspect of bringing a dog into your home. It is, simply, the responsible thing to do — for a new puppy or new adult. In this chapter, I tell you how to bond with your Chihuahua, read her body language, and help her gain confidence. You also find out how to teach your Chi to walk on lead and safely introduce her to the world. I even include a section on kindergarten puppy training, better known as KPT. Both of you will have some mighty good times as your little Manchita learns to share her Chi charm with an admiring public.

Building a Bond with Your Chi

Bonding can be relaxing for both you and your Chi. Chihuahuas love attention and body warmth, so holding your puppy in your lap is one of the better ways to bond with her. And she won't mind if you read or watch television at the same time! While you're holding your dog, you can condition her to be tolerant of touch. If she lets you handle every part of her body — from the tip of her nose to the pads of her toes (see Figure 9-1) — it becomes easier to groom and medicate her. Besides, all that touchy-feely stuff lowers your blood pressure (honest, petting dogs does that).

Is your Chi sensitive about having her tootsies touched? Many puppies are, but she'll get over it if you deal with it right away. No, don't force the issue. Instead, pet your puppy in places she enjoys until she's nearly asleep. As she becomes limp, continue stroking her body, but include her feet as well. If she tenses up, go back to petting only her body until she's sleepy enough that you can try her feet again. After she falls asleep (and she will), gently massage the toes of all four feet. Soon, your puppy will relax and let you touch her toes when she's awake, too, and that makes toenail trimming much easier (see Chapter 7). If she resists being touched on other parts of her body, use the same method to overcome those aversions.

Be yourself around your new dog and incorporate her schedule into your routine. If your pup is napping and you want to watch TV or play the piano, do it. Your puppy can sleep through normal household noises.

Figure 9-1: Pet your Chi from her ear tips to her toes.

Interpreting Body Language (And Preventing Anxiety)

Dogs may not talk (except on those amusing old Taco Bell commercials and in movies), but if you pay attention to your Chi's body language, you soon find out how to read her needs and even predict her next moves. Your Chi communicates through her facial expressions, using her ears, eyes, brows, lips, nose, and mouth. She also talks through her tail, coat (hackles), and body position, and she emits a variety of sounds.

Communicating with dogs comes naturally to many youngsters, but adults need to concentrate on it because they seldom take time to sit back and use their powers of observation. In fact, the older people get, the more they rely on verbal communication and lose their nonverbal skills. To give your Chi the best care, you need to know her intimately. Sit back and study the differences in her body language and facial expressions when she's happy, curious, anxious, proud of herself, and sleepy. Soon you'll be able to *read* your dog.

To start you off, here are some descriptions of general canine body language:

- ✓ **A relaxed dog wags her tail in a methodical, neutral position — her tail isn't high, tucked under, or stiff.** Her mouth may be slightly open, and her ears look relaxed (rather than fully alert). Her eyes appear soft, without a trace of threat or tension, and her weight is evenly distributed on all four legs.

- ✓ **A dominant or aggressive dog tries to appear larger.** She stands absolutely erect, holds her tail either straight out or up, and raises her hackles (the fur on top of her back). Her mouth usually is closed, and she makes eye contact with her adversary.

- ✓ **A submissive, shy, or frightened dog makes herself smaller by contracting her body.** She tucks her tail, flattens her ears, averts her eyes, and appears to shrink slightly.

- ✓ **When a dog greets you with her rear end up, front end low, a wagging tail, and lively eyes, she's play-bowing.** This is dog language for "Let's play."

- ✓ **If she flicks her tongue up to lick her nose over and over, a dog is uneasy about something.** Maybe she's checking out your new friend or concentrating hard to learn a new trick. In some cases, tongue flicking precedes snapping.

✔ **Mounting has more to do with dominance than sex.** Does your Chi ever mount another dog or stand on her hind legs with her paws on another dog's back? This is her way of saying, "I'm top dog here, and don't you forget it."

Okay, the following sections take it from here by presenting more behaviors and giving you more advice. And remember, although the body language in the previous list is universal, your dog will have many unique mannerisms all her own. Enjoy!

Understanding the "jitters"

A jittery dog acts frightened. You can recognize this behavior by her tightly tucked tail, contracted body (to appear smaller), and flattened ears. However, sometimes you won't see her body because she'll be hiding behind your legs or the sofa. Chihuahuas often shake all over when they're scared, but shaking alone isn't a good indicator of fear. Chis also may shake from cold or even from extreme happiness or excitement.

Some dogs are born nervous because of poor breeding, but most scaredy-pups act jittery because they weren't socialized at the right time. If a dog isn't socialized during its puppyhood, it never becomes as confident a companion as it can be (see the following section). You can understand an unsocialized dog's jitters by looking at the following scenario with a human child.

Imagine how a child (I'll call him Bobby) would react on his first day of school if he had been so overprotected by his parents that it was also his first experience away from home. Bobby's anxiety increases during the walk or drive to school. Traffic sounds startle him, and the sight of so many strange buildings, vehicles, and people confuses him. When he arrives, the big school building intimidates him — especially if he doesn't know how to navigate stairs. In the classroom, Bobby's fear of the strange adult called Teacher keeps him from focusing on the lesson. On the playground, he doesn't know how to respond to his high-spirited classmates. Feeling vulnerable and uncertain, he may back into a corner or become defensive and try to fight off the first child who approaches.

Here's another bad scenario: What if Bobby went on two outings before starting school? Both times, he visited his pediatrician for vaccinations. In his mind, leaving home, entering a strange building, and meeting a stranger all correlate to pain. Now Bobby can't relax or trust his teacher and consequently doesn't learn. A classroom observer who doesn't know Bobby's history probably labels him as shy or stupid — perhaps even stubborn.

Luckily for children, scenarios like that seldom occur because most parents take their kids out often. But puppies — especially Toy breed puppies — don't always have it so good. Some are raised like poor Bobby.

Good breeders socialize their puppies before selling them; the best refuse to sell a puppy before it's 3 months old. And don't worry. Even though the puppy loves its breeder, it transfers that love to you in no time. Besides, socialization is ongoing, and plenty of fun stuff is left for you and your puppy to do. Chapters 3 and 4 discuss socialization and buying from a good breeder. The rest of the sections in this chapter also dive deeper into dog socialization.

Using the first 16 weeks wisely

The first 16 weeks of your dog's life are critical to her social development. What a puppy discovers during that short time shapes her personality — making her outgoing or shy, happy-go-lucky or cautious. The brief time correlates to when wild animals explore outside the den for the first time, quickly learning lessons in survival. Absorbing everything in a hurry is a necessity, because a cub that makes a mistake in the wild rarely gets a second chance.

Although domesticated for centuries, dogs still arrive in the world programmed to relate to their surroundings during their first four months. In an ideal situation, a pup finds out how to behave around dogs during her first two months, which is why a good Chihuahua breeder keeps a litter together until the puppies are at least 8 weeks old. Between 8 weeks and 12 weeks, the youngsters become mentally mature enough to leave their canine family; this is the ideal age to settle into human families. From then on, their people shape their personalities.

If you're lucky enough to acquire a Chi when she's still a young puppy (under 4 months old), you can help her establish (or keep) an outgoing attitude. Introduce her to a friendly world and she'll grow up confident — a canine clown that shows off for your friends and likes finding out new things. But if you keep her secluded, she'll begin to fear anything unusual.

It's Party Time! Introducing Your Chi to Guests

Socializing has one big dilemma: Your Chi needs to meet plenty of people before she's 12 weeks old, but she's prohibited from going out in public places where she could encounter unvaccinated dogs until her series of shots is complete (see Chapter 13), which usually takes between 12 and 16 weeks. Breeders who keep their puppies for three months or more have their own socializing programs, but you may bring home a younger pup than that. No problem. The solution is simple — and fun. Let your dog meet new people right in your home by throwing a few puppy parties.

Introduce your Chi to men, women, and well-supervised children by inviting a small group of friends over for dessert or a video. Place a bowl of your pup's dry food on the goodie table so your friends can hand-feed her. Show your helpers how to hold a puppy (see Chapter 5) and ask them to take turns holding, feeding, and petting your pup.

Try to have several of informal get-togethers before your girl turns 12 weeks old, making sure you include men, women, and children of various ages (supervised, of course).

Going for a short drive every so often keeps your dog from associating riding in the car with receiving a shot. Ask your dogless friends or friends with well-behaved, healthy dogs if you and your puppy can stop by for a few minutes. Investigating new places and meeting new people is wonderful for your Chi, provided that there's no chance of contacting a doggie disease. By the time she's vaccinated and ready for real outings, she'll feel secure around strangers and comfortable in the car. In other words, she'll be ready to experience the world!

Leaving Home: Hello, World!

Every time your Chi meets someone new or leaves the house, she's socializing. Taking her with you when you visit a friend socializes her. So does meeting someone while out for a walk, playing with another puppy, or examining a beach ball.

The world is your Chi's playground, so she needs to get out and enjoy it as soon as she's safely vaccinated (see Chapter 13). Few people can pass up an adorable Chihuahua, and your pup benefits

Chihuahuas love to be loved and are true companion dogs. They need affection to thrive and socialization to cultivate their character.

Every Chihuahua should have her own snug bed, complete with a toy or two.

Some long-coated Chihuahuas have more hair than others. This one sports a thick coat.

The Chihuahua standard describes the breed as alert, with a saucy expression and terrier-like qualities.

What will these puppies be like when they grow up? They'll probably be a lot like their parents, so ask to meet their dam (mom) and any other family members the breeder has on the premises.

This charmer's eye-catching coat comes from good breeding, good nutrition, and good grooming.

Although they are too little to stop a thief, Chihuahuas are alert watch-dogs. If those big ears detect a stranger's footsteps, he'll race to the door, barking a warning.

MARY BLOOM

A nice thing about Chihuahuas is that they take up so little room on the furniture.

MARY BLOOM

It can take several weeks for puppy ears to become erect, and they don't always do it at the same time. Occasionally, the Chi's ears refuse to stand even after the pup is grown. The result is a dog that won't win in the show ring but can still be a super pet.

This puppy is performing a friendship dance and should soon have a partner.

Every Chi should know how to walk on lead and obey basic commands like sit, down, and come.

Chihuahuas are the ultimate housedog. They can get enough exercise indoors, but will gladly join you in any outside activity.

Even though Chis are small in size, they can still enjoy and excel on the agility course.

Chihuahuas have well-rounded heads, often referred to as "apple domes."

This Chi's a party animal ready to howl "Happy Birthday!"

Chihuahuas are very social animals. You can tell by his body language that this smooth coat wants to play.

Although Chis are too tiny to associate with toddlers, they are content in the arms of gentle school-age children (under supervision, of course).

Chihuahuas chill easily. A good sweater will keep her warm on a cold winter's day.

from these admiring people. She needs to meet senior citizens and gentle kids, bearded men and ladies in sun hats, teenagers carrying skateboards, and people pushing strollers.

Never, ever let your Chihuahua run free outside — not even for a second. Always put a leash on her when she's outside the safety of your home and fenced yard (see the later section "Walking on a Lead"). And no matter how outgoing your Chi is or how well she walks on a leash, always keep her in your arms when riding an elevator. If it gives a sudden lurch or people rush on without watching where they're going, she can get stepped on.

While safely outside (in your arms or on a leash), your Chi gets used to hearing motors, sirens, and the rumble of the garbage truck. Whatever you do, though, don't hold her all the time. She needs to walk on grass and pavement and find out how to navigate stairs.

If your house doesn't have steps, find some elsewhere and show your dog how to manage them. Start by putting her on the third step and encouraging her to come down to you. When she gets good at that, place her at the bottom of the stairs, sit on the third or fourth step, and encourage her to climb up to you.

The more people your Chi meets, the more she experiences, and the more sights she sees before she's 4 months old, the braver she becomes. And confident Chihuahuas are the most fun of all. The following sections explain how you can help your pup overcome fear of the world and how you can take her to class to help with your socialization efforts.

Helping your pup overcome fear

Think of socialization as a game with two rules:

1. Never pet your puppy when she's afraid.

2. Always praise your puppy for being brave.

When your Chi appears scared you'll want to comfort her, but that's a major mistake. Why? Because she interprets your pats and soothing words as praise. Anything a puppy is praised for she'll repeat again and again, so cringing behind your legs can become her learned reaction to anything new. On the other hand, never jerk her toward an object she fears. Treatment like that can turn a little trepidation into total terror.

Your Chi may be afraid of things in many different places. The following list gives you some tips for curbing your Chi's fear in different areas:

✓ **Objects in your home:** What do you do if your pup is afraid to investigate a new object in your house? Leave her where she is and go yourself. Handle the object like it's a winning lottery ticket and invite her to join you. Sitting down beside the feared object works especially well. Your puppy may start creeping toward you (and it), but hold your praise until she touches the thing with her nose. If the object isn't breakable or too large, roll it away from your puppy (never toward her). That may awaken her chasing instinct and entice her to play with the object.

✓ **A friendly person:** When your Chi fears a friendly person, follow these steps to make an intro:

1. **Give the person a dog treat and ask him or her to toss it near your dog and then ignore her and chat with you.**

2. **If your pup approaches, tell the person to kneel down but not to reach for her.**

3. **When the dog gets close, the person holds his or her hand low, reaching under the puppy's chin to tickle her chest.**

    Reaching over your Chi's head may make her back away in fright.

4. **If she doesn't approach the person, don't force her, but give her much more socialization.**

    Get many friends in on the act, and set up situations that entice your Chi to approach people on her own.

✓ **Loud noises:** If loud noises send your Chi behind the sofa, start announcing her favorite things with sound. For example, if she's an eager eater, mix her meal in a metal pan with a metal spoon. Just keep the noise within the realm of everyday life. The purpose is to help your pup handle her sound sensitivity, not startle or terrify her.

Sudden Fear Syndrome

Between the age of 8 and 11 weeks, suddenly becoming afraid of anything new isn't unusual for happy-go-lucky puppies. In fact, that behavior has a name — *Sudden Fear Syndrome*. If your Chi suddenly starts spooking, remember the rules of socialization: Don't try to cuddle her out of it, and praise her profusely when (and if) she does something brave.

Don't be surprised if your pup shies away from something as silly as a fire hydrant. During her fear phase, she may see the bogeyman everywhere. Although this isn't the time to take her to a Fourth of July celebration, it's best to keep taking her on regular outings. If you don't force her toward something she fears or soothe her silliness, the fear phase passes

Attending kindergarten for puppies

What's more fun than watching a puppy play? Watching several puppies frolic together and then your Chi being invited to join in. This treat awaits you after your dog has been immunized and can safely attend puppy kindergarten.

When your puppy is between 4 and 6 months old, she's fully developed mentally but not physically or emotionally, and she hasn't yet achieved an adult attention span. Often called *KPT* (Kindergarten Puppy Training) and geared to puppies between 12 and 16 weeks of age (some rules may vary), kindergarten classes usually run once a week for eight weeks. KPT classes provide excellent socialization by helping owners introduce their pups to people, places, things, and each other.

In addition to socialization, KPT prepares dogs for further education. Gentle training techniques encourage them to earn praise for a job well done and to learn respect for the word *"No."* Depending on the instructors, pups may also be introduced to basic commands such as Come, Sit, and Down (see Chapter 10), and may be taught how to walk on a leash.

KPT isn't just for puppies; it's for people, too. Instructors give advice on housetraining and answer questions about dog behavior. By the end of the course, you'll know how to solve minor problems before they become major issues.

To find a puppy kindergarten near you, check your local newspaper or yellow pages for kennel clubs or dog obedience schools. Some of these places offer puppy programs. You also can check with your veterinarian for recommendations.

Before enrolling your Chi in any class, talk to the teacher. Find out if he or she is experienced with Toy dogs, and inquire about safety protocol. For example, if the instructor turns puppies loose to play together, you want to make sure your Chi's group is composed only of other small pups.

Also, use your head when choosing playmates and play groups. Puppies don't know their own strength (although playing with other puppies helps them learn it). Don't overwhelm your 10-week-old Chihuahua by putting her with an 8-week-old Rottweiler. Instead, try to find other small puppies for her to play with. Sure, most puppies will probably be bigger than your Chi, but Chihuahua puppies can hold their own with other small-breed puppies of similar ages.

Walking on a Lead

If I were asked to list the mistakes Toy-breed owners make most often, teaching their dogs how to walk on a lead too late would definitely be near the top. It's so easy to carry a tiny dog that some people just don't get around to lead training. That never happens with a Great Dane!

Some breeders teach their puppies to walk on a leash before selling them. If your Chi willingly walks with you, you don't have to read the rest of this section. Instead, snap on her leash, step outside, and enjoy!

If your Chi doesn't know how to walk on lead, though, and isn't used to her collar or harness (see Chapter 5), follow these steps:

1. **Put the collar on her and play with her.** Is she a chowhound? Put the collar on her just before meals and let her wear it a little longer each time. After a few days, she'll ignore it.

2. **When your Chi is accustomed to her collar, attach the lead and let her drag it around.** Keep an eye on her so she doesn't catch it on something and start struggling.

3. **When she's nonchalant about dragging the leash (or if she's too busy playing with it to drag it), pick up your end and follow your pup wherever she takes you.**

    When leash-breaking a Chihuahua puppy, five minutes a day is enough, and more than ten minutes is too much.

4. **When she's comfortable with her collar and leash in the house (this may take a few days), put a few of her favorite treats in your pocket and carry her outside wearing her leash.** If you live in a crowded city, save leash-breaking for early on a weekend morning or for whenever the fewest people are out rushing around.

5. **Carry her about a quarter-block away from the house, put her down, and walk her home (it'll probably take plenty of verbal encouragement and a few treats).** If she pulls and rears like a baby bucking horse, wait until her tantrum subsides and try again.

   Keeping the experience a positive one is important, so ignore the rebellion and praise her when she walks with you (out in front, following behind, or beside you are all okay). Just watch your timing. Be sure to give her a treat when she's moving with you, not when she's balking like a belligerent mule.

   Does your Chi scream and turn herself inside out in a ploy to make you remove her leash? Just stay calm and keep trying. Whatever you do, don't give in and decide to put off training until she's older. When she's older, she'll be more set in her ways and will throw bigger tantrums.

6. **After she begins to walk home with you rather well, put gentle pressure on the leash to decide the direction both of you will go.** Instead of stopping in front of your house, continue past it for a few steps, encouraging her all the way. Gradually show her how to walk both toward and away from home. More important, keep your sessions short and upbeat.

   Does your Chi cough when you put the slightest pressure on the lead? She may have a collapsing trachea (see Chapter 15). Consult your vet. You can relieve that problem by having her wear a harness rather than a collar.

Socializing an Adult Dog

Oh no! People, including me in the previous sections, keep telling you how important it is to socialize a dog early, and you didn't even acquire your Chi until she was an adult. Worse yet, you think terrible things may have happened to her before you got her. Is it too late to socialize? Is your Chihuahua doomed to be insecure for the rest of her life?

No way. Dogs don't have to have ideal puppyhoods to become contented companions. Life may have been unkind to your Chi, but just look how her luck has changed! She has you now, and the rest of her life is ahead of her. Help her make the most of it by giving her training, not pity. Pity prevents progress.

To become a well-adjusted family member, your adult Chi needs self-confidence. You can help her find it. How? Show her how to please you. Begin with the basics (see Chapter 10) and then join a novice obedience class (see Chapter 11). You can use the commands during daily life and praise your Chi for every correct response — not by rote, but with feeling. Gradually, she'll gain enough confidence to stop avoiding life and start enjoying it.

Chapter 10

Establishing Good Behavior and Manners

Do you know why Toy dogs have a bad reputation for being yappy, hard to housetrain, and possessive? Because so many owners let little pets get away with rudeness. I'm sure glad you're not one of those owners. How do I know? Because you're reading about manners right here! After you train your Chihuahua with the tactics I present in this chapter, he'll become a good ambassador for this bright breed.

In this chapter, I help you raise your Chi to be a polite pup. You discover how to housetrain him — including crate training — introduce him to simple commands, and nip problem behavior in the bud before it becomes nasty habit. Not only will your dog love the positive attention that comes with training, but his well-behaved nature also will make him welcome in many more places. And going places together is one of the best parts of having a canine companion.

 Dog training methods go in and out of style almost as often as hemlines, but the positive motivation method that's so popular today has always been my favorite. Positive motivation works because dogs adore attention, and they'll perform encore after encore of any act that elicits your positive interest. Catching your dog doing something right and then praising him for it is the crux of positive training. See how many good habits you can instill in your Chi through praise, petting, and good timing.

Never punish your Chi for something he did when you weren't supervising. He won't know why he's being punished, which leads to all sorts of anxiety problems. If you didn't catch him in the act, let it pass. Keep it from happening again by using prevention, not punishment.

Making the Crate a Home Base

Besides serving as your pup's private den and his home away from home, your Chi's crate is your best housetraining tool. But before you teach him his bathroom manners, you should teach your Chi to accept, and even enjoy, being crated. Here are some simple steps to follow:

1. **Every time you put your dog in his crate, toss a favorite toy or special treat into the crate ahead of him.**

2. **Say "Crate" or "Kennel up" and gently, but firmly, put him inside and shut the door.**

3. **Now walk away. Don't wait around to see how he responds, because that entices him to react.**

   It won't be long before your Chi learns what "Crate" means and enters his little den on his own.

Your Chi may cry the first few times he's introduced to his crate, but if you leave the room and don't retrieve him until he settles down, he'll soon learn to relax in it. The worst thing you can do is rescue him when he cries, because that teaches him to control you by whining and howling. If he still complains in his crate after a week or two, head to Chapter 11 for help.

At night, make sure your pup relieves himself before you crate him and then put his crate in your bedroom, right beside your bed. No, a young dog won't make it through the night, but he should be okay for three or four hours. If he cries in his crate as soon as the lights go out, sing or whistle soothingly to him (to let him know that someone is near), but don't take him out of the crate. The first few nights are the hardest on him (and you), because your place won't feel like home yet. A young pup is used to snuggling with his mother and littermates, and he misses them most during the wee hours. Be prepared to lose some sleep.

Eventually, your dog will fall asleep and so will you, but expect him to wake you with his cries after a few hours. Like it or not, you must get up quickly and take your puppy outside to relieve himself. Dogs don't like to soil their sleeping quarters, which is why a crate is such a good housetraining aid. But if you ignore his plea to go potty, he'll have to soil his crate. Puppies just don't have much holding power. If crate accidents happen too often, he'll adjust to living with filth instead of maintaining the clean habits he was born with.

Never use the crate to punish your dog, and be careful not to use it too much. Your dog doesn't need to spend the majority of his time in a crate. How do you know if you're doing it right? Watch his reaction as he matures. Eventually, his attitude toward his crate should become neutral. If he either resists going into it or loves it so much that it's hard to get him out of it, something is wrong.

When your Chi matures, you may want to leave a crate in a corner of your living room with the door always open. He may appreciate a private place of his own where he can chew a toy or take a nap when he needs one. Let your kids and friends know that when he curls up in his crate, he's tired and wants to be left alone.

Housetraining — Avoiding Problems

Dogs are naturally clean critters, yet having accidents in the house is considered one of the biggest behavior problems in the Toy breeds. However, Toy dogs have an undeserved bad reputation when it comes to housetraining. The truth is, Toy dogs are every bit as bright as larger breeds (okay, often brighter), and they can control themselves just as well as big dogs. Thousands of Toys are extremely reliable in the home, and yours can be one of them — if you follow the guidelines in this chapter. Here I show you how to avoid the problems in the house and housetrain your Chi from the start.

Even if you're lucky enough to get your puppy while you're on vacation, you should introduce him to a schedule you can live with and stick to it (see Chapter 5). Don't confuse him by putting him on one schedule during weekends and vacation days and another on workdays.

Common Toy dog misconceptions

Do Toy dogs have poor plumbing systems? Not at all. Toy dogs are considered hard to housetrain because so many owners don't get around to training until their dogs have already developed bad habits. Then they face the enormous job of breaking the habits rather than the much easier task of establishing good ones. Here's why Toy dog owners let their puppies get away with leaving puddles and poops on the floor:

✔ Because the accident is so tiny that it can be cleaned up quickly

✔ Because the dog is so small, he probably doesn't understand

✔ Because he hates to get his feet wet and it's drizzling outside

✔ Because no one in the house feels ambitious enough at the time to walk the dog

People love to give those excuses when letting their little dogs do it on the floor just one more time. Bet they wouldn't think that way if a Saint Bernard just did his duty on the floor!

To clear your head of that kind of thinking, remember the following:

✔ The accident may be easy to clean, but do you want to clean up accidents several times a day for the next dozen or more years?

✔ Being small isn't the same as being stupid. Chihuahuas are smart. Your dog will understand if you take the time to teach him.

✔ Toy dogs are still dogs, and yours needs to learn to relieve himself in the right place, rain or shine. Most dogs do their duty real fast during bad weather.

✔ To housetrain a dog, you must train yourself.

Your Chi may take longer to be reliably housebroken than a big dog because Toy dogs see the world differently than large dogs do. As far as they're concerned, it's a long way from the kitchen to behind the living room sofa, so they can squat there and still consider themselves clean critters. Keep your dog close to you until he understands exactly where he's supposed to go potty (see the later section "Keeping to a routine"). And keep in mind that Toy dogs have to relieve themselves a little more often than large dogs.

Never train your pet when you're in a bad mood. Puppies are just learning how to learn, and your earliest teachings color their lifelong attitude toward training.

Keeping to a routine

The keys to housetraining are a regular routine and an alert trainer (that's you!). A housebroken dog is simply a dog with a habit — the happy habit of eliminating outdoors.

Simply put, you need to feed (see Chapter 6), water, exercise (see Chapter 8), groom (see Chapter 7), and take your dog outside to eliminate at the same times every day. Besides being healthier, a routine makes housetraining easier. Dogs are creatures of habit, so sticking to a schedule from day one helps your Chi make sense of his new environment. As he begins to recognize his daily routine, he'll learn to understand your expectations. And because puppies love to please, the habits he forms will be good ones.

When housetraining your Chi, take him to the same outdoor area to go potty every time, and repeat the same words — "Go Potty" for instance — as he eliminates. Routine is so important, so taking the same route to the potty place every time is a good idea (for example, go out the same door and turn the same direction).

If you live on the 20th floor of a building or in a place where the snow drifts as high as a Chihuahua's eye, you can try the litter-box method of training. Instead of using cat-box filler, line the box with several thicknesses of newspaper. Use the same housetraining routines I recommend in this chapter, but when I tell you to take your dog outside, take him to the litter box instead. Soon your Chi will be litter box trained. Pet shops also sell chemically treated pads that attract dogs and entice them to squat in the area you choose.

Chihuahuas are naturally clean dogs and don't want to soil their living quarters. When housetraining your Chi and establishing a routine, take advantage of that trait by confining him to a dog crate *every time* you're away or he's left unsupervised. Then as soon as you arrive home, take him outside and praise him for eliminating. If he soils his crate, clean up the mess immediately. Besides being dangerous to his health, a wet or dirty crate teaches your Chi to live with his mess — an attitude that hinders the housetraining process.

Training yourself, a.m. to p.m.

Staying on a schedule makes or breaks housetraining, so plan ahead. To adjust to housetraining your Chi, you may need to get up 15 minutes earlier; come home for lunch (or hire a dog walker); and come straight home from work until your pup is a little older. The following sections present a tentative schedule to keep with young puppy.

Morning

1. First thing in the morning, take your Chi outside for several minutes and praise him for a job well done.

2. When you bring him in, feed and water him (see Chapter 6 for tips).

3. Take him outside again after he eats breakfast. Young dogs almost always have to relieve themselves soon after eating.

4. Now he can spend time with you to exercise or have the run of a puppy-proofed room if you're at home but unable to supervise. If you're leaving for work, confine him to his crate.

5. Take him outdoors for elimination midmorning if you're at home.

Afternoon

1. Take your Chi outside as soon as you get home at lunchtime.

2. Give him lunch and fresh water.

3. Take him outdoors after he finishes eating. Confine him again if you can't keep an eye on him or must leave.

Evening

1. When you arrive home, take your Chi outdoors right away and enjoy a nice walk (weather permitting).

2. When you get back, let him watch you fix dinner or join you for the evening news.

3. Feed him for the last time each day between 6 p.m. and 7 p.m.

4. Take him outside after he finishes eating. After he relieves himself, enjoy his company for the evening.

5. Take him outside just before you go to bed. Confine him for the night.

Recognizing the signs of need

Sometimes (possibly many times), your Chihuahua must relieve himself more often than what the sample schedule in the previous section suggests. When housetraining, prevention works wonders, so watch him closely. Take your Chi outside immediately if he exhibits the following behavior:

✔ Begins walking in circles and sniffing the floor

✔ Starts panting when he hasn't been exercising

✔ Suddenly leaves the room

Play, heavy exercise, and a nice massage act as *on* switches for puppy plumbing. So if you just finished a playing or petting session, it's a good idea to take your Chi outside.

Does it sound like you'll be running in and out as often as a confused cat? Well, for awhile, you will be. But it isn't a life sentence. As your pup gets older, he'll need to eat only twice a day and his holding capacity will increase, so he'll need fewer trips outdoors.

Dealing with accidents

All puppies (and often dogs in new homes) make mistakes. If you get home too late and your Chi already had an accident, don't make a big deal out of it. Your puppy won't understand why you're so angry with him when he was so glad to see you, and that leads to far worse problems. Pointing at the poop while screaming at him won't help. You'll surely scare him, which may lead to anxiety-related problems.

If the dirty deed was done before you got home, take your pup outside anyway. Eventually, he'll learn to expect and to wait for the opportunity to go outside. Have patience and understand that he may still be too young to control himself for the length of time that you were away. Clean up the soiled spot as soon as you can, using an odor neutralizer or plain white vinegar.

Buy a good odor neutralizer and stain remover (UrineOff is a good one). Removing the evidence of your dog's mistakes immediately keeps your house looking and smelling like home, not a kennel. An odor-free floor is an important part of housetraining. Dogs tend to eliminate where their noses tell them they went before, so quick cleanups help prevent future accidents.

Never use any cleanup product containing ammonia, for the crate or the carpet. The odor of ammonia makes dogs seek out the same spot to go potty again.

If you catch your Chi in the act of an accident, you may be able to stop him mid-squat with a firm "No!" or a loud noise like clapping your hands. Pick him up, hurry him outside to the right spot, and praise him if he finishes what he started. Contrary to old wives' tales, swatting a dog with a rolled-up newspaper or putting his nose in his mess won't work. Punishment teaches a dog to eliminate behind the sofa where he thinks you won't find it, not to go outside and do it proudly in front of you.

Teaching Words that All Good Dogs Obey

Imagine how nice it is living with a dog that always comes when you call, sits and lies down on command, stays in place when told to, and respects the words No and Enough. Making this happen is easier than you think. I show you how in the sections that follow. Conditioning your Chi to respond to the commands Come, Sit, Down, Stay, No, and Enough can start at any age, but younger is better.

Conditioning Chihuahua puppies (or adult dogs) requires a trainer with an upbeat attitude — one who gives plenty of praise and positive reinforcement, with absolutely no punishment. If that's you, go ahead and get going! When teaching the meaning of the following commands, praise or reward your Chi every time he gives you the correct response, and simply ignore him when he doesn't. Dogs will do virtually anything for attention, so yours should quickly learn the lingo.

How often do you and your Chihuahua need to practice simple commands such as Sit, Down, and Come? Every day. But you don't need to set aside a special time for it. Instead, you can use the commands during daily life: Sit, for the dinner dish. Come, for a treat. Down, for petting. You get the picture.

Coming when called

Use bribery to teach your Chi what Come means. For instance, you can follow these simple steps:

1. Introduce the word at feeding time by saying his name and then the word "Come" in a happy voice ("Pepe, come!").

2. Show him his dinner dish.

3. Walk backward a few steps while holding it.

4. When your pup follows, praise him and then let him eat.

5. Repeat the process every time you feed him.

When conditioning your Chi to Come, call him only when you know he wants to come — not when he's sleepy or busy with food, a toy, or another person. Later, when your Chihuahua is older, you may want to attend obedience school (see Chapter 11). There you discover how to teach him to Come no matter what the distraction. In the meantime, practice often. Call him for all the good stuff — dinner, treats, and cuddles — and he'll soon respond happily.

How soon should you start training your puppy to Come? As soon as he settles in. He loves the attention, but keep the training sessions short (like puppy attention spans) and always be cheerful and upbeat.

Puppies love to chase, and chasing games help them learn what Come means. Touch your Chi on his rump playfully, say his name followed by the word "Come," and then run away a few steps while clapping (not too loudly) and talking happily. Let him catch you and then play with him for a few seconds before giving him another playful tap and starting over. Three times is plenty for one session.

Never sabotage your training by calling a Chihuahua of any age to give him a pill or chastise him for something. Go to your dog for the upsetting stuff, and keep his Comes carefree.

Sitting pretty

To teach your Chi what Sit means (see Figure 10-1), follow these simple steps:

1. **Hold a treat in front of his nose, say "Sit," and then move the treat upward and back over his head.**

   When his eyes follow the goodie upward, his head will tilt back and his rear end will lower until it reaches the floor.

2. **Give the treat immediately while he's still sitting and praise him.**

3. **Try it three or four more times, but be sure to quit while he's still having fun.**

A soft treat, such as a nibble of cheese (provided that your Chi isn't lactose intolerant), makes a good training tool. It's healthy, and a Chihuahua can eat it fast so you can continue training. Tiny pieces of soft, moist dog treats also work well.

Going down

To teach the Down command, start with your Chi in the Sit position (see the preceding section). Now follow these steps:

1. **Hold a tasty treat right in front of his nose and say "Down."**

2. **Make a movement shaped like a capital L by lowering the treat straight down, just in front of his paws, and then slowly pulling it forward at ground level.**

   As he reaches for the goody, the front half of your pup's body should move downward.

3. **If his body doesn't lower completely to the ground, put gentle pressure on his shoulders with your free hand, but don't mash him down.**

4. **The instant his whole body is in the Down position, give him the treat (see Figure 10-2).**

Teaching stay

Your Chi probably bounces up from his Sit right after you give him his treat, but now you'll prolong that process by teaching the Stay command:

1. **Stand on your Chi's right side, with both of you facing the same way, and hold a treat in your right hand.**

2. **Tell him to "Sit," but this time don't give him the treat as soon as his butt touches the floor. Instead, move your left hand sideways, stopping just in front of his nose (palm facing him), and say "Stay" at the same time.**

3. **Let a long second pass before giving him the treat.**

   Gradually — very gradually — work up to a ten-second Stay before presenting the reward. Decide how many seconds each Stay will be before you start, and vary the time. Otherwise, your Chi will soon outguess you.

What should you do if he moves before time's up? Absolutely nothing. Don't reward, don't pet, and don't punish. Just try again later and praise your dog when he does it right. After he learns to stay in place in the Sit position, you can use the same procedure to teach him what Down-Stay means.

Figure 10-1: Manchita sits on command with eyes focused on the reward yet to come.

Figure 10-2: Manchita downs for a treat.

Staying in place isn't a puppy's forte, so when conditioning your young Chi, begin with two- or three-second Stays and don't try to make him remain in place longer than ten seconds (use a watch; you'll be surprised by how long ten seconds actually is). If your ultimate goal is for him to stay in place for several minutes, an obedience school is your best bet (see Chapter 11).

Making "No!" and "Enough!" effective

Your petite pup may amaze your friends by walking on a leash like an obedience champ and performing Sits and Downs on command. But if he's a brat when show-off time is over, he isn't the pure pleasure he can be.

All dogs need to respond to two words: "No!" and "Enough!" No means "Stop that right now and don't ever do it again." If you bark out the word No in a sharp tone, your attitude won't be lost on your Chihuahua.

Just don't use No too often, or your Chi will get used to it. Reserve the word for really bad behavior like teething on a table leg or nipping at feet or clothing. If your voice isn't emphatic enough, clap your hands (once) right after you say No.

What if your Chi ignores you and continues chewing the chair leg? Go to him, pick him up, move him away from the temptation, and give him something he's allowed to chew. Then praise him for chewing the proper item. If he heads back to the forbidden object later, bark your firmest No yet, followed by a clap of your hands, if necessary, to get his attention. If he persists on trying to mouth the chair leg, tap his nose *lightly* as you say No, and then take him to a different closed-off room where he can play with his own toys.

Always keep your cool, and never touch your dog in anger. If you have a temper (you know who you are), stick with a verbal No.

"Enough" means "What you are doing was just fine for awhile, but you've been doing it for too long, so stop now." Use Enough when you don't want to pet your Chi anymore but he keeps pawing your hand. Say Enough if he gets too wound up during play or continues barking long after the meter reader leaves. Said firmly but without anger, Enough works on puppies, adult dogs, and the kids that play with them!

Preventing Common Problems

Besides housetraining issues, common puppy problems include destructive chewing, persistent barking, jumping, nipping, and possessiveness. Okay, that's the bad news. The good news is that if your Chi is still young, you can prevent most of the typical pitfalls

Techichis believed to be true soul mates

During the 12th century in Mexico, the Aztec Indians wiped out the Toltec nation but spared their dogs, the Techichis, because the dogs had such an impressive job description. Believed to be holy, their task was to guide their dead owner's soul to safety. This concept appealed to the Aztecs because they needed all the help they could get. After all, they believed the dead had to cross nine perilous lands and a treacherous underworld river before their souls reached safety. So when the Aztecs burned a dead warrior, they burned his dog with him. They thought the little holy dog would race on ahead, fight off evil spirits, and wait on the far bank of the raging river until it saw its master, and then swim back across, guiding him safely to the other side.

Sacrificing a dog with red skin by burning it along with a human corpse was also popular with the Aztecs. They believed the sins of the deceased were transferred to the dog and not taken out on the person. No doubt that's why archeologists discovered a number of graves in Mexico containing both human and Techichi remains.

of puppyhood. And prevention is a whole lot easier than correcting problems after they become bad habits. Yes, that's possible, too (see Chapter 11), but why do it the hard way when prevention is so much easier? The following sections help you prevent the common behaviors before they become problems.

All dogs need toys, but don't overdo it. A dog with too many toys may begin to believe that everything is a toy. Then he won't learn to discriminate between his toys and all the taboo items in the house.

Teaching what's okay to chew

Your puppy needs to chew, but teaching him what to chew isn't always easy. This section presents a nifty training aid, compliments of my friend Amy Ammen, director of Amiable Dog Training in Milwaukee, Wisconsin, and author of several dog training books. She calls this training exercise "Shopping Spree."

After your puppy knows how to walk on lead (see Chapter 9), teach him to discriminate between his toys and taboo items by taking him on a shopping spree right in your living room:

1. Choose a word that means "get that out of your mouth" (most people opt for "Out" or "Drop It").

2. Place some personal objects — such as a wallet, slippers, or purse — and some paper products — like napkins or a roll of toilet tissue — on the floor along with two of your puppy's toys.

3. With the props in place, put a leash on your puppy and let him explore the clutter.

4. When he picks up a taboo item, say your command along with giving a *tiny* jerk on the leash (just enough so he feels it — if it moves his body, it's too hard).

5. Walk toward an appropriate toy and encourage your puppy to play with it.

Take your puppy shopping a couple times a day and he'll soon take pride in leading you to one of his correct objects. When he does, be sure to praise him and let him keep his toy. And now that he knows the command for releasing an object, you should use that command, and only that command, whether he's holding a slipper, a finger, or a dead mouse.

Controlling barking

Chihuahuas make good watchdogs because they have excellent hearing and a loud bark, considering their size. Some barking is a good thing. Most people are glad when their dogs tell them that strangers are approaching their homes. But it's best to be glad quietly, taking your Chi's protective tendencies for granted instead of praising them. For example, the first time he goes into a prolonged barking fit at a door-to-door salesman, don't act like it's adorable unless you want him to bark long and hard at visitors all his life. Instead, let him know right from the start when he's barked long enough by saying "Enough." (I discuss this command earlier in this chapter.) It isn't barking, but rather *excessive barking*, that drives people mad.

The problem is, even if you take your Chi's warning barks for granted and don't bother to praise him for giving you advance notice when a visitor arrives, he usually feels rewarded anyway. That's because every time the meter reader or the salesperson leaves (after being barked at, of course), your Chi thinks he chased them away. And that makes him feel real macho.

Trying to thwart a Chihuahua's natural tendency to protect his family only frustrates him. Worse yet, he may learn to keep quiet no matter what instead of acting as your early-warning system. Countless Chihuahuas have alerted their families about fires and scared off burglars with their shrill bark. The trick is being able to turn off your live alarm on command.

Use the command Enough to let him know when he's done his duty and it's time to quiet down. If that doesn't work — and only as a last resort — buy a small spray bottle. Keep it handy and give him one surprise squirt, right in the face, to enforce the Enough word. You should avoid the tendency to threaten him with the water treatment, though. It's best if he thinks his barking, not you, flooded his face.

Don't punish your Chi after the fact. Not even if he has a guilty look. The truth is, dogs don't feel guilt. That's a people thing. Nor do they remember what they did five minutes ago. Sure, there's poop on the rug and your Chi looks worried, but what you're seeing in his eyes is confusion. He senses that you're angry with him, but he doesn't know why, which makes him apprehensive. Hence, the guilty look.

Deciding if jumping is okay

Only you can decide if jumping is an okay behavior for your Chihuahua. After all, Chis weigh hardly anything, so the danger of most people being knocked over is nonexistent.

Some people like having their dogs joyfully jump on them. If you're one of those people, nothing is wrong with jumping as long as you enjoy having your Chi jump on you no matter what you're wearing. Your Chi isn't clothes-conscious enough to understand that jumping on you when you're wearing jeans is okay, but it isn't okay when you're dressed to impress. The point is, don't let him do something one day that you don't want him to do another day. Decide right away if jumping is okay or not; if it isn't, read on.

You'll have to change your Chi's method of greeting people when you teach him not to jump. For instance, teach him to Sit on command (see the previous "Sitting pretty" section), and then tell him to sit (in a happy but firm voice) as soon as you open the door. When he does (even if you have to put him in the Sit position), kneel down to his level and give him plenty of praise. A Chi will want to jump on you for instant attention, but if you withhold your attention until after he's sitting, he'll soon learn to Sit for your approval.

Nipping nipping

Puppies use their mouths to investigate things, much the same way humans use their hands. They also use their mouths in play and sometimes to vent their high spirits. But needle-sharp teeth hurt, so you must teach your puppy that nipping isn't nice.

Resist the urge to jerk your hand away from your puppy when he clamps down on it. That's the canine version of an invitation to play, so pulling away just makes him come back for another nip.

How can you tell your pup that clamping down hurts? Say ouch! And say it like you mean it. Screech it out in a high-pitched voice that lets him know that he hurt you. Most pups will lick you in apology. If a week or two of yelping "Ouch!" doesn't make a difference, choose a command that means "Don't Bite." Say it every time your Chi touches you with his teeth, and put your finger on his button nose and press gently while you say it.

A last resort (use only on confirmed nippers) is dabbing a Bitter Apple spray on the part of you your puppy nips. This works especially well on shoelace and sock chasers.

Preventing possessiveness

Most puppy possessiveness starts over the food dish. That's because puppies compete with their littermates (brothers and sisters) for food. Sometimes they have to be deprogrammed when they enter a human family. Nothing to it. Just mix up these four choices — using one during one meal and a different one at the next meal, and so on. After a couple weeks, your Chi should stop being possessive of his bowl:

✔ Feed your Chihuahua his kibble a nugget or two at a time from your hand with your hand in his food bowl.

✔ Give him only ¼th of his dinner. Then just as he finishes the tiny portion, put the rest of his meal in the bowl.

✔ Put a cushion on the floor and sit down beside his food dish. Pet him for a minute or two as he begins his dinner, and then walk away and let him eat the rest of his meal alone.

✔ When he's nearly finished eating, walk up to him and place a tiny, but very special, treat in his dish. A slice of hot dog, a sliver of cheese, or a bit of burger will make him happy that you put your hand in his bowl.

I recommend dropping a very good treat into your puppy's food bowl as he's eating his food so that he thinks adults/children approaching his bowl is a good thing. This can prevent serious bites near a food bowl — especially if a baby crawls too close.

Chapter 11

Keeping Your Place as Head of Household

*U*h oh! Chief Chihuahua rules at your house. He growls when someone tries to sit in *his* chair, barks as loud and as long as he pleases, refuses to drop forbidden objects, guards his food with a vengeance, and sometimes even snaps to keep his spot on the bed. Obviously, a coup is long overdue. It's time to overthrow your tiny tyrant and put policymaking back in the hands of the people — namely, you! With dogs, a benevolent dictatorship works best. First, elect yourself president for life. Then read this chapter. It helps you turn your tiny tyrant into a true friend for life.

Curing Your Crybaby

Most puppies whine and bark the first several times their owners confine them to rooms or crates. Whatever you do, don't take your Chihuahua out of his place of confinement to stop the racket. That's exactly what he wants, and doing so makes him feel rewarded for barking nonstop. Instead, wait until he's silent for at least a minute; then you can go to him and let him out.

You can use some other tactics to squelch your Pepe's complaints. Try them in the following order, moving on to the next one in line only if you need to:

1. **The first few times you confine your Chi and leave him alone, try to put up with the noise for ten minutes without doing anything.** Some dogs simply quit sounding off when they realize they're dramatizing to an empty theater.

2. **Play a radio softly near him.** Music relaxes some dogs. Just be sure to keep both the radio and the cord out of his reach.

3. **If he is still mouthing off, make a sudden loud noise from another room.** You can stamp your foot or slap the wall. But be sure not to say anything. It's better if he thinks that his own racket, not you, caused the noise. As soon as he whines again, make the noise again. Repeat as often as necessary.

4. **From the room next to the one he's confined in, bang two metal pots together.** Do this once only every time he barks or whines.

5. **Fill a spray bottle with plain water, and every time he makes a racket, walk in silently and squirt him one time, directly in the face.** Then walk out again. When he's quiet for a minute or two, go to him without the spray bottle and pet and praise him. Repeat as necessary. It won't be necessary long! This is a last resort, because it's physical and your dog sees you do it, unlike the loud noise, which you hope he thinks he caused.

Your Chihuahua should always have a safe chew toy and something to snuggle under when he's confined. This will make him feel safe and may reduce his tendency to whine and cry.

Quieting Your Barker

Some Chihuahuas are noisy little dogs that seem to yip at the slightest provocations and mouth off nonstop when they want attention. Their tendency to vocalize makes them good watchdogs, so smart owners don't want to completely turn off their tiny noisemakers. But frenzied barking for attention or when someone walks near the house gets old real fast.

You want to scream when your barking dog drives you to distraction, but resist the urge. If you yell when your Chihuahua barks, he'll think you're joining in. Then the excitement of leading his best friend in a bark-a-long will egg him on all the more. Don't get exasperated and pick him up, either. All that does is make him feel even braver. Why? Because in your arms he's taller and protected by you.

The following sections explain what you *can* and *should* do in two specific situations: when your Chi barks at the door and barks for attention.

Mouthing off at the door

Your Chi needs to learn the command "Enough" (see Chapter 10) so you can appreciate his warning bark when a stranger comes to the door but turn it off on command (see Figure 11-1). You can also use Enough to stop him from barking for attention (see the following section). If your Chi wasn't taught to respond to Enough as a pup, try the spray bottle method I discuss in the previous section. It usually does the trick. In rare cases where it doesn't, try the following:

1. **Rather than plain water, pour a mixture of vinegar and water (a few drops of vinegar added to the water) into your spray bottle.**

2. **Have a friend ring the bell and/or knock on the door.**

3. **Let your Chi alert you (that's a good thing) and then tell him "Enough," firmly.**

4. **If the command doesn't stop his tirade, make him think twice by spraying him in the mouth with the mixture.**

   Be as discreet as possible. It's best if he thinks his tantrum, not you, caused the sour taste in his mouth.

   Repeat if you have to, but whatever you do, don't lose your temper.

One of the best ways to cure a Chihuahua that barks like crazy at the door is to set up situations in which friends bearing treats ring the bell. At the sound, put a leash on your dog, open the door, and invite the person in. Give the "Sit" command, and as soon as your dog shuts his mouth and sits, have the visitor give him a treat. This system may take several tries, but eventually your dog will figure out that the doorbell doesn't signal the boogeydog!

Figure 11-1: Cricket guards the entrance to *her* motor home but quiets down on command.

Yapping for attention

If your Chi barks incessantly for attention, don't give in and cuddle him; if you do, he'll discover how to manipulate a petting session whenever he wants one. Instead, either ignore him or use the "Enough" command (see Chapter 10) — reinforcing it, if necessary, with your spray bottle (one squirt only of plain water, directly in his face). Don't let him see the shower coming. He should think he triggered it by barking after hearing the word Enough. (See the first section for more on using a spray bottle.)

Housetraining a Stubborn Chihuahua

Because so much of housetraining is up to the owner, let me ask you a few questions:

Does the cliché, "When all else fails, read the instructions," fit you? Did you set up a routine, as suggested in Chapter 10, and follow it without fail?

Did you clean up every mistake right away (without using ammonia or yelling at your dog)?

Did you praise your Chi every time he relieved himself in the right place?

Did you give him an opportunity to go potty as soon as you got up in the morning, every time you arrived home, as well as after every meal, nap, and play session (up to ten times a day when totaled)?

Be honest with yourself. If your routine is haphazard or you're not taking out your dog often enough, it's *you* who are sabotaging housetraining. Get a crate, read Chapter 10, and start over.

Maybe it isn't your fault at all, however. If you did everything right and your Chi still leaves doggy-do on the carpet, keep the routine going but add the following. Also, check out the following sections, which explain different types of accidents. Knowledge is power!

✔ **When you come home, don't greet your Chi or give him any positive attention until after he eliminates in the proper place.** Then praise the devil out of him.

✔ **Learn to read your dog's bathroom language.** Most Chihuahuas (and other dogs) circle several times before squatting. If your dog starts circling, pick him up and head for the potty place. Then praise him for going there.

✔ **Control his intake of water.** Careful! Dehydration is dangerous! Give him free access to water during the day — especially with and after his meals and following activity — but take away his water dish about three hours before you go to bed.

   If it's hot in your house or if your Chi plays hard later in the evening, let him lap some ice cubes. That way he gets the liquid he needs without bloating himself.

✔ **Crate your Chi when you go out without him — even for just a few minutes.**

✔ **When you're home, keep your dog with you on lead until he's reliably housebroken.** That way he can't sneak a whiz behind the sofa.

   This technique also gives you a chance to catch him in the act. If you do, keep calm, tell him "No!" emphatically (without yelling), pick him up, and take him outside. Then tell him how wonderful he is for finishing the job in the right place.

Marking — it's a macho thing

Male dogs have an instinct to mark their territory, for which they use (you guessed it) urine. It's a macho thing. Dogs think their scent warns male dogs to stay away and attracts the ladies, but owners feel like bawling when their dogs lift their legs on table legs and bookcases.

Neutering provides the quickest cure. Otherwise, just keep your housetraining routine going, crate your Chi when you're away, and be patient. Housebreaking an intact (unneutered) male Chihuahua is possible, but it takes longer.

Sometimes, just as you relax and congratulate yourself on your housetraining accomplishment, your dog reaches puberty, learns to lift his leg, and must be reminded of his manners. A few weeks of keeping him on lead in the house (so he's always with you) and confining him when you're away often is all it takes to put him back on schedule.

Submissive urination

When you come home, does your dog greet you happily but with a hint of shyness, while squatting and dribbling several drops of urine? That's called *submissive urination*. Though often mistaken for a housetraining problem, this is really an anxiety problem and has nothing to do with housetraining at all. The tendency may be inherited, may be caused by harsh or too-frequent corrections, or even by abuse your Chihuahua suffered before you got him.

Between wolves in the wild, submissive urination means, "Hi boss. Sure hope I didn't do anything to upset you, but if I did, I'm sorry." Though it happens most often during a greeting, a dribble may also occur when you bend over him to pick him up or when you chastise him. The urination is a conditioned reflex to dominant treatment, and your Chi isn't doing it on purpose. In fact, he doesn't know he's doing it at all.

Never chastise your Chi for submissive urination, because that only makes it worse.

The easiest way to prevent a host of problems — including submissive urination, whining when confined, separation anxiety, and jumping — is to come and go without making a fuss. Long apologies before leaving and boisterous homecomings overstimulate many dogs, and excited dogs behave erratically.

Toss a treat for your Chi the instant you arrive home instead of bending over to pick him up. After he eats the treat, ignore him until he comes to you for attention. When he does, tickle under his chin or rub his chest (with your palm up) instead of reaching over his head or bending over him.

You also can teach him a few easy commands so he knows how to please you and earn praise. Then use a simple command, such as "Sit," when you greet each other (see Chapter 10). Now you've given him a positive way to express his devotion and earn your praise.

 Compliments from you are what eventually break the submissive urination cycle. Being praised for a correct response builds confidence, and confidence is what a Chi needs to conquer submissive urination.

Reinforcing the "Drop It" Command

Your Chihuahua is a portable vacuum cleaner with the mouth muscles of Jaws, Jr., and he loves what he shouldn't have. How can you get him to release forbidden objects without prying his tiny trap open? First, try taking him on a "shopping spree" (see Chapter 10). If he still refuses to drop taboo booty, put a drop of Bitter Apple spray (available in pet stores) on your finger, and then slide your finger along his gum line as you give the "Drop It" or "Out" command (choose a command and use the same one every time). He'll soon discover that it's smart to let go. (The "Trading for treats" section later in this chapter offers yet another technique.)

Humping (How Humiliating!)

Oh no! Your Chihuahua just humped Aunt Amelia's leg during the family reunion. Why does he do these nasty things? Rampaging male hormones are often to blame when he embarrasses you by humping someone's leg or puts on a sex show with a throw pillow. Dogs don't have sexual inhibitions like people do, so when the scent of a female in season wafts by and stimulates his libido, he tries to satisfy his frustrations with whatever is available. Because legs are close enough to the right height and width, many dogs mount them.

Neutering cures many males of mounting and relieves their frustrations, making them better pets in other ways as well. But if the humping is habitual, you may not notice a difference for a month or more after surgery.

Although neutering (see Chapter 13) is the cure of choice, some people may not want to neuter their Chihuahuas because they plan to use them for showing and breeding. Because dogs that mount legs are also displaying dominance (the urge to be boss), dealing with that urge may break the habit (see the following section).

You soon recognize when your dog's libido is becoming overactive. If he heads for a leg with that telltale vacant look in his eye, distract him by using a command such as "Sit" to stop him in his tracks. Keeping a shaker can handy also helps. (That's an empty soda can with a few pennies in it and a piece of tape over the opening.) If your Chi still tries to attach himself to his favorite throw pillow or your spouse's ankle, break his focus by tossing the can so it hits the floor near him (just don't hit him).

These techniques (and those that follow) also cure females that are so dominant that they have a mounting habit.

Don't get angry with your dog to teach him who's boss. All that does is teach him aggression. Withhold petting and praise until he earns it. Make him work for attention by obeying a command (such as Sit) or performing a trick (see Chapter 12), and give him more exercise (see Chapter 8).

Dealing with Dominance

If your Chihuahua has a tendency to be possessive, his behavior may extend beyond the food dish (see Chapter 10 for more). Some Chihuahuas (and other breeds) demand sole ownership of their favorite chairs, their end of the sofa, or even their snuggle spots on the bed. And when anyone tries to sit in *their* spots, the resentful dogs snarl a warning and, in some cases, may even snap. Granted, Chihuahuas tend to be sassy — but surly is unacceptable.

You should never, ever be afraid of your dog. Not even for an instant. Don't ignore or excuse threatening behavior because it ended quickly. If you do, next time your Chi's threat will be even stronger. And yes, if he got away with growling at you once, there *will* be a next time.

Most Chihuahua owners react with surprise the first time their petite pooches growl a warning at them. They don't realize that the growls (which, if unchecked, can escalate into snapping) only happened after their dogs established dominance over them in several subtle ways. For example, does your Chi badger you into petting him by pawing at you or nudging your hand? Do you sit where you did before you got him, or has he taken over your favorite corner of the sofa? Do you feed or give him treats when you want to or when he demands (or begs)?

If he's already calling some of the shots, you've lost round one; it may be only a matter of time before he's ready to test you at another level. Perhaps you'll be in a rush to clean up before company arrives, so you reach for his food dish before he licks the last morsel. He goes rigid and stands over the dish with his eyes looking directly into yours. You shrug it off and say something like, "Okay, just hurry up and finish it." You've just lost round two. When round three comes, it could be a growl. You now know there's a problem, but you'll probably think that he never did anything like that before.

Okay, now that you know what can happen, you can start preventing it immediately. The following sections show you how.

If possessiveness is becoming a problem, encourage other members of your household to make your Chi earn his rewards by obeying commands. Otherwise, he may learn to obey you but still challenge your spouse, for instance.

Possessive pup adjustment

The same techniques both prevent and cure possessiveness (but prevention is always the best policy). One of the best ways is to make your Chihuahua work for his food and privileges. If you haven't taught him the basic commands in Chapter 10, start now. If you did teach them, you're ahead of the game. Use them in everyday life. "Sit" when your dog wants food. "Down" when your dog wants petting. "Come" when he wants a treat. Sit and "Stay" before you allow him up on the sofa. "Enough" when you're tired of petting him and he paws you for more. You get the picture. At the first hint of possessiveness, make these acts privileges, not rights.

Establish dominance by inviting your Chi to sit beside you by saying "Come On Up" and patting the sofa when you say it. Then lift him up beside you if necessary. At the same time, teach him to "Get Down" by giving that command while pointing at the floor. He will figure out the signal if you place him on the floor every time you say it. Eventually, he'll jump up and get down on command under his own steam.

Young puppies can't jump up on the sofa themselves and shouldn't be allowed to jump down because they can damage their legs or shoulders. Using the cues Come On Up and Get Down before your puppy matures is a good idea, but place him on the furniture and always lift him down while he's young.

Changing your attitude

Is possessiveness already a problem? You need to change your attitude as well. Instead of taking the path of least resistance, like backing away when your Chi growls (which teaches him that growling gets him what he wants), resolve to take command of the situation. Make him work for every bit of attention. Use the commands from Chapter 10 often, and give your dog affection and praise only for complying. If he growls when he's on the bed, don't allow him on the bed. The same applies to the sofa, chair, or wherever he displays dominance (see Figure 11-2). After several days of making him earn attention, you can let him share your chair again. But only on your terms — by invitation only — from now on. It could take months of not allowing him on your bed or chair before the behavior changes.

Don't pity him because he has to go through this. You're doing him a favor. When you train your Chihuahua and let him know how to please you, he becomes happier and more content. After all, he can relax. The household is in good hands — yours!

Figure 11-2: Possessive dogs defend "their" chairs, but Tiko hopes her owner will join her.

Dealing with hard cases

If your dog has been the boss for a long time and is serious about biting when you try to reform him with the tactics I describe here, don't try to deal with him yourself anymore. A Chihuahua may be small but he can still do damage — especially if he snaps at your face. Instead, ask your veterinarian to recommend a professional trainer or behaviorist. The investment you make is worth it. A good pro puts your relationship back on the right track and teaches you how to maintain it.

Trading for treats

Some Chihuahuas become possessive over treasured objects — anything they have that you want to take from them, such as a pencil that fell off your desk. You can try to prevent possessiveness over objects by teaching your Chihuahua what "Out" means:

1. **Get a small plastic container with a lid, break up a few of your dog's favorite biscuits, and place them inside.**

2. **Shake the container, open it, and give him one treat.**

   Do that two or three times a day until the mere sound of the shake excites him.

3. **Graduate to shaking the container while he gnaws on his favorite toy.**

4. **Say "Out," give him a treat when he drops the toy, and walk away without touching the toy.**

5. **After several days of this, pick up the toy when you give him the treat, hold it for a second or two, and then put it down again.**

   Soon you'll be able to get him to open his mouth and trade any object for a treat.

When the object is a taboo item, be sure to keep it after making the trade and then show your Chi his own chew toy. For an alternative method, often used for habitual offenders, see the section "Reinforcing the 'Drop It' Command" earlier in this chapter.

Home Alone and Feeling Frantic

Most mature dogs catch a nap when their owners leave the house, but some anxious dogs pitch a fit when they're left home alone. They may chew on the carpet, shred the toilet paper, urinate, bark nonstop, or unleash any combination of destructive behaviors. You're probably thinking, "poor owners," but believe it or not, the destructive dogs are miserable, too. They have a problem called *separation anxiety.*

To better understand separation anxiety in dogs (see Figure 11-3), consider the phobias people have. Some people are afraid of heights, others are afraid of tight places, and still others are afraid of the water. Well, dogs are social creatures, and some of them are afraid of being alone. They panic, pure and simple, and then make noise or destroy stuff to release pent-up nervous energy.

The following sections help you understand the condition even more and provide some tips for alleviating your dog's nerves.

Figure 11-3: Dogs hate to be left alone, but most eventually get used to it — within reason.

Adjusting your exits and entrances

Some dogs seem to be born with tendencies toward separation anxiety. Others develop it after a major change — the owner's divorce or being given up for adoption. But a surprising number of dogs catch the problem from their owners. It goes something like this:

> "Oh, poor poor Pepe. I'm leaving now. Are you gonna miss me? Are you? I'm gonna miss you. Poor sweetums. You'll be all alone (kiss, kiss). Now you'll be a good boy, won't you? Give

mama a kiss. That's my boy. Poor baby. I'll be back soon. I promise (kiss, kiss)."

And then the owner leaves.

Now, what does Pepe make of all this? He just got a lot of attention and sympathy and then his human left. Maybe she's not coming back. Maybe he'll never see her again. Maybe he'll never see anyone ever again. No wonder he feels anxious!

The best way to prevent separation anxiety is to make your comings and goings low key. Ignore your Chihuahua for ten minutes before you leave and take him for granted when you return. Don't make the mistake of thinking that your dog has human emotions. He doesn't tear up the house out of spite because you left him alone. And he certainly doesn't have fun doing it. He's actually miserable. Separation anxiety is comparable to a person with claustrophobia getting stuck in an elevator. Your Chi needs help, not punishment.

The following section details what you can do for a dog that already suffers from the problem.

Alleviating the anxiety

Okay. You know your dog already has a problem with separation anxiety. Perhaps you could've prevented it, but no need to fret over that now. Just don't set up your dog for another dreadful day of demolition. Instead, crate him comfortably when you leave the house (see Chapters 5 and 10 for tips). In addition to keeping him out of trouble, being in his den may calm him. Yes, I know, that's just a quick fix and doesn't actually cure the problem. But it's a start, and you're keeping your dog out of trouble so he doesn't sense your aggravation.

Now that you have the destruction under control, you can work on alleviating your Chi's anxiety problem when he has the run of the house (or even a whole room). To do this, you must leave the house frequently for short periods of time. Eventually, that teaches him that comings and goings are unimportant because you always return. Here's how to set up your scenarios:

1. **Take Pepe outside to eliminate about ten minutes before you leave.**

2. **Turn on the radio and make sure two of his favorite toys are available.**

3. **Leave Pepe's crate in its normal place with the door open so he can go inside if he wants to.**

4. **Don't say goodbye or reassure Pepe in any way. In fact, don't give him any attention at all for several minutes before you leave.**

5. **Leave, close the door behind you, and count to ten. Open the door, go inside, and ignore Pepe for a minute or two. Then tell him to "Sit" and praise him for obeying (see Chapter 10).**

6. **Gradually increase the amount of time before you come back in. Make progress slow at first. Take two weeks to go from ten seconds to ten minutes.**

   If you find a puddle or the beginning of any destruction, don't call it to Pepe's attention; make a mental note of how long you were gone. Next time, decrease the amount of time you stay away. Then gradually work your way back up.

With a lot of practice (and patience), you may be able to work your way up to spending a few hours away from home without your Chi having an anxiety attack. Unfortunately, this doesn't work with every dog. If your dog doesn't learn to accept separations, he may need professional help. Ask your vet for referral to a behaviorist (if you're lucky, there may be a board-certified veterinary behaviorist in your area). The solution will include desensitization work and may include a temporary prescription of a drug to help keep your dog calm as he completes his desensitization program.

If your dog used to suffer from separation anxiety but overcame it, be sure to put him in a reputable boarding kennel when you go on vacation instead of hiring a dogwalker or housesitter. Otherwise, leaving home and not returning for a week or more could make him regress.

Now that you know what to do, here's what you shouldn't do: If your Chihuahua becomes a demolition demon when home alone, the worst — yes, the absolute worst — thing you can do is punish him when you get back. This simply gives him additional anxiety. Instead of being scared only when you leave, he'll be terrified of your return, too. That means double trouble.

Chapter 12

Training Your Chi for Canine Events, Tricks, and for Show

Do you want to show the world your wonderful Chihuahua? Would you like to partner with your dog to bring a little light into someone else's life? Does competition bring out the best in you? If so, this chapter contains plenty of ideas to help you and your Chihuahua find sports and hobbies you can participate in together.

Some Chihuahua owners enjoy making the most of their dogs' intelligence and dexterity by participating in dog sports like obedience and agility. Others like to show off their dogs' beauty in the wondrous world of dog shows. Chihuahuas can also earn Canine Good Citizen Certificates and serve as therapy dogs. In this chapter, I tell you about some activities you and your Chihuahua can participate in as partners — activities that will benefit your Chihuahua and make her a better companion. I also give you a short course in trick training, for fun and functionality.

 Sporting events for dogs may occur indoors or outside in all kinds of weather. Be aware that your Chihuahua won't be allowed to wear a sweater during competition. Your Chi won't do her best when she's chilled, so plan to attend dog events during the warm months unless the trials take place indoors.

If your dog is a Chihuahua mix or a purebred without papers, she can still participate in every event in this chapter with the exception of dog shows. The AKC (see Chapter 17) will grant an Indefinite Listing Privilege to spayed/neutered, unregistered, purebred dogs to allow them to compete in obedience and agility. The UKC also welcomes spayed/neutered, unregistered, purebreds and mixed breeds. And three out of four organizations that sponsor agility events welcome mixed breeds, too. Therapy dogs, Canine Good Citizens, and temperament-tested dogs may be any breed or mix.

Beginning Obedience Training

I like to call obedience *companion dog training,* because it teaches the dog how to be a happy and responsive partner and the owner how to train, understand, and enjoy the dog. During classes, your Chi discovers how to work with you despite distractions like strangers and other dogs. The happy result is enhanced companionship. Some simply call it teamwork. Whatever you call it, obedience training provides a great background for any other activity you may want to do with your dog.

If an obedience instructor suggests a training method or correction that doesn't feel right to you, don't do it. It's your dog, and you have the final say in her training.

Years ago, common knowledge said that dogs shouldn't attend obedience school until they're at least 6 months old. Back then, obedience exercises (such as the long sit; see Figure 12-1) were just tools people practiced on the training field once a week and for a few minutes a day at home. Today, obedience schools are modernized. Contemporary classes concentrate on practical training, and up-to-date instructors tell their students how to incorporate the training into everyday life. Modern instructors also emphasize positive reinforcement rather than punishment so younger dogs learn without becoming stressed. We also know that 4 months is an ideal age to enter your Chi into a novice class (although dogs profit from the training at any age).

Reviewing obedience basics

In a novice obedience class, a Chihuahua learns how to

✔ Heel (walk in the traditional position by your left side) on and off lead

✔ Sit when you stop

✔ Go down on command

✔ Stand quietly while a friendly stranger pets her

✔ Come when called

✔ Remain in both the "Sit" and "Down" positions amid distractions from other dogs

Best of all, provided that the training is positive and upbeat (don't stick around if it isn't), your Chi gains considerable confidence from the classes.

Dog clubs and private instructors offer obedience classes. They're advertised in the Yellow Pages or the newspaper. Your veterinarian may also have info about nearby classes, and some pet supply stores offer them right inside the stores.

Although the ultimate goal of obedience is a happy partnership with your dog, obedience also is one of the more popular dog sports. If your Chihuahua enjoys the training, you can turn obedience into a hobby and enter trials. When she qualifies for her novice title, she officially becomes Manchita, CD (in other words, the title becomes part of her registered name — Manchita, for instance). The CD stands for — you guessed it — Companion Dog.

In addition to the CD, the American Kennel Club (AKC) obedience titles include the CDX (Companion Dog Excellent), the UD (Utility Dog), the UDX (Utility Dog Excellent), and the OTCH (Obedience Trial Champion). The United Kennel Club (UKC) also offers a series of obedience titles.

Jumping into advanced competition

The fun doesn't have to end after your Chihuahua earns her Companion Dog title. She can accomplish plenty of challenging exercises in advanced competition. Among them are retrieving a small dumbbell, jumping various hurdles, discriminating between your scent and a stranger's, and responding to hand signals rather than verbal commands. Are you worried about your Chi making it over the jumps? If she has a sound body, she won't have a problem. Your Chihuahua gets measured before she enters the ring and the jumps are set at the right height for her size.

Choosing an obedience instructor

Shopping around is a good idea when it comes to obedience — not for a bargain but for the best school for you and your Chihuahua. Your Chi needs an instructor who has experience with dogs of all sizes — especially tiny ones.

Believe it or not, you'll recognize a first-rate teacher even though you don't know much about dog training yet. How? By your powers of observation. Watch a session or two of each beginner class offered in your area before signing up for one. Top-notch teachers have several attributes in common. Look for the following traits:

✔ **Good instructors are safety conscious.** They demand that all dogs be vaccinated (see Chapter 13). They don't crowd too many students into too small a space, and they provide a training area with sufficient traction and no hidden obstructions.

✔ **Good instructors are masters of positive motivation.** They show their students how to use praise, petting, and toys to encourage correct responses.

✔ **Good instructors are flexible.** They adapt their methods to fit their students' needs.

✔ **Good instructors are approachable, friendly, and helpful.** They have upbeat attitudes.

✔ **Good instructors are creative.** They vary the drills by initiating group games so handlers and dogs have a good time while performing the necessary repetitions.

✔ **Good instructors are attentive to all their students.** They work well with handlers and dogs of all sizes, shapes, ages, and genders, and they aren't prejudiced against any breed or mix.

✔ **Good instructors have lesson plans.** They discuss training goals and explain how to work each new command into everyday life. Their classes are never chaotic.

✔ **Good instructors keep the class moving.** They don't allow one student to monopolize the lesson.

✔ **Good instructors respect their students and have empathy.** They're aware that everyone in the class has feelings — including the dogs.

One of the really cool things you discover in obedience and agility school is that dogs, because they're closer to the ground, see things differently than humans do. When a student's dog seems leery about something, a good instructor will tell the student to get down and look at it from the pet's perspective. Try it sometime.

Figure 12-1: Maxie and Ginny demonstrate an obedience exercise called the long sit.

Passing the Good Citizen and Temperament Tests

According to the AKC, "A Canine Good Citizen is a dog that makes its owner happy without making someone else unhappy." That means Canine Good Citizens behave at home, are good neighbors, and are polite in public.

The Canine Good Citizen (CGC) test is pass-fail and noncompetitive. It evaluates practical training, not your dog's formal obedience. Your Chi is tested on how she behaves during everyday situations like being touched by a friendly stranger, walking on a crowded street, meeting another dog while out for a stroll, and coming when called. She also gets graded on her reaction to distractions and her attitude when you're out of sight (she shouldn't show separation anxiety). In addition, she must obey simple commands such as "Sit" and "Down" (see Chapter 10), but not with the precision of a competitive obedience dog.

All CGC tests are performed on lead. If your Chi passes a ten-part test, she earns a certificate proclaiming her a Canine Good Citizen.

Why go for the CGC honor? While preparing for the CGC test, owners find out how to train their dogs, and their dogs become better companions. Many dog clubs and private obedience schools offer short courses in CGC training, and some of them give the test as their graduation exercise. In addition, the AKC offers free info to help people train for the test. For CGC training material and information on how to find a test site near you, contact the AKC through e-mail at info@akc.org or call Customer Service at 919-233-9767.

The American Temperament Test Society (ATTS) also offers a ten-part test and rewards dogs that pass with a Temperament Tested, or TT, Certificate. The test takes no special training but requires a well-socialized dog with self-confidence and a reliable disposition. During a walk that simulates several situations, your Chi encounters friendly, neutral, and threatening scenarios and is evaluated on her reactions. The ATTS provides free information about the test. To discover more, go to www.atts.org or call 317-288-4403.

One of these honors isn't better than the other; they're just different and give you something to do with your dog. Of course, breeders use the titles to prove how smart, reliable, trainable, and beautiful their breeding stocks are.

Owners of dogs that earn CGC and TT certificates or belong to therapy dog clubs traditionally use the letters after their dogs' names — as in Manchita, CGC, TT, TDI, for instance. These titles don't become an official part of the dog's registered name, however.

Getting Active in Agility

How much fun can you handle? If you're thinking "a whole lot," agility may be the sport for you and your dog. Thousands of dog owners swear that agility is the most fun you can have with a dog.

At agility trials, dogs are timed as they navigate a course that resembles a colorful playground. They soar over hurdles, weave through poles, stride across balance beams, sprint up A-frames, play seesaw, and crawl through tunnels. Meanwhile, their handlers point out the next obstacle in the path (dogs must take obstacles in the correct order) and direct them through the course. Audiences at agility trials are always encouraging, but when the crowd sees a Chihuahua, the applause always amplifies!

Many owners do agility training with their dogs just for fun, but plenty of titles await you if competition is your thing. Your Chi could add so many titles to her name that it would take two breaths just to say it!

Few people want to landscape their yards with agility equipment (at least not at first), so most agility enthusiasts attend a private instructor's classes or join an agility club. Besides having the attributes that a good obedience instructor possesses (see "Choosing an obedience instructor" earlier in this chapter), a good agility teacher also

- ✔ Provides sturdy obstacles with neither rough edges nor a hint of a wobble
- ✔ Goes slow and keeps the obstacles low, making sure every dog and handler in the class has a firm foundation
- ✔ Provides new challenges by building on that foundation

 Smart handlers know the rules of the game before they play. Rulebooks for obedience and agility are available through the organizations that sanction these events. Four major (and some smaller) organizations offer agility. For more information and to find a teacher/club near you, ask your veterinarian for a recommendation, get info at your pet supply store, or check your phone book for local all-breed dog clubs.

Therapy Dogs: Delighting the Elderly and the Infirm

A couple decades ago, the scientific community found that interacting with friendly animals is therapeutic for people. Since then, polite pets have been welcomed at nursing homes and other institutions of healthcare.

Well-socialized Chihuahuas make top-notch therapy dogs because they're world-class lap-sitters. Lap-sitting is one of the most important tasks of a therapy dog. But becoming qualified to perform pet therapy isn't easy. This special service calls for a pet that keeps her cool in an institutional setting.

 Therapy dogs must have dependable dispositions and impeccable manners. Although a Chi's main assignment is lap-sitting, she still needs plenty of confidence to remain relaxed in an institution. After all, she'll be sitting on strange laps amid the distractions of hospital equipment (like wheelchairs and walkers), institutional odors, crowds, and noise.

Serving the hearing impaired

Chihuahuas can and do help the hearing impaired through *hearing dog programs.* After a training regimen where she learns to alert her handler to the doorbell, telephone, alarm clock, smoke alarm, oven timer, or baby crying, the dog is paired with a deaf person. The two practice obedience commands together, and the owner is taught how to care for the dog. They then go home together and the dog serves as the person's ears. Because they're so small that they fit anywhere and so smart that they easily take to the training, Chihuahuas are popular hearing dogs.

Hundreds of clubs across the United States are dedicated to pet-assisted therapy. These groups prepare their members through classes and tests. At least two national organizations — the Delta Society (www.deltasociety.org; 425-679-5500) and Therapy Dogs International (www.tdi-dog.org; 732-340-0728) — have local clubs or certified instructors in many cities. These resources are eager to help owners prepare their pets for therapy work. Your local dog club also may have a volunteer program.

The test used most frequently to certify dogs for therapy work is the AKC's Canine Good Citizen Test (see the section "Passing the Good Citizen and Temperament Tests"). Some organizations modify the test to include institutional equipment. A health certificate from your veterinarian may also be mandatory (see Chapter 13).

Requirements vary among organizations and institutions, but the rewards remain the same: Bored eyes light up and tired faces break into smiles at the sight of your Chihuahua. And the warm feeling remains with you and those you help for hours. But don't take my word for it. Give it a try!

How to Teach Your Dog a Trick or Two

Close your eyes and visualize your Chihuahua greeting people with a paw shake, waving hello and goodbye, asking for a cookie (or better make that a taco?), even dancing on her hind legs while you whistle. Does that image make you smile? Good. Chihuahuas love showing off, and it will surprise you how fast your Chi will learn tricks when you start teaching her. So what are you waiting for? Put some treats in your pocket and call your Chi. In this section, I teach enough tricks to tickle your family and friends.

The tricks in this section build on each other, so you should start with the first one and move on only after your Chihuahua can reliably perform the trick.

The benefits of trick training

Chihuahuas like learning tricks. After all, during training, they have what they want most — your full attention, plus praise and treats. A Chi thinks trick training was created just to make her feel special, but you reap rewards, too. Besides giving you a chance to have fun and impress your friends, teaching tricks enhances your Chi's vocabulary, encourages closer bonding, and leads to better behavior.

Another advantage to trick training is that it makes your Chi an impressive ambassador for her breed. Many people believe tiny dogs are brainless and lack character, but a Chi that waves and barks on command changes their thinking in a hurry.

Besides, after a shy Chi learns how to pull off a trick or two, she'll have something other than fear to focus on in social situations. And making people laugh improves her confidence.

Pushing your dog's performance buttons

When it comes to motivation, the happier your Chi is about learning a new move, the faster she'll perfect it. So, if you're a good motivator, your dog can be a terrific trickster in no time.

What's the key to effective motivation? Praise. But praising your Chi works only when your tone is sincere and maybe a little silly — okay, mighty silly with some dogs. Praising your pet in a drab monotone won't turn her on. It will sound similar to elevator music.

How can you make the praise so powerful that your Chi wants more? Give it with gusto. Give your Chi a big smile when you say, "Good girl!" If she's a little lethargic, accentuate your praise with a little applause. Use joyful words that come naturally to you, and say them in an excited voice every time she willingly gives a trick a try. Don't become boring by using the same praise words and treats every time. You can surprise her with new words. "Way to go, girl!" "All Right!" "Yes, Yes!" Scratch her back. Give her a taste of cheese, a sliver of hot dog, a bite of burger, or toss her a toy.

Read your Chihuahua's reactions to rewards. Your praise should make her eager to continue the lesson. Don't make it so shrill that it scares her or so invigorating that it distracts her.

Soon, you'll discover which phrases inspire your Chi to try harder, which treats she finds most tempting, and whether she'd rather chase a squeaky toy or have a back rub. In other words, you'll identify your Chi's buttons. Pushing them makes her happy, and when she's happy, she's willing to try the trick again.

Putting her in the mood

Because treats are an important part of trick training, try to train when your Chihuahua is hungry — before, not after, her meals. Before beginning a training session, take her outdoors and give her an opportunity to relieve herself. When you get back inside, let her watch you prepare and pocket some treats. When you have her undivided attention, start with something she knows. Have her Sit for a tidbit (see Chapter 10). That sets the tone and puts her in a cooperative mood to learn her first trick.

Don't try trick training until your Chi can sit on command. Sitting is a prerequisite to most tricks.

Using praise and treats wisely

When teaching tricks, use praise and treats/toys to motivate your Chi, and don't bark out "No!" when she makes a wrong move. When she does something right, reward her. When she does something wrong or does nothing at all, don't reward her. It's as simple as that. Neither force nor punishment should ever be involved.

Reward every correct move, no matter how tiny or tentative, when your dog is learning something new.

Shaking Hands or Gimme Five

If the Sit command is second nature to your Chi (see Chapter 10), you can teach her to Shake Hands or Gimme Five (see Figure 12-2).

Just follow these simple steps:

1. **Kneel down to your Chihuahua's level after telling her to Sit and say the cue word you choose.**

    Be creative. It doesn't matter what verbal cue you use as long as you use the same one every time.

2. **Pick up one of her forelegs, lift it from underneath, and gently release it.**

Praise her as soon as you drop her leg, and give her a tiny treat.

3. **Repeat the process five times and then try it again later or tomorrow.**

4. **After she's comfortable with you picking up her leg, gently move it up and down before releasing it.**

   The big breakthrough comes one day when your Chi lifts her leg as soon as you say the cue word. When she does, let her know how happy you are!

Gradually wean her away from expecting a treat every time, but always tell her what a good girl she is. And even after she performs reliably for praise, surprise her with a treat occasionally. After she has this trick down pat, you can have family and friends practice it with her (but not more than five tries at a time).

Figure 12-2: Glad to meet you, Manchita!

Waving hi and bye

When your Chihuahua is able to shake hands as easily as a state senator, you can start teaching her how to Wave. Use these simple steps:

1. **Use your cue words and ask your Chi to shake hands (see the previous section).**

2. **Just as she lifts her paw, pull your hand away while repeating your cue words in a happy voice.**

   Most dogs wave their paws in the air in an effort to make contact with their humans' hands.

3. **The instant your Chi waves even a little, say "Wave" and give her a treat.**

   Keep at it, making her wave just a bit longer each time before she gets her reward. When she starts to master the wave (see Figure 12-3 for an example of a master waver), you can eliminate asking for the handshake by going directly from Sit to Wave. Finally, you can wean her off the treat by giving it only once every few times. But continue praising her for every wave.

It's also fun to hold your Chihuahua at chest level in both hands and ask her to wave at someone. You can teach this trick the same way, except that you need a helper. Hold your Chi while your helper walks up; he or she should ask her to shake hands and then pull the hand away to elicit a wave. Some Chis will wave with both front legs when in their owners' arms.

Figure 12-3: This well-trained Chi waves at a friend.

Use the command Wave rather than the more obvious "Hi" or "Bye" because it's more versatile. You can cue your Chihuahua to wave hi and wave bye, and you can personalize the trick by telling her to "Wave to Aunt Amelia," for instance.

Speak and Shhhh

Time to get silly! Here's your chance to teach your Chi how to speak with the following steps:

1. **Start by showing your Chihuahua her favorite treat.**

   Wiggle it right in front of her but don't let her take it.

2. **Get her all wound up by teasing her with the treat.**

3. **As she prances around, say "Speak" excitedly, over and over.**

   The object is to get her to make a sound (any sound).

4. **When she makes a sound (even if it's a wimpy squeak), give her the treat and plenty of praise.**

   After she eats the treat, try again. Stop after five tries no matter how much fun she's having.

It won't be long before your Chi makes the connection and barks as loud as she can when you say Speak and show her the treat. That's a good start. Continue using the treat until you have to say Speak only once. Gradually wean her off the treat.

 The real fun begins when you get creative. "Speak to Me." "If you want a cookie, Speak." "Speak to Aunt Amelia!" "Speak Spanish!"

Some Chihuahuas anticipate this trick and begin barking before you can say the cue word. Every time your Chi tries that, tell her "Shhhh" and don't give her the cue (or the treat) until she quiets down. Have her stay quiet for several seconds. After repeating this process, she'll learn that Shhhh means hush — an extra bonus trick that can really come in handy if your dog is a problem barker (see Chapter 11).

Dancing the tango

Chihuahuas make marvelous dancers, with moves that are the envy of larger breeds. To teach your Chi the tango (or the waltz, jitterbug, two-step, or mambo), turn on your favorite tune or hum a few notes. Hold a treat several inches above her head and say "Let's dance!" The object is to get her to walk a few steps on her hind legs, so move the treat forward slightly after she rears up.

When she realizes what you want, it still may take several weeks until her leg and back muscles are developed enough to let her dance on her hind legs for several seconds. As soon as she can balance on her hind legs rather well, start moving the treat in a circle above her head to teach her to turn. Soon, she'll be pirouetting in either direction!

What do you do with a dancing dog? Join in, of course! As your Chihuahua swings and sways on her hind legs, start moving to the music along with her. Having a partner encourages her to make up steps of her own. She may soon add hops, skips, and jumps to her dancing repertoire.

Touring the Dog Show Circuit

If you want to see more than a hundred breeds of gorgeous dogs gathered in one place, treat yourself to a dog show. Besides seeing beautifully groomed and trained representatives of all your favorite breeds, you become acquainted with rare breeds that few people ever get to see. Agility and obedience trials often are held in the same venues as dog shows, too. Dog shows are fun regardless of whether or not you understand the judging procedure, but a little knowledge will make your first experience more rewarding. In this section, I tell you about the basics of dog judging so you understand what the exhibitors and judges are doing. Then I give you the upside and the downside of the "dog game," and I help you get started in the dog show game if you want to become a player.

Dogs not entered in competition aren't allowed at dog shows, so leave your Chi at home when you go to a show just to check it out. Rather than a dog, put a notebook on your lap and jot down your impressions of why certain dogs won. Later, if you get into the dog game, dig out that notebook and read what you wrote. Your first impressions may help your handling.

To be eligible to show in conformation, your Chihuahua must be

- ✔ At least 6 months old
- ✔ AKC registered with full registration (see Chapter 4) or registered with the club sponsoring the event
- ✔ Unaltered (spayed or neutered dogs aren't eligible to show)

When exhibitors compete at dog shows, they say they're showing their dogs in *breed* or *conformation*.

How dogs are judged and other show basics

Dogs don their finest fur when competing at a dog show, and with so many gorgeous creatures to choose from, your first reaction may be to pity the poor judge. But a dog show judge has help in the form of guidelines, called the *breed standard* (see the Chihuahua standard in Chapter 2). The standard describes an ideal specimen of the breed. The judge's job is to select as the winner the dog that most closely conforms to this written description of physical perfection.

In other words, no matter how many dogs compete in the show ring, the winner should be the dog that most closely resembles the ideal dog described in its breed standard. Second place goes to the next closest dog, and so on.

When watching a show, you see dogs of the same breed judged together early in the day. But later, you see the winning dogs of each breed competing against each other. That's when novices really get confused. After all, how can a judge choose between an animated Chihuahua and an elegant Pekingese? Well, the judge isn't really comparing the Chihuahua to the Pekingese. Instead, he or she is comparing how close the Chihuahua matches its breed standard with how close the Peke matches its standard.

The following sections explain the order of the dog show classes, how the elimination contest works, and what it takes to get that coveted Champion title for your Chihuahua.

When you arrive at a dog show, buy a show catalog right away. Then you can match each dog's catalog number with its handler's armband number, thus finding out who's who.

Winning or losing — it's the judge's call

Your first experience with subjective dog show judging may make you feel a little confused. Most of the better-known sports are judged objectively. During games of baseball, basketball, football, golf, or tennis, you always know the score. But it's different at dog shows, where winning or losing depends on the judge's opinion. This concept can be confusing at first, especially when you see a dog get a "Best of" prize one day and not even place in its class the next.

The more you discover about canine conformation and the Chihuahua standard (see Chapter 2), the better you'll understand how each judge picks his or her winners. One judge may be a stickler for movement. A superior head may sway another. Because judges interpret the standards in their own unique ways, different dogs may win under different judges. And that's a good thing because it lets many excellent dogs have their days in the sun.

Plus, dogs are judged *on the day,* or, to be more precise, in a moment of time — something like the way humans judge themselves when they confront their images in the mirror each morning. On Saturday, you may smile and congratulate yourself on looking years younger, but then on Sunday you may appear drawn and weary. Well, dogs have good days and bad days, too, and a judge can only go by what dogs look like during the few moments they're exhibited. So, if the owners of yesterday's Best of Breed Chihuahua kept superdog up too late while they celebrated, he may look like sleepydog during the next day's competition.

An elimination contest

Shows where dogs are judged on their conformation are *elimination contests*. The process of an elimination contest has many steps, which I list here:

1. **To begin with, all the dogs of a single breed (or variety of a breed) compete with others of their sex in one of the regular classes — Puppy, 12-to-18-Month, Novice, Bred-by-Exhibitor, American-bred, or Open.**

2. **First-place winners of the same sex from each of the classes compete against each other for Winners Dog and Winners Bitch.**

3. **These two winners are awarded points toward their championship (see the section "Becoming a champion" later in this chapter) and return to the ring for Best of Breed (or Variety) competition.**

   Dogs that are already champions are called *Specials,* and they also compete for Best of Breed or Variety.

4. **Three awards are presented in the final elimination contest at the breed level:**

   • The top specimen is awarded Best of Breed or Variety.

   • The best dog of the opposite sex than the Best of Breed is presented with the Best of Opposite Sex (BOS) ribbon.

- The best of the two class winners is named Best of Winners (BOW).

   Sometimes, a class dog (a dog that isn't a champion yet) goes to the top and takes Best of Breed or Variety, as well as Best of Winners.

5. **When Chihuahua judging is complete, all but the Best of Variety winners are finished for the day. The Best of Variety Chihuahuas are now eligible to compete in the Toy group.**

   The Toy group is where all the Toys that won Best of Breed or Variety compete for group placements.

6. **Following a group judging and elimination, only seven dogs — the first-place winners from each group — are left in the show. During the climax, they compete for Best in Show (BIS).**

   When the show is over, only one undefeated dog remains — but a couple hundred dogs may have earned points toward their championships, and many others thrilled their owners by placing high in their classes.

 Only two Toy breeds, the Chihuahua and the English Toy Spaniel, are represented by two varieties in the Toy group. The two Chihuahua varieties are the long coat and smooth coat. Two other Toy breeds, the Manchester Terrier and the Poodle, also come in varieties, but only the Toy Manchester Terrier and the Toy Poodle compete in the Toy group. Their larger counterparts compete in other groups.

Group classifications

For purposes of showing, the American Kennel Club (AKC) divides dogs into seven groups as follows:

- ✔ Group 1: Sporting Dogs

- ✔ Group 2: Hounds

- ✔ Group 3: Working Dogs

- ✔ Group 4: Terriers

- ✔ Group 5: Toys

- ✔ Group 6: Non-Sporting Dogs

- ✔ Group 7: Herding Dogs

Becoming a champion

To become an *AKC champion* on the dog show circuit, your Chihuahua must win 15 points, including points from at least two major wins (*majors* are shows where three or more points are awarded). The two majors must be awarded by different judges, and at least one of the remaining points must be won under a third judge.

The number of points your Chi may be awarded for going Winners Dog at a show varies. It depends on how many Chihuahuas competed, the schedule of points established by the AKC, and whether your Chi goes on to win Best of Winners, Best of Variety, her Group, or even Best in Show (see the previous section). The most points ever available at a show is five, and the fewest available is one. Your Chi must win points at a minimum of three shows to earn a championship. Five-point majors are few and far between and competition is keen, so most Chihuahuas are shown several times before becoming champions.

When a dog *finishes its championship,* it's permanently recorded as a champion of record and is entitled to the word "Champion" before its name. The AKC abbreviation is *Ch,* as in "Ch Manchita."

The ups and downs of showing dogs

All hobbies have their good points and bad points. In the sections that follow, I list some of the things, both positive (upside) and negative (downside), you may want to consider before deciding you want to show your dog.

The upside of showing dogs

Here are the many benefits that come with competing in dog shows:

- ✔ Competing with your dog is fun and exciting.
- ✔ You can make new friends with people who have similar interests, and you may be invited to join dog clubs.
- ✔ Many obedience schools offer conformation classes where you and your Chihuahua can both make new friends.
- ✔ Depending on your goals, it can be a casual or an absorbing avocation.
- ✔ Showing dogs is educational. If you go in with an open mind, you'll discover something new every time you attend a show.
- ✔ You get to meet the top Chihuahua breeders.

✔ Becoming seriously involved means you may become a breeder (at least occasionally).

✔ Training your Chihuahua for the show ring strengthens your bond.

✔ Showing involves traveling.

✔ You get the opportunity to learn from your losses to make you a better competitor.

✔ Winning feels wonderful!

The downside of showing dogs

Here's the other side of the coin — the disadvantages of joining the dog show circuit:

✔ Winning at dog shows means you'll need a dog with superior conformation.

✔ Showing dogs is expensive and requires some special equipment.

✔ The alternative to training and showing your own dog is hiring a professional handler, which is expensive.

✔ Training your Chihuahua for the show ring is time consuming.

✔ Showing can be stressful to dogs and their owners.

✔ Showing involves traveling.

✔ When you become seriously involved, breeding dogs becomes a probability (at least occasionally).

✔ The sport can take over your life. Between conformation classes, club meetings, dog shows, and breeding, showing dogs can become all-encompassing.

✔ Losing feels lousy (until you learn to turn losses into learning experiences).

Getting started in showing

I hate to be the bearer of bad news, but no matter how handsome you and your friends think she is, if you didn't buy your Chihuahua as a potential show dog, chances are she won't win at dog shows. Some dogs are rare exceptions, of course, but your Chi is probably tops at exactly what you bought her for — companionship.

Eventually, you'll need another Chi if you want to take up showing, but in the meantime, make your companion Chi your compadre for learning the ropes. Take her to conformation class and discover how to train and handle her in the ring. She'll love the attention, and you can make your novice mistakes on her. This way, you become a better handler for your next pup — the one you buy with showing in mind.

Take your time purchasing a show-potential Chihuahua. Study the breed standard (see Chapter 2) and attend a couple shows. Watching the judging helps you develop an eye for a show-quality dog. Soon, you'll find out which attributes are more important to you, and which breeders' dogs are strong in those traits. Then talk to the breeders whose dogs you most admire and check out their available show-potential pups. But don't expect to get one right away. You may have to put your name on a waiting list and fork over a deposit (money alert!).

The following sections help you dive even deeper into the world of dog showing.

For more information on showing, go to the AKC's Web site (www. akc.org). Magazines, such as the *AKC Gazette,* also keep you up-to-date on dog shows held all over the United States. Many excellent books on showing and how dogs are judged are available.

Preparing for what show dogs do

Assuming your Chihuahua is show quality and has full AKC registration — a requirement for showing — what's next?

Besides possessing physical beauty and a steady temperament, your Chi must take travel, crowds, noise, and strange dogs in stride. She also must

- Stand still for grooming

- Pose while the judge examines her

- Circle the ring at a smooth trot in a line with her competitors

- Gait solo in the designated pattern

- Keep her cool from the first burst of applause through the hush that settles over the arena just before the judge points to the winner

Yikes! You know what to expect after watching a show or two, but how will your Chi get used to all that? And how will you ever be able to handle her in the show ring? Easy. You take lessons together. Dog clubs and private instructors offer *conformation classes* where you become familiar with the finer points of handling. At the same time, your dog gets used to stacking (posing) and trotting (gaiting) around other dogs and people. Check the Internet and ask your vet and breeder where quality show training is available.

When you attend conformation classes, you find out when matches take place in your area. *Matches* are practice dog shows — much like the real thing except they're informal and no championship points are awarded. Matches are great for honing your handling skills and getting your dog used to the show atmosphere.

Of course, many people hire professional handlers *(agents)* to show their dogs. If you decide to hire a handler, choose one who has an excellent reputation for taking care of and winning with Toy dogs. Your dog's breeder may be happy to help you locate and choose a handler.

Where's the show, and how do I enter?

Your conformation instructor will know where shows are scheduled in your area, but you need some written material when you're ready to enter. The *Events Calendar,* a supplement to the *AKC Gazette,* and a few other dog magazines (sold by subscription and also found in pet shops, bookstores, and newsstands) list upcoming AKC shows. They also include the names and addresses of the show superintendents you need to contact if you want to receive show information.

The superintendents will make your mailbox bulge with premium lists about shows in your area, complete with entry forms, fee information, and closing dates for entries.

If your Chihuahua is ready to show, enter well ahead of the closing date so you aren't disappointed. Late entries are not accepted.

Speaking dog show lingo

Every sport has its unique terminology, and dog showing is no exception. When studying the breed standard (see Chapter 2) or evaluating dogs with other fanciers, certain words always come up. Knowing and understanding these terms early in the game is a good idea. The following sections present many common terms that float around whenever dog showing is the topic du jour.

Type

Type is what sets one breed of dog apart from every other breed. The concept of breed type is easiest to understand if you remember that each breed has only one correct type. It's type that makes you instantly recognize the features that combine to make up a Chihuahua. Type enables people to differentiate your dog from a Papillon, Miniature Pinscher, or any other breed.

And in the show ring, the *most typey* dog is the one that comes closest to matching the characteristics described in its breed standard.

Soundness

Soundness is the ability to function well, and it includes physical and behavioral characteristics such as a correct skeleton, proper musculature, and a stable temperament. Also, no handicaps, temporary or permanent, should inhibit the dog from using these attributes. A dog that's deaf, blind, lame, overly aggressive, missing a testicle, or painfully shy is *unsound.* If a sound dog steps on a smoldering cigarette and limps because her burned pad hurts, she's *temporarily unsound* and can't be shown. But as soon as she heals enough to move normally, she becomes sound again.

Not all faults in a dog are considered unsound. For example, your Chi's ears may be on the small side (the standard specifies large) yet function just fine. Because having smallish ears doesn't interfere with her ability to hear, the characteristic doesn't make her unsound. However, small ears are uncharacteristic of the Chi breed, so she lacks type.

Balance

Balance means that all parts of the dog fit each other without exaggeration of any single part. The size of the head corresponds with the size of the body, and height, width, and weight are proportionate. If people look at your Chihuahua and say, "My, what long legs she has," or "Doesn't she have a big head for her size?" chances are she lacks balance.

Don't fret over balance too soon. Puppies often go through stages when they're temporarily out of *proportion,* another word for balance. When your Chi is young, her head may look too big for her body. She may have a well-developed front and a wimpy rear, or she may seem to be walking downhill because her back legs grew faster than her front legs. However, by the time she matures into a good show dog, all her parts must be balanced.

Condition

When it comes to condition, the ball is in your court. You can't control whether your Chihuahua matures typey or balanced, but her condition depends on you. A Chi is in *condition* when she

Manchita's showy story

Show breeders sell their top-quality puppies as *show potential pups*. That means the pups appear to have all the attributes necessary to become champions. But potential is only potential. As a dog matures, things may change. That's what happened to my Manchita, a show-potential puppy that I got when she was going on 4 months old. At 6 months, she still looked mighty fine, so we entered a show. She won the Puppy class and then beat the other class winners for Winners Bitch. That day, Manchita was awarded her first (and last) championship points. During the next few weeks, her bite changed big time, and she matured with a wry mouth and the habit of letting the tip of her tongue dangle. So much for showing!

Manchita's breeders guaranteed her for show potential, as many top breeders do. When her mouth went wry, the breeders were prepared to trade for a different pup and place Manchita in a pet home. But we wanted to keep her (and the timing wasn't right for raising a second pup), so we never asked them to honor the guarantee.

carries the right amount of weight for her size (see Chapter 2) and has an immaculate coat with a healthy sheen, good muscle tone, clean ears, and clear eyes (see Chapter 7).

Style and showmanship

Style and *showmanship* are similar terms with respect to the show ring, but they're not quite identical. *Stylish* is the dog show term used to describe a dog that carries itself elegantly and with pride; a *good showman* indicates a dog with a pleasantly bold attitude that performs well during the judging.

If your Chihuahua has showmanship and style, she shows off her breed characteristics, making the most of her typeness. Judges recognize a dog like that easily. She steps out with pride — neck arched, head up, aspect bold, happy, and eager — yet remains under control. A good showman that lacks style, however, may still be appealing because of her saucy, outgoing manner, but she'll never fool a knowledgeable judge.

At a dog show, style often separates the superior from the good and the winners from the losers — especially when all other points are nearly equal. Style or elegance is a quality you can't give your Chi. She was either born with it or wasn't. She may be typey, sound, well balanced, and in fine condition, yet still lack style. That doesn't mean she won't win, because a correct dog — especially one with showmanship — wins her share of champion points. However, what it does mean is that when competing against an equally correct dog that's also stylish, your Chi will come in second.

Unlike style, which you can't instill into a dog through training, you can help your Chi grow into the best showman she can be:

✔ Give her plenty of socialization to bolster her confidence (see Chapter 9).

✔ Lead-break her with praise and patience (see Chapter 9).

✔ Keep your training periods upbeat and brief so she doesn't become bored.

Follow this advice and you'll elicit your dog's best attitude.

Part IV

Chihuahua Care and Concerns

The 5th Wave   By Rich Tennant

Dr. Doug and his Chihuahua shared a unique companionship.

C'mon Misty — scissors, scissors! That's a scalpel. You know that!

In this part . . .

Selecting a skilled and caring veterinarian is the most important step in keeping your Chihuahua healthy. This part shows you how to find that special person, how to make the most of your visits to the vet, and how to preserve good canine health at home. I also outline all the ailments your Chihuahua could suffer from and how you can take measures to prevent sickness. Finally, you discover how to handle emergency situations and serious illness, and I give you advice on coping with the death of your beloved pet.

Chapter 13

Visiting the Vet

*N*ext to you, no one is more important to your little Pepe's health than his veterinarian. That's why choosing his vet is one of the more important decisions you'll ever make for him. This chapter helps you find a veterinarian you can trust with your Chihuahua's life.

But it takes two to save a sick dog — one to diagnose the illness and prescribe the treatment, and the other to follow up at home. Because the other is you, I also help you become the kind of client every caring veterinarian wants — one who prevents problems whenever possible, sees the signs of sickness before they become severe, keeps calm (uh oh), remembers instructions, and carries them out exactly as prescribed. Finally, I cover other important health topics, from your dog's first exam and his all-important vaccinations to altering your Chi and fitting him with an ID.

Choosing Your Chihuahua's Veterinarian

By now you know that all dogs aren't the same. Toys like Chihuahuas have special needs, and sometimes specific problems. Therefore, you need a veterinarian who likes and understands Toy dogs. Depending on where you live, you may have several excellent choices right in town, or you may have to drive 50 miles to visit the vet most of the Toy owners in your community trust. Near or far, picking your dog's vet is a major decision. Someday, his life may depend on the doctor's diagnostic ability.

Here are some of the better ways to find a good veterinarian:

- ✔ Ask your Chi's breeder. If the breeder lives within a reasonable distance, try his or her vet first. Even if the breeder lives far away, he or she may have sold pups to other people in your area and can tell you how to contact them for referrals.

- ✔ When you see people walking Toy dogs in your neighborhood, ask them who they use and if they're satisfied with the quality of care.

- ✔ Call the nearest major veterinary hospital or the local or state veterinary association (you can find them in the phone book) for recommendations.

- ✔ Look for a veterinary hospital with AAHA (American Animal Hospital Association) accreditation. These hospitals voluntarily meet a high standard set by the AAHA and undergo regular inspections to make sure they maintain standards. Going to www.aahanet.org can help you find a local hospital that goes this extra step. When you find a candidate, ask for a tour of the hospital. If the staff is friendly and happy to show you around, this is a good sign. If not, stay away.

Let your mouth, not your fingers, do the walking when looking for a good veterinarian. Asking Toy dog breeders and members of a local kennel club beats looking in the Yellow Pages.

After you choose a vet with an awesome reputation and make the first appointment for your Chihuahua, you must decide whether you're satisfied with your choice. The right veterinarian will do or have the following. (If the vet you visit doesn't do or have these things, you may opt to discuss your dissatisfaction with the vet or simply change veterinarians. Many vet offices accommodate several vets, so you may be able to change to one you feel more comfortable with in the same office.)

- ✔ **Handle your Chihuahua with professional proficiency.** Whether your dog is everybody's pal or shy with strangers, your vet should handle him gently but firmly. A complete physical examination needs to be performed carefully but with practiced ease (see Figure 13-1). Steer clear of any vet who seems rushed or rough or says or does anything that leads you to believe he or she may not like Chihuahuas.

- ✔ **Weigh him and take his temperature and a complete history.** This should include where you got him, how long you've had him, his age, diet, vaccinations, wormings, activity level, appetite, and previous illnesses.

✓ **Explain the examination and discuss the results with you.** A caring vet may give you tips on how to improve your Chi's condition or keep him healthy over the long term.

✓ **Answer your questions thoroughly in language you understand.** Any vet who purposely talks over your head or has an arrogant attitude doesn't need you (or me) for a client. Good vets answer their clients' questions in everyday language without talking down to them.

✓ **Make provisions for emergency care during weekends, holidays, and the middle of the night.** Some veterinarians handle emergencies themselves; others refer their clients to services that specialize in emergencies. If your vet opts for the service, make sure a vet knowledgeable in Toy dogs is always available.

✓ **Have a pleasant receptionist and staff and a clean waiting room.** The exception is the small-town vet who cheerfully operates a tidy, one-person office.

✓ **Have an organized and well-equipped facility.**

✓ **Discuss fees.** Although most clinics expect you to pay for regular office visits right away, you may want to ask about their policies for unexpected, expensive emergencies.

✓ **Be caring.** If you sense coldness or indifference in the vet or his/her staff, your pup is in the wrong place.

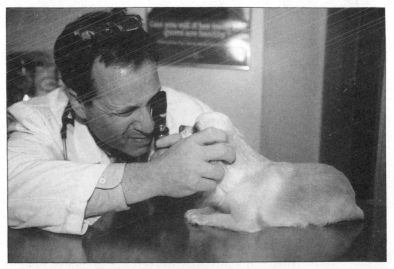

Figure 13-1: Your Chihuahua needs a vet who likes and understands small dogs.

Being the Best Kind of Client

If your Chi becomes ill or injured, it takes more than an excellent vet to cure him. It also takes you — a conscientious and composed client. A dog does best if his veterinarian and his owner work together to pull him through a crisis. The following list explains how you can be the type of client a veterinarian is glad to have on his or her team:

- ✔ Calling and making appointments for routine visits, such as annual exams and booster shots.

- ✔ Arriving to appointments on time.

- ✔ Not asking your vet to diagnose your dog over the telephone.

 Why no phone diagnosis? Because it can't be done. A variety of canine illnesses display similar signs. It takes a hands-on examination, and possibly some tests, to find out what's causing the problem and to decide on the best method of treatment.

- ✔ Having an understanding attitude when the vet runs late because he or she had to drop everything to take care of an emergency.

- ✔ Knowing your dog's normal behavior and calling the clinic immediately if something doesn't seem right.

 Write down your dog's normal vital signs and keep them handy. Yes, your vet should keep a record, but your Chi may get sick while you're traveling, and knowing what's normal for him helps an emergency vet make a better diagnosis.

- ✔ Bringing along a written list of recent behavior changes, if any exist (for example: excessive thirst, loss of appetite, change in activity level, unexplained fear or aggression, and so on).

- ✔ Bringing the health and vaccination records the breeder gave you (for your first visit; see the following section).

- ✔ Keeping your dog on leash on your lap or in his crate in the waiting room. Don't let him play on the floor or sniff strange dogs. It's easy for pups to pick up germs.

- ✔ Being honest. When your vet asks if your Chihuahua has been on any medication, don't be ashamed to admit that you tried an over-the-counter medication from the pet shop. Admitting a mistake may make you feel like a fool, but your vet has to know exactly what your dog has ingested to make a correct diagnosis. Not only that, but mixing medications can be fatal.

Also, if your Chi seemed slightly sick for several days and you kept hoping that he'd get better on his own, admit that, too. Don't try to make yourself look better at your dog's expense.

✔ Making a list of your dog-care questions and bringing it along. Your vet should be glad to answer appropriate questions about feeding, grooming, toenail trimming, and anything else related to your Chihuahua's health; however, he or she doesn't have time to listen to you ramble on about how Grandma Mildred thinks your Pepe should be a television star.

✔ Taking notes when the vet gives you instructions.

✔ Following all instructions exactly. You must give medications at the right time and in the correct dosage or they won't work. If you don't understand how to administer a medication, ask. Your vet can explain or demonstrate.

Never increase the dosage of a medication (not even a little) in the hopes of making your Chihuahua feel better faster. Medication doesn't work that way. In fact, what cures at the proper dosage can kill when overdosed.

✔ Staying as composed as possible, even during an emergency. The more serious the injury or illness, the more your vet needs you as a clear-thinking partner in your Chihuahua's treatment.

No matter how frightening the emergency and how fast you want to get your dog to the vet, you need to secure his crate for the trip so it doesn't roll or slide while you drive. The last thing a sick or hurt Chihuahua needs is a terrifying tumble.

✔ Not being argumentative or belligerent. Most vets care about their clients and understand how deeply people love their dogs. But vets aren't magicians; they can't guarantee that a badly injured or gravely ill dog will recover, no matter how skillfully they treat it. If you lose confidence in your vet, the best thing to do is change clinics.

✔ Paying your bills according to clinic policy.

The Ins and Outs of the First Exam

The best time for a Chihuahua and his veterinarian to meet is within 48 hours after you acquire him. In fact, breeder contracts usually tell owners how soon the dogs' initial exams must take place; ignoring these contracts voids the guarantees. Although most puppies purchased from reliable breeders are healthy (see Chapter 4), the timely first examination is especially important for three reasons:

✓ Your veterinarian either confirms that your dog is healthy or gives you the bad news if he isn't (I'm talking major problems here, not a minor infestation of worms or a loose baby tooth that needs attention). If something is seriously wrong, finding out while you can still return the Chihuahua is better than falling hopelessly in love with a puppy so sick that it can never live a normal life.

✓ So the clinic can establish a permanent record of what's normal for your dog (assuming he's fine). If he ever shows signs of sickness, tests can quickly disclose deviations. Besides, why not get to know your vet when your Chi is healthy instead of entrusting your dog to a total stranger during an emergency?

✓ Your new dog probably needs vaccinations, a checkup for internal and external parasites, and medicine to prevent heartworm. I tell you more about preventative medicine later in this chapter and in Chapter 14.

Unfortunately, people don't always get to decide when to visit the veterinarian. In case of an emergency, take your dog to the vet ASAP. Speedy treatment often is the difference between death and complete recovery. Call the clinic first and explain what happened so the staff can prepare.

Here's to hoping your first visit will be routine and painless. The following sections dig deeper into the visit details.

Getting organized

Here's a checklist of what to do before your pup's first visit to the veterinarian so you can get organized:

✓ Feed your Chihuahua a couple dog biscuits an hour or more before driving him to the veterinarian. That may keep him from getting carsick.

✓ Put a roll of paper towels and a container of wet wipes in your vehicle in case a quick cleanup is necessary.

✓ Prepare a copy of your dog's health record to take along.

✓ Collect a recent stool sample. You can use a resealable plastic bag. (Some vets want you to bring one along for the first exam. Be sure to ask about that when making his appointment.)

✔ Transport your dog in a crate. Secure the crate to make sure it doesn't take a tumble if you have to swerve or make a quick stop.

✔ Bring cash or your checkbook. Vets get paid at the time of treatment, and some of them don't take credit cards.

Making the most of your first visit

Surely you have questions about dog care before your first visit. The initial visit is the time to ask. Write your questions down at home as you think of them so you don't forget anything. To get you started, here are a few questions new Chihuahua owners often ask:

✔ When is it safe to start taking my dog to public places?

✔ What do normal bowel movements look like?

✔ How often should my dog have a bowel movement?

✔ What's a good balanced diet for my Chihuahua?

✔ How often can he have treats, and what makes a good treat?

✔ Does my dog need a vitamin and mineral supplement?

If you want to buy health insurance for your Chihuahua, the insurance is readily available. Discuss this option with your veterinarian or search for Pet Health Insurance on the Net. You'll find many options. Before buying a policy, be sure you know what it does and doesn't cover, what percentage it pays, and how to make claims. For example, some pet policies are for emergency care only; others offer wellness plans that cover annual examinations.

No coddling allowed

Even if the thought of your dog getting his first shot makes you cringe, don't let him know that. Be friendly with the veterinarian, not nervous, or your dog will feel your tension and get scared. The ideal attitude for the first visit (and those thereafter) is patient but matter-of-fact. Hold your Chi in place gently but firmly for the examination and talk to him in a happy tone, without letting sympathy creep into your voice. Consoling and coddling your Chihuahua will only make him sure that something terrible is going to happen. Your dog takes his cues from you, so if he senses that you're relaxed and like the vet, he'll relax and like the vet, too.

Home again and more confused than ever

You and your dog visited your vet for the first time, and now you're home again, filled with new information — some of it different from what you've read in this book. What should you do? Who should you believe?

Trust your veterinarian. This book is a general reference, meaning that it contains good, solid information about Chihuahuas in general. But your dog is an individual that just had a thorough examination, and now you have personalized instructions. Follow them. They're meant especially for your pup.

Understanding Those Vital Vaccinations

Sorry in advance for all the gloom and doom, but for your Chihuahua's sake, you must know the worst conditions your pup can contract. The good news is that modern dog owners are lucky. They don't have to worry about losing their pets to the host of deadly diseases that wiped out dogs by the thousands just a few canine generations ago. Today, the main focus of dog care is preventative medicine. The vaccinations your vet schedules are the best safeguards to keep your Chi from contracting a variety of potentially fatal diseases. This section breaks down all the vaccination knowledge you need.

Although vaccines often are referred to as permanent shots, don't believe it. No canine vaccine gives permanent immunity, which is why dogs should get booster shots throughout their adult lives.

Different vaccines for different lifestyles

If it has been awhile since you had a new puppy, you may think all vaccinations programs are similar. They used to be, but they aren't anymore. Today, dog vaccines are divided into core and non-core. *Core vaccines* are the ones recommended for all dogs in a particular area. *Non-core vaccines* give dogs additional protection in special circumstances. For example, if you live in the northeast part of the United States and your dog is pretty much a stay-at-home pet, your vet will recommend one series of shots. But if you and your dog will do a lot of traveling, your Chi will need the extra protection of non-core vaccines (see the section "Just say 'No!' to other deadly diseases" for more on extra protection; the other sections deal with the most frequent core group).

If you plan to travel a great deal with your dog, tell your vet because exposure to strange dogs and new places may demand extra precautions. Don't take your Chi on any outings until you're sure his puppy series of inoculations is complete. Following his puppy series, he needs a booster shot every year of his adult life.

Taking extra precautions for Toy puppies

Don't be surprised if your Chihuahua's vaccination schedule is different from the plan your friend follows for her Doberman Pinscher puppy. Chihuahuas and other Toy dogs are more likely to have allergic reactions to some of the common combination vaccines. In fact, sometimes they come through their first vaccinations just fine but then get sick from the second or third round. That's why many vets separate the shots and give tiny dogs their parvo shots alone rather than in combination with other vaccines. The leptospirosis vaccination also is an issue with Toy dogs, so discuss this vaccine with your veterinarian. Depending on your lifestyle, it may not be included.

Your puppy's vaccinations must never be closer than two weeks apart. Three to four weeks apart is ideal. Your vet will recommend the proper schedule for your pup.

If your dog is allergic to a vaccine, a reaction (swelling around the muzzle, difficulty breathing, or even collapse) usually occurs between 20 and 30 minutes after the shot. If you live far from your clinic, don't drive home immediately after your dog is vaccinated. Instead, stick around for about an hour (read a book or listen to music in your vehicle with your dog on your lap). That way, immediate help is just seconds away.

An allergic reaction to an injection is called *anaphylaxis* or *anaphylactic shock*. The sooner treatment to counteract the reaction begins, the better the chances of survival. Discuss allergic reactions with your vet during the first visit.

What does DHLPP mean?

Although your Chihuahua may not get the whole combination in one shot, one of the most common vaccines given to dogs is a combination shot known as the *DHLPP*. The following sections break down what the letters mean.

D is for distemper

Distemper, a highly contagious airborne disease, is the number-one killer of unvaccinated dogs. Its victims usually are puppies, although older dogs may come down with it, too. Because distemper manifests itself in various forms, it can be difficult even for experienced vets to diagnose. Symptoms include some but not all of the following: diarrhea, vomiting, reduced appetite, cough, nasal discharge, inflamed eyes, fever, convulsions, exhaustion, and lack of interest in toys, games, or attention. Although dogs with distemper occasionally recover, they may suffer permanent damage to the brain or nervous system. Dogs that receive treatment immediately have the best chance of survival.

H is or hepatitis

Infectious hepatitis in dogs affects the liver just as it does in humans, but humans don't catch the canine form. In dogs, it spreads through contact with an infected dog's stool, saliva, or urine. Intense thirst is one specific symptom, but all the other symptoms are similar to those of distemper. Hepatitis progresses rapidly and often is fatal, so prompt veterinary treatment is critical.

L is for leptospirosis

Leptospirosis (or *lepto*) is caused by a *spirochete* — a microorganism that's often carried by rats. A dog that has contact with a rat can become infected, as can one that eats something contaminated by rats. The result is a bacterial infection that's capable of causing permanent kidney damage.

P is for parvovirus

Parvovirus (or *parvo*) attacks the stomach lining, lining of the small intestine, bone marrow, and lymph nodes, and in young puppies, even the heart. It's highly contagious and spreads through contaminated stools. Your dog may encounter the stools via their paws or your shoes. Beginning with depression or exhaustion and a loss of appetite, symptoms soon progress to vomiting, diarrhea (sometimes bloody), and fever. Puppies with infected hearts *(myocardial parvovirus)* often die suddenly or within a day or two of contracting the disease. Those few that recover may suffer chronic heart problems. How severely adult dogs are affected depends on the individual. Some dogs become extremely ill, and others just lose their appetites and lower their activity levels for a day or two.

P also is for parainfluenza

Parainfluenza, also known as *infectious canine tracheobronchitis* and most commonly called *kennel cough,* spreads rapidly from dog to dog. It's caused by several different viruses, as well as a bacterium. Symptoms are a frequent, dry, hacking cough and sometimes a nasal discharge. Other than that, the dog appears to feel fine; many dogs infected with parainfluenza don't even miss a meal. Dogs vaccinated against parainfluenza sometimes get the condition anyway, but they usually have milder symptoms than unvaccinated dogs.

Although the disease usually runs its course, it's more dangerous to puppies than it is to mature dogs. Puppies should be kept in a warm, humid room while recovering. No matter how old your Chi is, though, your vet probably will prescribe antibiotics to prevent complications and medication to control the cough.

Whether he's 9 weeks or 9 years old, your dog needs to see your vet right away if he starts coughing. It could be a sign of something serious.

Rabies

Rabies always is fatal to dogs. And a dog with rabies is a danger to humans and other animals, which is why law mandates rabies vaccinations. *Rabies* is a virus that can infect dogs that come in contact with cats, raccoons, skunks, foxes, or other warm-blooded animals that already have the virus. It affects the nervous system and is generally passed from animal to animal or animal to human through infected saliva — usually from a bite. Rabies also can infect a victim through cuts or scratches that come in contact with saliva from a rabid animal.

One of the first signs of rabies is a difference in disposition. A gentle dog may start to act aggressive, or an independent dog may suddenly crave affection. Soon, the dog's pupils may become dilated and light may seem to cause him pain. Eventually, the dog won't want any attention and may develop stomach trouble and a fever.

As the disease progresses its symptoms can include bared teeth, random biting, lack of coordination, twitching facial muscles, and loss of control of the facial muscles, resulting in an open mouth with the tongue hanging out. The dog's voice may change, and it may drool, paw at its mouth, and cough. Finally, it will slip into a coma and die. All warm-blooded animals are susceptible to the disease, so anyone bitten by a dog (or any other animal) needs to see a doctor right away.

Rabies vaccine prevents this dreaded disease. Your vet will give the rabies shot to your Chi separately, not in combination with other vaccines. Some rabies vaccinations are good (and legal) for longer than a year, so be sure to ask your vet when your dog's shot should be renewed.

Just say "No!" to other deadly diseases

Besides the diseases you read about in the previous sections, your vet may also recommend vaccinations against Lyme disease, Bordetella, Giardia, Corona, and Adenovirus, depending on where you live and your lifestyle:

- ✔ *Lyme disease* (spread by the deer tick) attacks nerve tissue, joints, the heart, and, occasionally, the kidneys. Its symptoms include lameness due to joint pain, loss of appetite, and fever. Lyme disease is more of a danger in some parts of the country than in others. Not only that, but veterinarians aren't in agreement about how well the vaccine works. Discuss Lyme disease with your vet and trust him or her to make an educated decision about whether your Chihuahua should be vaccinated.

- ✔ *Bordetella* is a contagious and potentially serious respiratory disease that breaks out most often during the summer months when many dogs spend a week or so at the boarding kennel.

- ✔ *Giardia* is an intestinal parasite that dogs can pick up by drinking water contaminated by feces.

- ✔ *Corona* is a virus that's transmitted via the stool of an infected dog. It breaks out most often when many dogs are kenneled in the same facility. Dogs that travel a lot also pick it up much more often than those that remain near home. Although this virus can cause dangerous diarrhea in puppies (dangerous because of the possibility of dehydration), adult dogs usually shake it off in a matter of days. Let your vet decide if your Chi needs protection from coronavirus.

> ✔ Two types of *adenovirus* exist. One causes a respiratory infection and the other causes hepatitis, which can lead to liver and kidney damage. Adenovirus vaccine may be the hepatitis part of the core vaccines your veterinarian recommends.

These days, your Chi can be vaccinated against all these diseases. But just because a vaccine exists doesn't mean your dog needs it, so let your veterinarian decide after consulting with you. (In addition to your vet's vaccination schedule, your Chihuahua needs to be on a regular program that prevents heartworm. I tell you more about this in Chapter 14.)

Administering Medicine the Correct Way

If you can get away with it, giving pills in food is the easiest medicating method. My American Staffordshire Terriers gobble up a cheese-wrapped pill instantly. It usually takes two people to give a Chihuahua a pill, however. My Chi, for instance, eats the cheese and leaves the pill on the floor! With your helper holding your Chi firmly, open his mouth and place the pill as far back on the center of his tongue as you can. Then hold his mouth shut while tilting his head upward (careful, don't cover his nostrils). Stroking his throat gently during this step may induce him to swallow. After he swallows, look inside his mouth to make sure the pill went down.

Opening a puppy's mouth and giving him a treat on a daily basis, from the first day you bring him home, will make it easier to give him pills later in life.

Liquid medication probably will be easier on both of you, so opt for it if your vet gives you a choice. Use an eyedropper to give your Chi liquid medication. Lift his lips slightly and place the eyedropper in the back corner of his mouth, where the upper and lower lips form a pocket. Hold his head up and his lips shut and squeeze the eyedropper. Keep holding his muzzle, tilting it slightly upward until you're sure that he swallowed the medicine. Gently stroking his throat may help.

If you get your Chi used to taking delicious liquid from an eyedropper, administering liquid medication becomes a cinch. Occasionally, melt a teaspoon of vanilla ice cream, put it in an eyedropper, and give it to your Chi just as if it were medicine.

Spaying or Neutering for a Happier, Healthier Dog

If showing in conformation (see Chapter 12) isn't your game, the nicest thing you can do for yourself and your Chihuahua is to have your dog spayed or neutered. The following sections tell you why.

Prime time for spaying or neutering is when your Chihuahua is between 4 and 6 months old. Avoid waiting until 8 to 10 months of age to spay or neuter. Many dogs experience a fear development period at this time, and a surgical hospitalization can plant an ingrained fear of going back to the hospital. It can also lead to aggression.

Spaying

Females spayed before their first season (usually around 6 months of age) are at much less risk of developing breast cancer than unspayed females. And because spaying removes the female's reproductive organs, spayed females never suffer cancers or infections of the ovaries or uterus. In addition, they don't have unwanted pregnancies and won't drip blood all over your carpet and furniture for several days twice a year!

Spayed females also are nicer to live with. Her sexy scent won't entice males to serenade in chorus on your front lawn, and she won't suddenly develop a desire to roam. Spaying helps to keep a female's disposition consistent and lets her participate in competitive events such as obedience and agility without taking three weeks off every six months (because females in season are banned from performance events). In short, spaying your Chi when she's young gives her a healthier life, presents you with fewer hassles, lessens the risk of a big dog mounting her, and doesn't add to the pet overpopulation problem.

Please don't breed your female Chihuahua so you can get back your initial investment or so your children can witness the miracle of birth. A beloved female may need an emergency Caesarean section or even die giving birth, leaving you with traumatized children and orphan puppies. And as far as your investment goes, any emergency will result in big vet bills, and raising even healthy puppies is an expensive endeavor.

Plus, even if all goes well with the whelping, it's common for one or more seemingly healthy puppies to die one day to four weeks after birth. This also can be very traumatic to children.

Neutering

Neutering your male dog before he's a year old can save him the pain of prostate problems when he ages, including cancer, and it makes him easier to live with.

Male hormones make dogs desire every female in season whose scent wafts by on the wind, and some of the males perform Houdiniesque feats to escape and find the female. Male hormones also make dogs more aggressive toward other dogs and may contribute to housetraining problems, such as scent marking (when the male urinates on objects inside the home to stake out his territory).

Frustration (also caused by male hormones) is what may make a dog embarrass you by making love to Aunt Amelia's leg during Thanksgiving dinner. Although neutering won't immediately cure a frustrated, aggressive escape artist with a housetraining problem, it will eliminate the production of male hormones, which almost always will start your dog on the road to improvement.

Myths and old wives tales about altering

Several myths and old wives tales about spaying and neutering began circulating long ago, and every one of them is wrong. Here's the real story:

✔ Spaying or neutering does *not* make a dog fat and lazy. Overfeeding and lack of exercise do that. The truth is, altered pets are often the top performers in competitive events. Neutered males can keep their minds on their work, and spayed females can compete throughout the year without losing several weeks because of being in season. In fact, almost all service dogs (hearing dogs, guide dogs for the blind, and dogs that help the physically handicapped) are spayed or neutered.

✔ Spaying or neutering does *not* prevent a dog from being an alert watchdog. Neutered males concentrate on their homes better than males that have the scent of sex on their minds. And spayed females alert to strange sights and sounds every bit as quickly as unspayed females.

✔ Male dogs don't get sad or resentful about being "castrated." In reality, dogs don't have human feelings about romantic love and sex. Males never miss the hormones that made them feel frustrated and constantly steered them toward trouble, and females don't feel unfulfilled because they didn't have litters. In fact, altered dogs usually become closer to their human families, which is where dogs really want to be.

Slapping an ID on (Or in) Your Dog

The traditional form of doggie identification is a tag inscribed with the owner's name and telephone number attached to the dog's collar. Perhaps this would be enough for the nice family down the block to see whom your Chi belongs to if he ever wanders out the door unseen. But collars can come off and tags can get lost, so this section presents two newer and better ID methods to discuss with your veterinarian. They ensure that your Chi carries his identification all the time.

Sporting a tattoo

No, you shouldn't decorate your Chi's handsome bod with hearts or eagles. *Tattooing* is a relatively painless procedure that permanently places an identification number on the inside of your dog's ear or high on the inner thigh of his back leg — out of sight unless someone looks for it. Animal shelter personnel and other humane workers know where to look to find a dog's tattoo.

The tattoo links your dog to a registry where his ID info is on file. Another plus is that laboratories can't use tattooed dogs. Just don't forget to sign on with the appropriate national registry (database) as soon as your Chi is tattooed. Excellent registries include the following:

- ✔ **AKC CAR (Companion Animal Recovery):** Contact AKC CAR at www.akc.org/lostfound or by calling 800-252-7894.

- ✔ **Tattoo-a-Pet:** You can access Tattoo-a-Pet at www.tattoo-a-pet.com or call 800-TATTOOS.

- ✔ **The National Dog Registry:** You can get info at www.nationaldogregistry.com or call 800-NDR-DOGS.

If you want to have your dog tattooed and your veterinarian doesn't offer the service, contact your local kennel club. Some dog clubs conduct tattooing clinics, where a veterinarian or a trained club member tattoos pets for a reasonable fee. Even if your local dog club doesn't offer the service, its members can tell you where they've had it done.

Fitted with a microchip

The newest method of permanently identifying dogs is the *microchip*. This tiny device (about the size of an uncooked kernel of rice) is encoded with your pet's identification information and implanted under his skin (usually at the juncture of the neck and the withers) by your veterinarian. The procedure is similar to receiving a vaccination.

If your Chi becomes lost and ends up in a shelter, a device called a *scanner* reads the microchip and identifies him. Although more and more humane facilities are acquiring scanners, the problem remains that not all of them own a scanner yet. Also, if the person who finds him has never heard of microchipping, he or she won't take him to be scanned.

To be on the safe side, have your dog microchipped and use another form of identification as a backup.

Chapter 14

Debugging de Dog

In This Chapter

▶ Battling internal worms

▶ Banning bugs and other external thugs

A host of creepy-crawlies are looking for a free lunch and a cozy condo, compliments of your Chihuahua. Some prefer camping under a tent of hair; others want to set up housekeeping indoors and homestead in the intestines, bowels, and even (horrors!) the heart. In this chapter, I unmask these intruders and tell you how to protect your dog from parasitic invasions.

The dictionary defines a *parasite* as an organism that relies on another living thing for its survival but contributes nothing to the host organism. That's true as far as it goes, but many parasites do contribute something in a negative sense — they hand their hosts an array of afflictions.

 Parasites that live inside their hosts are called *internal parasites*. Those that stay on the skin are called *external parasites*. For example, worms are internal parasites, and fleas are external parasites.

Just Say "No Way!" to Worms and Other Internal Bugs

Don't be embarrassed if your Chi gets intestinal worms. No matter how carefully you look after her, she can still become infested with them. Heartworms, however, are a different story. These deadly dependents are preventable, so if your dog is unlucky enough to be diagnosed with them, someone screwed up. Here's the poop on the nasty critters that may try to munch on your Chi.

Heartworms

Heartworms are transmitted by mosquito bites. As the worms mature inside the dog (a process that takes about six months), they migrate to the large blood vessels of the lungs and eventually to the heart where they reproduce, blocking blood flow. Heartworms grow so big that as few as two can kill a Chihuahua. A single heartworm can grow up to 14 inches long.

Many dogs die without showing symptoms. Prevention is the only defense, and it must start as soon as you get your Chi and continue all her life. If you acquire her as a puppy, ask your veterinarian to put her on a heartworm prevention program and then stick to it without fail.

Even after she starts preventative medication, your Chi still needs an annual blood test for heartworms. Why? Because prevention is the best thing going, but it isn't 100-percent perfect (and neither are we, the people who have to remember to give our dogs pills). In fact, if you slip up for any reason, you should have your Chi tested before resuming her monthly prevention program. Why? Because if a dog already has heartworms and takes preventative medication, the combination can be fatal. In fact, if you acquire her as an adult dog, your vet must give her a blood test before prescribing preventative medicine.

What if you acquired your Chi as an adult and she tests positive? Now that's a real bummer. On the plus side, you caught it while she's still breathing — and where there's life, there's hope. You can have plenty of hope if you caught the problem early. Treatment needs to start immediately. Unfortunately, the procedures to rid a dog of heartworms are dangerous, although less dangerous than the deadly worms. Many (but not all) dogs survive the treatment. Good luck. After your dog is heartworm free, rely on preventative medication to keep her that way.

Roundworms, hookworms, whip-worms, tapeworms — yuck!

Many puppies are born with roundworms, and some get hookworms and/or roundworms from their mothers' milk. In fact, your Chi can pick up one of several species of worms, including hookworms and whipworms, when simply out for a walk. She may even ingest a tapeworm while nipping at a flea that suddenly sprang from the grass and landed on her well-groomed back, because fleas play host to tapeworms. So what's a dog owner to do?

Prevention through maintaining clean quarters and the quick removal of internal parasites are the best policies. Prevention works best if start as soon as you get your puppy. In addition to vaccinating your Chi (see Chapter 13) and putting her on a heart-worm prevention program, your vet also needs to examine her stool to find out if she has intestinal parasites. After she checks out negative for worms, take a stool sample to your vet at least twice a year (three times the first year). That way, if one comes up positive, you'll get rid of the new worms before they become overwhelming and endanger her health.

The symptoms of roundworms, whipworms, tapeworms, and hook-worms are similar:

- ✔ Dull eyes
- ✔ A rough, dry coat
- ✔ Weakness
- ✔ Weight loss despite an enormous appetite
- ✔ Coughing
- ✔ Vomiting
- ✔ Diarrhea (sometimes bloody)
- ✔ A big belly (all the time, not just right after eating)

Most dogs have only two or three symptoms; others totally lose their appetites when harboring worms. Occasionally, a dog may show no symptoms at all but then suddenly becomes severely anemic from a heavy infestation. Hookworms, for example, are bloodsuckers and can kill a dog as tiny as a Chihuahua puppy within weeks.

Don't try to diagnose and worm your Chihuahua by using over-the-counter medications. Many symptoms of worms also are signs of other serious illnesses. Not only that, but different worms demand different treatments. The amount of medicine is determined by your dog's weight, and medication is downright dangerous if misused.

On the bright side, getting rid of intestinal worms is a routine veterinary procedure. If your vet discovers that any of these worms are living inside your Chi, he or she may give her a shot or prescribe medication and schedule a follow-up treatment. Don't overlook or reschedule the follow-up visit, because timing is important.

Giardia

Giardia are found in lakes, ponds, and other outdoor water sources. Chihuahuas seldom contact Giardia because the *protozoans* (one-celled microscopic organisms, not worms) are most often ingested by thirsty hunting dogs and dogs accompanying backpackers — not comfort-loving critters like Chis. However, your Chi can ingest Giardia by an act as simple as lapping water from a puddle.

After a dog ingests them, Giardia chew on the inner lining of the small intestine. Naturally, this creates irritation, which is accompanied by the following:

- Inflammation
- Stools coated with mucous
- Weight loss
- Diarrhea
- Bloating

If you travel with your dog, Giardia should convince you to carry water from home. But dogs can pick up the protozoa from licking an affected dog's stool (yes, sometimes dogs do yucky stuff like that). If your Chi gets diarrhea after eliminating at highway rest stops, let your vet know that Giardia is one possibility. Prompt treatment is important.

Coccidia

Coccidia, another protozoan, lay their eggs in animals' stools. And dogs sometimes get up close and personal with poop. After they get inside your Chi, coccidia line her intestinal tract, causing

- Watery stools and bloating
- Straining during elimination
- Vomiting
- Weight loss
- Streaks of blood on the stool

Is there any good news? Yes. Coccidia are easily diagnosed by your vet and quickly eliminated when treated early.

It is best to pick up all feces as soon as your puppy goes to help prevent your yard from becoming contaminated and a constant source of reinfestation for your puppy.

Controlling the External Pests: Fleas, Ticks, and Mites

Fleas, ticks, and a mixture of mites are the most common external parasites that annoy and endanger dogs. In the following sections, I explain what you need to know to keep your Chi safe from a variety of bloodthirsty bugs.

Defeating the terrible tick

I give you the good news first. If you walk your Chihuahua in the sunshine during the warm months and keep her away from tall grass and profuse plants, chances are she won't pick up any ticks. Why? Because like Dracula, these bloodsuckers prefer darker areas — especially the woods. But occasionally ticks appear in unexpected places, and because they're so dangerous, your best bet is to check your Chi's body daily from late spring through the end of summer. It takes several hours for a tick to do its dirty work, so if you remove a tick quickly, your dog probably won't come down with any of the dire diseases ticks can cause.

Dogs seldom get all, or even half, the symptoms that a particular disease can cause. If you've found a tick on your dog within the last two weeks, just one or two symptoms of a tick-related illness warrant an immediate trip to the veterinarian.

Scanning for and removing ticks

When checking for ticks, pay special attention to your dog's head, face, neck, and the inside of her ears. Those are a tick's favorite lunch counters. Another choice spot is between the toes. But a tick can cling to any part of a Chi's body, so run your fingertips everywhere — up and down her legs, under her pits, and down her back, sides, belly, and tail. It sounds like a big job, but you can easily complete the whole exam in a minute. Now aren't you glad you chose a Chihuahua?

If you find an attached tick, don't try to pull it off by hand. The safest way to remove a tick is with a preparation recommended by your veterinarian. If you're far from the veterinary clinic and don't have a preparation on hand, remove the tick with a pair of tweezers. Some pet shops sell special tweezers just for that purpose, but unless you live near the woods and have to remove ticks often, the tweezers in your medicine chest will do just fine.

Grab your tweezers and follow these steps:

1. **Separate your Chi's hair so you can see where the tick embedded itself in her skin.**

   The embedded part is the tick's head.

2. **If you have rubbing alcohol handy, put a drop of it right on the tick.**

   That makes some ticks release their hold.

3. **Use your tweezers to clamp down as close to the head as possible and pull it out slowly.**

   Ideally, you'll remove the entire tick, head and all.

4. **Put a dab of alcohol on your Chi's skin where the tick had been.**

   Uh oh. You did everything right, but the tick's head broke off and stayed under your pup's skin. If that happens, play it safe and call your veterinarian for further instruction.

If you're sure you removed the tick within an hour or so of when it attached itself, your dog is probably home free. But it's a good idea to keep the tick in an escape-proof container so your vet can identify it in case your dog shows signs of sickness. Watch her closely for the next couple weeks and take her to the vet if something seems wrong. You'll know the signs after you read the next few sections. They tell you all about the many miseries ticks carry.

Tick Bite Paralysis

The American dog tick (sometimes called the Eastern wood tick) and the Western Mountain or Rocky Mountain wood tick all inject toxins into their hosts through their saliva. Early signs of sickness are weakness, fever, a change in the dog's voice, vomiting, dilated pupils, and lack of coordination. The clinical signs usually disappear gradually after you remove the tick. But if the tick remains undetected, paralysis, difficulty breathing, and death may follow these symptoms.

Rocky Mountain Spotted Fever

Rocky Mountain Spotted Fever is a deadly disease brought to your dog by the same ticks that can cause paralysis. It occurs when a tick injects a particular protozoan under the skin. Signs of this disease are a high fever, a tender abdomen, water retention (look for swollen legs and feet), blood in the urine or stools, nosebleeds, difficulty breathing, and general weakness. Symptoms may not show up until two weeks after the tick bite.

Lyme disease

Transmitted by the deer tick, _Lyme disease_ occurs when a carrier tick transmits a particular bacterium into a dog (or person) through its saliva. An estimated 50 percent of deer ticks are carriers. These ticks are also more difficult to find on your dog because they're small. The good news is that they must be attached for nearly two days before infection can occur.

A dog with Lyme disease may become lame, depressed, weak, and feverish; suffer painful joints; and be reluctant to move. If you live in a rural area known for having a large population of deer ticks, your veterinarian may suggest vaccinating your Chihuahua against Lyme disease.

Lyme disease has currently been diagnosed in 47 states. It also attacks people, so check yourself and your dog after a walk in the woods. A preventative vaccine for humans is available and is probably a good idea if you live near a wooded area. Ask your doctor about it.

Fleas are no circus

I wish I could offer you a quick and easy method for getting rid of fleas, but unfortunately, eliminating fleas isn't easy . . . not even with all the new formulas that are marketed every year. The truth is, fleas quickly become resistant or actually adapt to insecticides. That's why new flea dips, powders, and sprays appear on the pet shop shelves annually.

With a dog as small as a Chihuahua, using any over-the counter flea remedies isn't a good idea. Instead, discuss your Chihuahua's lifestyle with your veterinarian, and he or she will prescribe a safe and effective program to keep fleas from moving in on your Chi.

With fleas, prevention is key and earlier is better. Those bad little buggers are capable of producing another generation every 21 days, and one female flea can produce thousands of eggs in her lifetime. Not only that, but fleas itch something awful, often cause an allergic reaction that turns into an oozing *hot spot,* and can carry tapeworms. Dogs react to fleas in a variety of ways. A dog with a fleabite allergy is miserable with just one or two fleas on her, but another dog may have a severe infestation without even bothering to scratch. Chances are, your Chi will let you know when she has fleas. Most Chihuahuas scratch themselves silly when fleas bite them.

The only way to control fleas is to eliminate them not only from your dog, but also from inside and outside your home . . . and from your vehicle if your dog travels with you. Fleas don't live on dogs all the time — they just feed on them and ride around for awhile. Then they hop off and camp in the carpet, dog bed, or grass until they get hungry and want to hitch a canine ride again. The best way to terminate fleas is to interrupt the fleas' life cycle through an insect growth regulator (commonly called a *flea tablet)* that your dog eats once a month.

You can incorporate this tablet in with the monthly heartworm preventative. If you live in a heavily infested area, such as Florida, a monthly tablet and a monthly topical in combination is the most effective way to prevent your home from becoming a flea hotel.

Flea tablets are prescription medicine, and insecticides for the home and yard must be used with great care — especially when you own the smallest of all breeds. Don't try to come up with a flea management program on your own. The use of more than one product often is necessary, and your vet knows which ones can be safely used at the same time and which products become toxic when combined. And if you're like me and prefer natural products, tell your vet.

An easy test for fleas in the house

Finding out if your home has fleas is easy. Fill a large, shallow pan with water and add some liquid dish soap. Before retiring for the night, put the pan on the floor and place a desk lamp right next to it with the light cocked over the water. After you go to bed, and the lamp is the only light on in the house, fleas will jump at it, fall in the water, and sink immediately, because dish soap makes the water soft. If you find drowned fleas in the pan the next morning, you know your home has been invaded. Some people set this flea trap every night during the summer and say it's a big help in controlling fleas.

Your vacuum cleaner is your best friend when fighting fleas. Besides inhaling the adults, it also sucks the eggs and larva right out of the carpet and upholstery. Vacuum every room often when fighting fleas. Just be sure to throw the vacuum bag away when you finish.

Managing mites

A myriad of microscopic mites, including one commonly called *walking dandruff,* feed on the skin, blood, and even hair of a dog. Your Chihuahua may never be bothered by any of them, but it's smart to be familiar with the symptoms. Chances are, your dog doc will do a skin scraping (it's painless) to find out what kind of mite is making Manchita miserable. Don't try to diagnose and treat skin problems yourself. Some of them have such similar symptoms that even your vet won't be sure how to proceed without a test, and each mite demands different medication.

Saracoptic mange

Saracoptic mange, sometimes called *scabies,* is caused by crab-shaped mites that literally get under your dog's skin. After burrowing in, they sip your Chi's blood, mate, and lay eggs. These mange mites make her itch. Symptoms are relentless scratching, tiny red bumps, and patchy crusted areas. Visit your veterinarian before she suffers hair loss or a bacterial infection. Scabies responds to medication.

Follicular or demodectic mange

Commonly called *red mange,* follicular or *demodectic mange* is caused by a different type of mite. Because itching is a symptom in some dogs but not in others, look for small, circular, moth-eaten-looking patches. They're usually found on the head, or along the back, sides, and neck.

In young dogs, red mange often is stress related. Anything that produces anxiety — such as going through the hormonal changes of adolescence or staying in a boarding kennel for the first time — can trigger a minor outbreak. So, do mites crawl around with miniature blood pressure cuffs so they can tell when a dog is stressed out? Not exactly. The truth is, most dogs have some of these mites on them all the time and never have a problem. But when they're under stress, their defenses break down and the result is a small patch of demodectic mange (sometimes called *juvenile mange*) — easily treated by your veterinarian.

Generalized outbreaks of red mange are another story. If your Chihuahua ever gets a case of mange that covers much of her body, have her spayed or neutered (if she isn't already). Never breed a dog with a generalized case of mange — the disease and its misery can be passed on to the puppies. Severe cases of demodectic mange are treatable, but the treatments are much more intense, may include antibiotics, and should be performed at the veterinarian's office.

Ear mites

Does your dog continuously scratch her ears or shake her head? She may have ear mites. These critters move into the ear canal and proceed to eat the outer layer from the walls of their cottage (yup, that's your dog's skin). Wipe gently inside her ear with a cotton ball. If it comes out with rusty-brown or blackish goop on it, your Chi has mites. These bugs are easily treatable when caught early, so go see your veterinarian.

Walking dandruff

Yes, the walking dandruff mite has a real name. If you want to remember or pronounce *cheyetiella,* may the Force be with you. But to return to earth, does your Chi try to turn her body into a circle so she can nip and nibble along her spine? Does she lie on the rug upside down and wiggle around in an effort to scratch her back? Have you noticed an abnormal amount of flaking when you groom her? Those signs all point to walking dandruff, a mite that devours the skin along a dog's spine (and sometimes other places, too). Your veterinarian can get rid of these itchy critters, but it may take several treatments. You'll have to clean all your dog's bedding and favorite rugs, too.

Chapter 15

Dealing with Sickness, Injury, and Other Considerations

- -

In This Chapter

▶ Watching for signs of sickness or injury

▶ Dealing with emergencies and transportation

▶ Popping your Chi's pills

▶ Understanding ailments specific to Chihuahuas

▶ Maintaining your old dog's comfort

▶ Facing the facts of life and death

- -

*A*lthough prevention is still the best plan when it comes to health care, being perceptive and prepared run a close second/third. The sooner you seek help for a sick dog, the better his chance of recovery. This chapter helps you sense the earliest signs of sickness or injury. It also describes some hereditary ailments that occasionally inflict Toy dogs and shows you the first-aid basics so that you can act in an emergency until professional help is available. With luck, this chapter has more info than you'll ever need. I hope you never have to use it, but it's here for you just in case.

I do hope you have to use one section of this chapter, however. It's about taking care of a golden oldster. All pet owners hate seeing the signs of aging in themselves or their pets. Yet, as the cliché goes, getting old is a whole lot better than the alternative. So don't let a little gray on your dog's muzzle depress you. Your sassy senior can enjoy a high quality of life for many years, and this chapter helps you keep him in super shape.

Finally, I discuss the most painful fact of life: death. Losing a precious pet is heartbreaking enough without having to make sudden decisions, so I discuss options such as euthanasia and different methods of caring for the body. I also include some info on the stages of grief and healing.

Recognizing the Signs of Sickness

Many signs of sickness in Chihuahuas, although subtle at first, are symptoms that you may sense rather than actually see — the way a mother instinctively knows when something is troubling her spouse or child. So, if something seems wrong but you can't figure out what it is, don't chalk it up to an overactive imagination. The difference is probably an early warning, which is the best kind of warning; quick treatment, before your Chihuahua weakens, has the greatest chance of success.

If something doesn't seem right, even if that *something* doesn't appear in this chapter, trust your intuition and take your Chi to the vet for a checkup. The following sections present a tiered approach to recognizing signs and taking action.

Wait and see (but not very long)

Some problems go away on their own, but your Chi needs medical attention if any issue continues longer than 24 hours. If your Chihuahua has any of the following symptoms, watch him carefully:

- ✔ Refusing to eat anything at all but having no other signs of sickness

- ✔ Limping, or refusing to put weight on one of his legs, yet eating normally and showing no obvious signs of a fracture or other pain or sickness

- ✔ Changing personality or activity level but exhibiting no other signs of pain or sickness

- ✔ Mild diarrhea

   The stool is loose but not liquid and doesn't have any blood in it. No signs of straining or stomach pain.

- ✔ Vomiting two or three times but showing no other signs of sickness (plenty of perfectly healthy dogs vomit after eating grass)

A little less hop in his step? Call the vet

Years ago, when I showed American Staffordshire Terriers, I had a female named Frankie who bounded over obedience jumps with several inches to spare. One day, at a Chicago show, she seemed a little less spirited than usual during breed judging, but she still started the morning on a high note by winning Best of Breed. Later on, she also earned a qualifying score in open obedience competition; however, I noticed that she just cleared the jumps with no room to spare. I wanted to attribute her sedate attitude to a muggy Midwest afternoon, but it nagged at me on the long drive home.

The next morning, I called the vet for an appointment, telling him only that something about Frankie didn't seem quite right. It turned out that she had a uterine infection. Because I caught it early, it was easily cured, but if I had waited for more evidence of illness, her problem may have become serious. What's the moral of the story? No one knows your dog better than you do.

> ✔ Scratching or nipping an itchy spot or two but not hard enough to break the skin

> ✔ Drinking and urinating more than usual but showing no other signs of sickness

 The average dog's temperature is between 100.0°F and 102.5°F. He has a pulse rate between 80 and 120 beats per minute and takes 20 breaths per minute.

To take your Chi's temperature, use a rectal thermometer with a rounded end. Shake it down below 100 degrees Fahrenheit, smear it with petroleum jelly, and insert it carefully between 1 ƒ 1/2 inches. Talk soothingly while holding him firmly, in a standing position, for two minutes (don't let him sit). Remove the thermometer and check the reading. Disinfect the thermometer before putting it away.

Call your vet now

If your little Pepe has any of the following problems, call your vet immediately and explain the symptoms in detail. You'll probably need a same-day appointment:

> ✔ Refusing to eat and seeming depressed or lethargic. He may also be suffering from stomach pain.

> ✔ Suffering an eye problem. This includes excessive tearing; an eye swollen shut or partially shut; or an eye that looks cloudy or off-color.

✔ Breathing that's labored or fast and shallow. May or may not be in combination with a cough.

✔ Vomiting frequently, combined with depression or exhaustion.

✔ Incessant diarrhea. A liquid stool, combined with a terrible odor and possibly pain and straining.

✔ Swallowing of an object without choking. A swallowed object can turn into a life-threatening problem if your Chi can't pass it. The sooner your vet assesses the situation, the better.

✔ Swelling on any part of his body. It may feel hard and hot to the touch or be infected and oozing.

✔ Scratching and/or biting at the skin until it's inflamed, with possible hair loss brought on by intense itching.

✔ Injuring himself, like a deep puncture that can become infected, a cut that needs to be stitched, or severe lameness with no indication of a fracture.

Emergency!

A real emergency is a situation so scary that your Chihuahua needs the attention of your vet or veterinary hospital immediately — no matter if it's Sunday, New Year's Eve, or three o'clock in the morning. The following lists outline the many emergency situations you may encounter; for more on handling these issues, see the following section.

Emergencies resulting from accidents include

✔ Broken bones

✔ Heavy bleeding

✔ Severe trauma (possibility of internal bleeding and/or shock)

✔ Burns from fire, scalding, or chemicals

✔ Poisoning

Emergency illnesses include

✔ Seizures

✔ Staggering and/or falling down

✔ Uncontrollable diarrhea (sometimes bloody)

✔ Frequent vomiting

- ✔ Breathing problems

- ✔ Allergic reactions

- ✔ Obstruction in the throat (choking)

- ✔ Obstruction in the intestine or urinary tract (straining to eliminate)

- ✔ Paralysis

- ✔ Heatstroke

- ✔ Bloat (extremely rare in Chihuahuas)

Handling Serious Issues: First Aid and Transportation

Emergency situations demand the service of a veterinarian ASAP. In the meantime, handling your Chihuahua properly until he's in the hands of a pro is important. Keeping calm is the hardest part. If a wave of panic doesn't rush over you when you first see your sick or injured pet, you're stronger than I am. But panic won't help him, so take a deep breath and resolve to stay calm and think straight. Then get to work.

If your Chi has an emergency, call your veterinary clinic (or its emergency number) immediately and tell the receptionist (or who-ever answers the phone) what happened. That way, the clinic can prepare for his arrival. Then give him first aid and transport him to the clinic. The following sections address this process with various emergency situations.

Unless the clinic gives you other instructions for transporting your Chihuahua, put him in his crate with a lot of clean, soft bedding, secure the crate in your vehicle so it won't slide or roll, and drive to the clinic. *Note:* Be careful when handling a dog that's in pain or panicking. He will bite.

If you suspect that your Chi has been poisoned by ingesting or inhaling poison, absorbing a toxic substance through the skin, or by injection (snake, scorpion, or spider bite), get professional help immediately. If you're far from a vet, call the National Animal Poison Control Center hotline at 900-680-0000. The fee is charged over the phone.

Heavy bleeding

Use a pressure bandage (not a tourniquet) to control heavy bleeding or blood spurting from any part of your dog's body. It's best if you have a helper so one person can keep the pressure bandage on your Chi while the other drives to the clinic.

If you have two people, follow these steps:

1. **With clean hands, apply direct pressure to the wound by holding a gauze pad firmly against it for 30 seconds.**

2. **If bleeding continues, apply a second gauze pad on top of the first and continue applying pressure.**

3. **Wrap your Chi in a clean towel, and with one person carrying him and holding the gauze pad(s) in place, go to the veterinary clinic.**

If you don't have a helper, follow these steps:

1. **Wrap a wide adhesive bandage around the wound and the gauze pad.**

2. **Put your Chi in his crate with a towel or blanket around him.**

3. **Secure the crate in your vehicle so it won't slide or roll and head for the clinic.**

   If the clinic is many miles away and the adhesive bandage is around one of his legs, stop and check the foot below the bandage after half an hour. If it's swollen or cold, loosen the bandage but leave the gauze pad in place.

 Resist the urge to clean or wipe a wound while it's still bleeding. Stopping the bleeding is your first priority, and cleaning the wound often makes it bleed even harder.

Choking

If your Chihuahua paws at his mouth, drools, seems unable to close his mouth, coughs, tries to vomit, strains for breath by stretching his head and neck, or appears frantic, he may be choking.

If he's getting enough air to sustain himself, put him in his crate and take him to the clinic immediately. If he appears on the verge of passing out or if his tongue is turning blue, follow these steps:

1. Wedge something (the handle of a small screwdriver works well) between the top and bottom molars on one side of his mouth to keep it open.

2. Use a flashlight or put him under good lighting and look into his mouth and down his throat.

3. Pull his tongue straight (careful, he may try to bite) to see if the offending object is on top of it.

4. If you find the problem, remove it with your fingers or a pair of long-nosed pliers.

5. If all else fails (you can see the wedged object but your Chi can't catch his breath), hold him upside down by his hind legs and shake him (or pat him on the back if you have a helper to hold him).

   With luck, that will dislodge the object so he can breathe again. Visit the vet anyway. Your Chi just suffered a major trauma. (If you can't see the object, follow the instruction in the next section.)

Can't catch breath

If your Chihuahua is gasping for air, his tongue is turning blue, his breathing is loud and labored, or he's not breathing at all, you don't have a second to spare. If he's getting enough air to sustain himself, transport him to the vet immediately in his crate. But if he isn't breathing, start mouth-to-nose resuscitation right away. Here's how:

1. First try the methods recommended in the preceding "Choking" section.

2. If he still isn't breathing, lay him on his right side on a table. Close his mouth and tilt his head back.

3. Keeping his mouth closed, place your open mouth over his nose (you can do it through a handkerchief if you prefer) and breathe five or six shallow (short) breaths into it.

   Of course you're terrified, but try to control your breathing. Your dog is small, so he doesn't have much lung capacity. If he starts breathing, you've saved his life. Now take him to the vet for observation.

4. If he still isn't breathing, keep giving him mouth-to-nose resuscitation. Try to give him approximately 20 shallow breaths per minute.

Keep trying for a full ten minutes. When he starts breathing by himself, go to the clinic. If breathing doesn't resume by then, he's probably dead, but at least you know you did everything possible to help him.

Broken leg

When treating and transporting a dog with a broken leg (or any broken bone), your job is to get him to the clinic without making the injury any worse on the way. Steady the limb (without pulling on it) by wrapping absorbent cotton around the entire leg. Then use gauze bandage, held in place with adhesive, to keep the leg from moving during transport.

Heatstroke

Symptoms of heatstroke include rapid or heavy breathing, a bright red mouth and tongue, thick saliva, unsteadiness (possibly falling over), diarrhea, vomiting, a hot and dry nose with legs and ears hot to the touch, and complete collapse — often combined with glassy eyes and gray lips.

Dogs don't sweat. The only way they can regulate their body temperature is by panting.

To save your Chihuahua during a case of heatstroke, you must start cooling him immediately — even before you call the clinic:

1. **Take him to a shady or air-conditioned place.**

2. **Soak a towel in cool (not ice) water, wring it out, and apply cold compresses to his belly and groin.**

3. **Lay the cool towel on his back and gently wet his head with it.**

4. **Let him drink a small amount of cool water at intervals — not all he wants at one time.**

   If he's too weak to drink, wipe the inside of his mouth with the water.

5. **Call the clinic, put the cold, wet towel in the bottom of his crate, and take him to the vet.**

Although most emergencies are the result of bad luck rather than bad management, heatstroke is absolutely preventable. Don't overexert your Chi on a muggy day or leave him alone inside your vehicle. The temperature inside a car or truck, even one parked in the shade, usually is 25 degrees hotter than outside the vehicle. Every year, hundreds of pets die from being left alone in parked vehicles for just a few minutes.

Reviewing Veterinary Issues Specific to Chihuahuas

Although Chihuahuas have fewer genetic defects than many breeds (maybe because so many breeders try hard to eliminate problems), no breed is perfect. In the following sections, I present some idiosyncrasies — a few serious issues but most not — that are sometimes seen in Chihuahuas and other Toy breeds.

Subluxation of the patella

Subluxation of the patella, or *luxating patella,* is a relatively common problem in small breeds and some large ones as well. In dog lingo, this defect is called "slipped stifles" or "loose kneecaps." When it occurs, the kneecap (we're talking about the rear legs) slips out of its groove — sometimes often and sometimes rarely, depending on the severity of the problem. If your dog is unlucky enough to have his kneecaps slip often, surgery may be the solution. A dog with a mild case can live a normal life, kind of like a person with a trick knee.

Hypoglycemia

Hypoglycemia refers to low blood sugar and is a common problem in young Toy puppies. Most of them grow out of it before they're old enough to leave the breeders, but for a few, it's a danger throughout their lives.

Symptoms of low blood sugar include a staggering gait, glassy eyes, and sometimes limpness or rigidity. If the dog doesn't receive immediate help when the symptoms show, he can suffer seizures, unconsciousness, and, finally, death. Treatment involves putting some sugar in your dog's mouth, calling your veterinarian, and heading for the clinic.

When you know that your dog has a tendency to develop hypoglycemia, you can prevent future attacks by changing his feeding schedule. Give small amounts of food several times a day and avoid sugary treats (check the ingredients before buying dog treats). Too much sugar in his food can put your Chi on a roller-coaster ride of sugar highs and lows instead of keeping his blood sugar nice and level. (For more on diet, head to Chapter 6.)

Collapsing trachea

Collapsing trachea is a problem for Toy dogs of many breeds — mostly in dogs older than 5 years, but occasionally a puppy has it from birth. The symptoms include coughing, shortness of breath, and exhaustion. To understand the condition, think of the trachea as a straw made of cartilage that carries air from the neck to the chest. When the cartilage collapses, breathing becomes difficult — kind of like sipping soda through a flattened straw.

Your vet can treat the condition with medication, but if you smoke, your Chi's prognosis may be poor. Secondhand smoke is a proven contributing factor to the problem, and smoke tends to settle low, where a little dog's nose is.

Heart murmur

Heart murmurs are relatively uncommon in Chihuahuas. Thankfully, even those that have one usually have the functional type. As in people, that means they can be as active and athletic as they want and live long, normal lives. If your Chihuahua is unlucky enough to develop a severe murmur, your vet will detect it during his annual exam. Further tests, such as an ultrasound and an EKG, may be recommended, and your vet will discuss treatment options with you.

Molera

The Chihuahua's *molera* (or *fontanel*) is considered a breed characteristic and not a condition or defect. Most Chihuahuas (80 to 90 percent) have a molera — a soft spot on the top of the head similar to a human baby's soft spot. But unlike babies, most Chihuahuas don't outgrow it. It usually shrinks as the dog matures and ends up between nickel- and dime-sized. Your Chi's molera won't be a problem as long as you're gentle when petting or handling his head.

In rare cases, the molera remains quite large and can be a sign of a serious problem called *hydrocephalus*. The good news (for the worrier, I suppose) is that hydrocephalus has several other signs besides a larger-than-usual molera.

Hydrocephalus

A dog with hydrocephalus (also called "water on the brain") may have an unusually large head for his size caused by swelling. Other signs of this fatal condition are frequent falling, seizures, a lot of white showing in the eyes, an unsteady gait, and east-west eyes (the opposite of crossed eyes). A dog with this condition is in pain and won't live long, so euthanasia is the humane solution (*euthanasia* is the medical term for a humane, vet-assisted death).

Going under anesthesia

The possibility that your dog may someday need anesthesia is one main reason why you need to choose a veterinarian who's accomplished in treating Toy dogs (see Chapter 13). Although deaths from anesthesia are rare and are usually the result of an allergic reaction, the use of a sedative is potentially dangerous. Your vet uses anesthesia only when necessary (before surgery, for example).

Prevention is the best course of action. Be sure to read about how to clean your Chihuahua's teeth (see Chapter 7) so that cleaning them under anesthesia won't be necessary. And when your dog *has* to go under anesthesia (during spaying or neutering, for example), ask your vet if any necessary dental work (such as pulling impacted baby teeth) can be done at the same time.

Be sure your vet uses one of the modern gas anesthetics. They're much safer than the old-fashioned intravenous products. The most modern gas is Sevoflurane.

Watching those eyes

An eye injury certainly isn't a "condition," but because Chihuahuas have big eyes and live close to the floor, they're prone to eye injuries. Put several drops of saline solution in your dog's eye if an injury seems minor. That's often all it takes to flush out a foreign object that was accidentally kicked up by someone's shoe. If that doesn't relieve the problem or if the injury appears more serious, take your Chi to the vet right away.

Keeping Your Senior Sassy

Oh no! Your Pepe is getting gray hairs. Even though he's healthy, rambunctious, and still in his prime, seeing the first signs of aging is scary. But it doesn't have to be. Keeping your oldster healthy and happy isn't hard at all. If you're lucky enough to share your life with a golden oldie, you can help him stay feisty by keeping his infirmities in mind.

If you prefer homeopathic medicine for yourself, you may want to find out if it will help your Chihuahua. Excellent information is available at www.hpathy.com/veterinary/index.asp. Acupuncture also has been known to relieve many disorders — especially arthritis. You can read all about it at www.acupuncture. com/animals/dog.htm.

Aid for your aging dog

Dogs age much like humans do. Even if your Chi has led a worry-free life, one of the first signs that he's becoming a senior is sprouting gray (white) hairs (see Figure 15-1). They appear first on his face, encircling his eyes and giving his muzzle a grizzled look. Don't let them spook you. Chances are your Chihuahua will have gray hairs for several years before feeling the first creaky joint of old age.

Figure 15-1: Manchita is 11 years old and has gray and thinning hair (compare this to her picture in Chapter 1). But she still plays like a pup!

Other signs of aging include dental problems, including the loss of teeth. Eventually, your Chi may no longer be able to crunch his kibble (dry food). One solution is to soften it by soaking it in warm water for several minutes and mixing it with canned meat. If he develops kidney trouble (or other organic or allergic problems), your veterinarian can prescribe an easily chewed food made especially to ease such difficulties.

While recovering from an accident or illness or when suffering the dental problems that may come with old age, your Chihuahua may welcome baby food. You can find boxes of rice cereal and jars of strained meats in the baby-food section of the supermarket. A combination of rice cereal and strained meat (warmed slightly) may entice your dog to eat when nothing else works.

Older dogs often are less tolerant of cold than even puppies are, so be sure that

- ✔ Your senior Chi has a warm sweater for outings.
- ✔ You keep him away from drafts.
- ✔ You put an extra baby blanket in his bed.

And speaking of his bed, he may start spending more time in it, preferring an afternoon nap to a brisk walk. I'm sure you've heard the saying "use it or lose it," and that advice applies to dogs as well as people. An older Chi still needs his exercise, although you shouldn't expect him to take part in strenuous activities. Make your walks together leisurely rather than lively, and when playing indoor exercise games (see Chapters 10 and 12), don't be surprised if he shuffles rather than speeds through the house!

No matter what speed your Chi chooses, playing helps him stay mentally sharp and keeps his muscles oiled, too. Not only that, but exercise helps him avoid obesity — a serious health problem in older dogs.

Aching joints and other signs of aging

Arthritis often attacks older dogs, and although nothing cures it, your veterinarian may be able to provide relief. Some ancient Chihuahuas may not have severe enough cases to require medicine, but they may need a little more help at home. If your Chi can't jump on and off the sofa anymore, lift him up and down. Same with walking the stairs. And if he can't reach his traditional easy chair he sits in when he's home alone, make sure that he has a place to nap and stay warm while you're away. Either build (or buy) a ramp so he can reach his favorite spot or place a doggie bed by it for comfort.

If your Chi were an older human, he would need bifocals and a hearing aid. The problem is, this equipment isn't made for dogs. So if your Chi always came when you called him but he suddenly starts to ignore you, chances are he has a hearing (not a behavior) problem. And if he was on the same elimination schedule for a dozen years and then starts waking you up at 4 a.m. to take him outside, he's not just looking for attention.

Your Chi may become a crotchety old codger, too, detesting even minor changes and become unwilling to make new friends (perhaps because of failing senses or twinges of arthritis). Report sudden changes in routine and disposition to your vet. Many problems can be relieved. Others can't, and some of them probably bother you more than they bother your Chi. After all, dogs don't agonize over the signs of aging like people do. As long as your Pepe still enjoys life and isn't suffering severe pain, he'll be happy as long as you love him.

The branch of medicine called *geriatrics* treats problems peculiar to aging; *gerontology* is the study of aging in people or their pets.

Coping with the Death of a Pet

Owners often know in advance when death is threatening their pets, but sometimes dogs die without warning, leaving owners saddened and shocked. Complicating the process are the decisions you may have to make concerning euthanasia and a final resting place. Understanding your options in advance may make things a little easier. I hope this section will help you with your planning and grief.

Is euthanasia ever the best ending?

Euthanasia is the most humane ending if your Chihuahua is in severe and constant pain with no hope of recovery. It consists of a lethal dose of a strong anesthetic, humanely administered by your vet. The injection puts your dog to sleep instantly and stops his heart. Only you can decide when the time is right, but it won't be as hard as you think. Trust your instincts and what your dog is showing you. These factors tell you when ending your dog's misery is the most merciful thing you can do for him.

After you make that painful decision and make your final trip to the vet, the receptionist will ask if you want to leave your dog or stay with him during the procedure. Staying may be harder on you in the short run, but it's best for most people in the long run. Take care of all the paperwork first so you won't have to handle it through your tears. Then hold your Chi in your loving arms while the vet administers the injection. That way you'll know for sure that your dog didn't suffer, and he'll die peacefully, nestled against your chest.

Do you ever get over it? Well, no. You'll probably always miss your Pepe. But someday you'll be able to talk about his antics without a tear in your eye or a catch in your throat. Instead, you'll smile as you relate some of your favorite Pepe stories. And you'll know that the good times you had together will never be gone. They'll always remain in your mental bank of happy memories.

Handling your dog's body

Many people choose to leave their departed pets' bodies at the veterinary clinic. Usually the clinic notifies a service, which picks up the body and cremates it. Several dogs usually are cremated at the same time, and the *cremains* (ashes) are buried in the earth. Don't be shy about asking your vet how he or she will dispose of the body. Some clinics have their own facilities for cremation, and others have different procedures.

Let him die while he's living

One of the saddest sights I ever saw was an ancient Chihuahua named Sadie lying on her side in a puddle of urine, with her hind legs and tail soiled by feces. Sadie's owner loved her too much to have her put down. When the owner had to spend a couple days in the hospital, she asked my friend to care for Sadie, warning her that the poor puppy (Sadie was 16) couldn't stand up anymore and would have to be cleaned up and force fed. My friend asked me to come along on her first visit, and although we expected it to be bad, it was worse than we expected. We bathed and dried Sadie, cuddled her, pushed prescription pills down her throat, got some strained chicken down her throat the same way, gave her water from an eyedropper, and covered her with clean blankets. Through it all, Sadie's expression remained blank. Her spirit was gone, leaving her miserable shell of a body behind. Please don't love your dog so possessively that it makes you selfish. To paraphrase a Jimmy Buffet song, let him die while he's living, not live when he's dead.

Private cremation is another option. The ceremony may be handled at a pet cemetery, a private pet crematorium, or your veterinary clinic. You can keep your pet's ashes in an urn, bury them, or scatter them in a place your pet loved.

Some people prefer to bury their dogs in their own yards. You can mark the spot with a beautiful perennial plant. This is an excellent option, provided that it's legal in your area. If not, pet cemeteries offer burials, which can be as simple or as elegant as you choose (and can afford). Because not all pet cemeteries are created equal, look for one that's neat, clean, and has been around for a long time.

Helping Yourself and Your Family Heal

Shock, disbelief, anger, alienation, denial, guilt, and depression are all stages of grief. Most people go through every one of them, although not always in that order. To help yourself through these painful stages, you need to

- **Understand that mourning the loss of a beloved pet is natural.** Your Chi wasn't "just a dog." He was *your* dog. You had a strong bond with him, and broken bonds cause broken hearts.

- **Take time to mourn.** Don't tell yourself to "get over it" and then bury your grief so deep that it eats you up from the inside. No guidelines exist for working through the stages of grief. Some people need more time to mourn than others.

- **Make a few changes in your habits and decor.** Put your Chi's bed, bowls, crate, and toys out of sight. Take his treats out of the cookie jar and his leash off the hat rack. Because walking him was probably one of the first things you did each morning, create a new morning routine.

- **Talk about your feelings.** Find an understanding ear — someone who also adored your Chi or who loves his or her own dog deeply — and discuss your feelings of loss. Many cities have support groups that help people through the pain of losing a pet. Ask your vet for a recommendation.

  In the days that follow your Chi's death, don't be afraid to say that you miss him in front of your family. Encourage your kids to talk about their feelings, too. Look at pictures of him together and recount his hilarious escapades. Tell the kids (more than once) that he will always be part of them, because the good memories they have of him are theirs forever.

Sometimes sadness may sweep over you at work, and your co-workers may notice. If they ask you what's wrong and you don't want to talk about it, or you aren't sure how they feel about pets, just tell them that you recently lost a good friend. After all, it's the absolute truth.

✔ **Read a book about pet loss.**

✔ **Give your other pets extra attention.**

✔ **Consider getting another dog.** No, not a replacement. It's impossible to replace your Chi because he was an individual and no other dog will be just like him. But you *can* love other dogs, as long as you don't expect them to act like your Pepe. If you think you'll have a problem with that, you can buy a different color Chihuahua or a different breed entirely. That will help you learn to love your new dog's unique personality.

Also, be sure to tell your children that Pepe can't be replaced, but that learning to love another dog is okay. In fact, some say the greatest honor you can give your dog is to love another of his kind.

If your Chihuahua's death was preventable, forgive yourself but learn from the experience. Maybe you didn't feel up to walking him one morning, so you turned him loose "just that one time" and he ran in front of a car. Or maybe you lost track of when his booster vaccination was due and he caught a deadly disease. If you contributed to his death, you're probably beating yourself up with guilt. But that won't bring him back. Instead, face what you did, learn from it, and go on. Give his death meaning by resolving never to make that mistake again. After all, no one is a perfect pet owner. Pet owners are just people who love their dogs but are occasionally prone to poor judgment.

Helping your spouse and your children cope with the loss of a pet can be soothing to you at the same time. One of the ways families come to terms with the finality of their situations (and then go on) is by combining their efforts and creating memorial ceremonies for their dead dogs. You can hold a ceremony regardless of whether you have remains to scatter or a body to bury, and you can perform the ceremony indoors if you don't have a yard.

Explain the ceremony to your family as a celebration of your Chihuahua's life and all the joy he brought to your family. Ask each family member to think of why they loved your dog or something funny that he did so they can tell it during the ceremony. (Youngsters who have a problem expressing themselves may want to begin a contribution with "Thanks, Pepe, for . . .") Before the ceremony, the family may want to go out together and choose a plant (indoor or outdoor, depending on the situation) to grow in your Chi's memory.

Never use a pet's death to make a point to your children. Even if you had to nag little Julie when it was her turn to walk your Chi, resist forever any urge to say something like, "If you hadn't made him wait so long to go potty, he may not have had kidney failure." Grieving kids need compassion, not guilt.

Part V
The Part of Tens

The 5th Wave   By Rich Tennant

"We're very careful about grooming. First I'll check his teeth and nails, then trim any excess hair from his ears, nose, and around the eyes. After checking for fleas and parasites, I'll let Roger go off to work so I can begin grooming the dog."

In this part . . .

Part V contains a few little topics that I think are important (or fun) enough to have their own special space. Here I include a list of ten questions to ask a breeder when you're looking for a new dog. I present ten sources where you can find much more information about Chihuahuas on the Internet. Finally, I shine a spotlight on celebrity Chis or famous people who have come to love Chihuahuas.

Chapter 16

Ten Questions to Ask Chihuahua Breeders

The best place to buy a healthy Chihuahua is from a breeder. Beware of puppies being sold by middle-people. For example, no matter how clean the pet shop seems, that appealing pup in the window may have been born in a puppy mill (an overcrowded and filthy facility that breeds and sells hundreds of puppies of various breeds). The combination of poor breeding practices and lack of human attention during the formative weeks can cause lifelong complications. I concede that may not always be the case, because the pet store could be getting its pups from a caring breeder. But you may not be able to tell for sure. So, buyer beware — and buyer be sure to get answers to all the questions in this chapter to ensure that the seller is reputable and cares about the breed.

When dealing with a rescue organization, chances are employees won't know where the dog originated, but the person fostering the dog can tell you the circumstances of the rescue and everything that's known about the dog's health and temperament. Chapter 4 goes into much more detail about buying from breeders and adopting from other organizations.

How Many Litters a Year Do You Breed?

Okay, you've found some potential Chihuahua breeders. But how do you recognize a good one? For one, the best breeders specialize in only one or two breeds, and they never breed more puppies than they have time to care for. And that means plenty of individual attention. Good breeders adore their pups, give prospective owners the third degree, and may exhibit their stock at dog shows. Their facilities are clean, their puppy play areas contain toys, and their dogs enjoy being handled.

When a breeder houses more puppies than he or she has time for, it usually shows. Two of the surest signs are spooked, unsocialized puppies and dogs living in unclean quarters.

Can You Tell Me All about This Dog's Personality?

Some breeders are more talkative than others, so if the seller you visit needs some help getting started, ask about a prospective pup's position in the litter or how she's been socialized. Good breeders know all about each and every one of their pups, and most of them will be happy to fill you in on a particular puppy's life story. Beware if the breeder hesitates when asked whether the pup is dominant or submissive with its littermates, or hems and haws about how she was socialized. Caring breeders can tell plenty of stories about puppies no more than a few weeks old because they're observant when the puppies play together and make time to give each one individual attention.

May I See the Pup's Family?

After you've found a puppy or adult dog that twangs your heartstrings, it's time to meet your prospective pet's family. Expect to see at least the *dam* (that's mom in dog lingo) and the pup's littermates (siblings). With luck, you may also see an aunt or uncle, and maybe even a grand-dam or an adult brother or sister from an earlier litter. Don't be disappointed if you don't see the *sire* (papa). He may live far away, but his picture and pedigree will probably be available. There may not be any aunts, uncles, or older sibs on the premises, but buyer beware if you don't at least meet the puppy's dam.

May I Test This Pup's Temperament?

If the breeder believes that you know how to hold and handle a tiny dog (see Chapter 5), he or she will likely be willing to let you test the puppy's temperament. This involves taking the puppy away from its dam and littermates, and possibly out of sight of the breeder — for example, into another room or around the side of the house. You can take this book with you; easy instructions for temperament testing are in Chapter 4.

May I Have a Copy of the Chi's Schedule and Records?

Many breeders give new owners a copy of the puppy's feeding schedule and health record. If the breeder only offers to tell it to you verbally, write down all the information. Making sudden changes to a dog's diet can be dangerous (see Chapter 6). Also, your veterinarian needs to know what vaccines your dog has already received and when they were given so he or she can set up a vaccination and worming schedule (see Chapter 13).

What Kind of Health (Or Show) Guarantee Do You Offer?

Most reputable sellers offer some type of health guarantee with their pups, giving you a certain amount of time (usually 24 to 48 hours) to take the dog to your vet for a complete physical. When buying a show-potential puppy (one you plan to exhibit in dog shows; see Chapter 12), find out if the breeder will offer a replacement pup if the dog isn't show quality at adulthood.

Is This Pup Eligible for Full or Limited AKC Registration?

A filled-out and signed registration application should accompany every breeder's AKC registrable dogs. The form also has a section for you to complete when you purchase a pup. Do it ASAP, enclose the required fee, and send it to the American Kennel Club (the address should be on the form). A registration certificate will soon arrive in the mail. Then, and only then, do you own a registered dog!

If your puppy has limited registration, that means it isn't a show dog (although it can still compete in obedience, agility, and other sporting events) and its offspring won't be eligible for AKC registration (see Chapter 4 for more).

Will I Receive a Registration Application When I Buy?

If you want an AKC-registered dog and the seller doesn't have a registration application ready to go with your puppy, proceed with caution. Yes, it's possible that the paperwork is still at the AKC offices and will arrive soon. If you trust the seller enough to take the puppy with papers pending, you should request a bill of sale signed by the seller that includes your dog's breed, date of birth, sex, and color — as well as the registered names and AKC numbers of the dog's sire and dam, and the full name and address of the breeder. If the important paperwork doesn't show up in a week or so and you want to contact the AKC, you'll be able to identify your dog with all the information from the bill of sale.

Most breeders automatically offer a copy of the puppy's pedigree. The *pedigree* is the Chi's family tree, and it gives more information than just names. If any of her ancestors were illustrious in the show, obedience, or agility ring, abbreviations of their titles may be included, too. For details, check out Chapter 4, or ask the proud breeder to decipher the mysterious letters.

What Dog Clubs Do You Belong to and Recommend?

Most (but not all) good breeders belong to a dog club or two. For example, Chihuahua breeders often are members of the Chihuahua Club of America, and possibly local all-breed dog clubs as well. Membership in a dog club is a good sign that you're dealing with a serious breeder, but not everyone is a "joiner." So, don't pass up a puppy that makes your heart sing just because its breeder didn't join a dog club.

May I Call or E-mail You for Advice After We Get Home?

Make sure the breeder you choose is willing to be a source of information after the purchase — someone who can give you advice about the breed, its training, and so on. A caring breeder may ask *you* to keep him or her posted on the puppy's progress. Steer clear of any that hem and haw when you ask if you can use them as resources to help you raise your new puppy.

Chapter 17

Ten Web Sites Where Chihuahua Lovers Gather

In This Chapter

▶ Finding clubs for Chihuahua lovers

▶ Gathering info on Chis and Chi breeders

▶ Adopting a homeless Chi

▶ Enjoying just-for-fun stuff for people and their dogs

*T*he Internet is often called the "Information Superhighway" because you can find info about everything and anything while cruising along its wide lanes. But, like the gorgeous Alaska Highway, the Net can suddenly disintegrate into dirt and deep ruts, so you need to navigate with care and avoid some sites altogether. The problem is, people can say anything they please on the Net because they don't have editors to make sure the info is useful or even correct. When I type the word Chihuahua into a search engine, I come up with 1,280,000 matches. Naturally, that figure changes daily. In this chapter, I present a few of my favorite sites to start you on your way. I'm sure you'll find many more worthy sites as you cruise along, so keep on trucking (I mean, clicking!).

The Chihuahua Club of America

The Chihuahua Club of America (www.chihuahuaclubofamerica.com) is the national parent club for the Chihuahua breed under the American Kennel Club (AKC; see Chapter 2). The site includes the breed's official standard, breed rescue referral, and myriad helpful articles about topics such as puppy care and health. For added interest, you can read the club's official statements on the molera (the soft spot on top of many Chihuahuas' heads) and the use of the term "tea cup" when describing a Chihuahua's size.

 Traveling with your Chihuahua? Check out the CCA's guidelines for staying in hotels/motels with your dog.

The American Kennel Club

Settle down and get ready to surf at the American Kennel Club's site (AKC; www.akc.org). Here you can find information on dogs in general, as well as Chihuahuas in particular. The site includes info on every one of the over 150 AKC-recognized breeds, help with AKC registration, downloadable forms, breeder referrals, breed rescue info, and upcoming events (including dog shows, obedience, and agility trials; see Chapter 12). And that's just the beginning:

- ✔ You can click on Customer Service for a wealth of help, including an advice column.

- ✔ If you have children, they'll enjoy the fun facts and activities on the Kids Corner page, where Bailey the Beagle answers readers' questions about dogs.

- ✔ Do you have animal-loving kids in high school? Teenagers planning a career that involves dog care will benefit from the For Juniors section, which includes scholarship info.

Truth is, after you click on the AKC site, you can spend several entertaining hours reading about purebred dogs and their activities. Have you ever seen a Spinone Italiano? No, it isn't on the menu at the Olive Garden. Look it up at the AKC site — a fact-filled, fun place to learn about dogs.

Chihuahua FAQ

The Chihuahua FAQ site (www.chihuahuafaq.com) is written by Michele Welton, an obedience instructor and behavioral consultant. On the site, she answers frequently asked questions about buying, training, and living with a Chihuahua, as well as dogs in general. She also discusses Chihuahua rescue and has a Chihuahua blog where she discusses various topics about the breed at her own discretion.

Chihuahua Rescue and Transport, Inc.

Chihuahua Rescue and Transport (CRT; www.chihuahua-rescue. com) is a network of volunteers dedicated to the welfare and rescue of Chihuahuas in the United States. On the site, you can see photos and information about the Chihuahuas currently available for adoption. Besides rescue and adoption information, the site provides an online newsletter.

It's also a super site for finding that special something to show off your favorite breed. Merchandise includes a Chi Gang Beach Party T-shirt, a Chi Pride T-shirt, tote bags, towels, and even Poppy's Pouch — a beloved bed for many Chihuahuas. The profits help homeless Chis, too! Beware: When reading CRT's rescue stories, be sure to have a box of tissues handy. You'll need them. If you want to be a part of this caring group, read the site's info on becoming a volunteer.

Canadian Chihuahua Rescue and Transport

Canadian Chihuahua Rescue and Transport (a sister organization to CRT; www.ccrt.net) rescues, fosters, and provides veterinary care for homeless, abandoned, and abused Chihuahuas in Canada. Its site provides detailed profiles of dogs available for rescue, matches homeless Chis with carefully screened adoptive homes, and provides follow-up support for new owners. Educating the public about the Chi breed is a high priority. And for a good read, you can check out the heartwarming stories of successful rescues. If you want to help, the site provides info about becoming a volunteer; it also posts a link to CRT in the United States.

Everwonder

Remember when restaurant chain Taco Bell's ads featured a sassy, talking Chihuahua? Well, her name is Gidget and she was a girl dog playing a boy dog! At the Everwonder site (www.everwonder.com/ david/tacobelldog.html), Gidget fans can view old Taco Bell commercials to their hearts' content. Features on the site include audio and video clips of all your favorite ads, tales of Gidget and her body doubles on the set, and much more.

Breeders.net

Looking for a good Chihuahua breeder? Go to www.breeders.net, click Find Dog Breeders, and then click Chihuahua from the breed list. Now enter your zip code and click Fetch! The site will provide a list of the Chi breeders nearest you.

If you're shopping for your first dog, read the information on the How to Find a Dog page. The authors of this site explain the differences between good and bad breeding practices, give you tips on selecting the right dog for you, and remind you that being listed on this site is no guarantee of quality. In other words, you need to check out potential breeders for yourself. But that's okay. You can find out how to do that in Chapter 4.

Agility Ability

Discover the exciting sport of agility — including its history, a description of the obstacles, and some of the terrific dogs that have garnered great scores — at www.agilityability.com. To see photos of Chihuahuas training for agility and of the few fearless Chis that have earned agility titles, click on Agility Chihuahuas. (For more on agility and other competition, see Chapter 12.)

Chihuahua Savvy

At the Chihuahua Savvy site (www.chihuahuasavvy.com), you'll take a short course on Chihuahua puppy and adult care and training. You also can find info on the Chi personality and more, including breeder and rescue advice, tips, and a blog.

Wikipedia and Wikimedia Commons

If you search for Chihuahuas in Wikipedia (www.wikipedia.com), the free Internet encyclopedia, you'll find a wealth of breed info, including temperament, health, and fame articles. It's always a good idea to double-check anything of importance that you read at this site, though. You can also scroll down to the Wikimedia Commons box, click Chihuahuas, and get rewarded with plenty of lovely photos of your favorite breed!

Chapter 18

Ten (Or So) Famous Chihuahuas

....

In This Chapter

▶ Meeting Chihuahua actors, performers, and "authors"

▶ Catching up with an inspiring Chihuahua

▶ Discovering dog stars and stars' dogs

....

*T*hanks to television and movies, most of today's pop culture
enthusiasts admire, or at least are amused by, famous
Chihuahuas. Yet, artists and entertainers adored this bright breed
long before television was invented and movies made over 100 million dollars in a weekend. In this chapter, I tell you about diminutive dog stars and celebrity Chi owners. But choosing only ten of
them is just too hard, so I cheat a little and stuff several human
stars and their Chihuahua companions under one heading!

Tinkerbell Hilton

Hotel heiress Paris Hilton has Tinkerbell, a Chihuahua that shares
plane rides and goes to restaurants and interviews with her.
Tinkerbell was a familiar character on the old reality show *The
Simple Life,* and has even "written" a book, *The Tinkerbell Hilton
Diaries: My Life Tailing Paris Hilton* (Grand Central Publishing),
as told to D. Resin.

Bruiser

In the movie *Legally Blonde,* Elle Woods, played by Reese Witherspoon, attends Harvard University with her plucky Chihuahua Bruiser (whose real name is Moonie). Bruiser/Moonie also is featured in *Legally Blonde 2,* where he's present in the courtroom while his mistress pleads cases!

Wheely Willy

The subject of two best-selling children's books (including *How Willy Got His Wings* [Doral], by Deborah Turner), Wheely Willy is a real-life paraplegic Chihuahua that gets around via a canine "wheelchair," which allows him to move freely on his front legs while wheels roll on behind him. Originally found abandoned in a box with a cut throat and spinal injuries, Willy was eventually adopted by pet groomer (and author!) Deborah Turner. She tried to rig something that would give Willie the gift of autonomous movement, but she failed until she saw an ad for the K-9 Cart. Now Willy's can-do attitude inspires others as he visits hospitals and institutions around the globe and participates in local events (he's from Long Beach, California), such as the Los Angeles Marathon and the Cystic Fibrosis Fun Walk. Willy has also made several appearances on the Animal Planet television network!

Gidget

Gidget, Taco Bell's talking dog star, retired from the advertising business in 2000 after a long and successful career as chief spokesdog for the fast-food chain. But it seems like only yesterday!

She played a cool-guy role and did her own stunt work, which included riding on Godzilla's tail, running up a fire escape, riding a skateboard, and jumping on a taxi cab. She loved riding in limos, and she had her own line of drinking cups, T-shirts, and talking toys. She even had two male stand-ins! But despite all her fame, this diva was easily pleased and willingly worked for chicken and steak bits. Ay Chihuahua!

Gidget was born December 8, 1994, and is owned by animal trainer Sue Chipperton, who acquired Gidget as a pup and trained her for stardom. Her expressive face appeared in a print campaign for The Limited, and she had a "carry on" role in the movie *The Fan* with

Robert De Niro before becoming the hottest commercial canine since Spuds McKenzie. Following her Taco Bell adventures, Gidget appeared in another movie. She played Bruiser's mother in *Legally Blonde 2!*

Mojo

Perhaps you've seen the gutsy Chihuahua called Mojo in the action movie *Transformers*. His name is Chester in real life, and he's quite the spark plug. One of his several scenes included him lifting his leg and relieving himself on an evil transformer's foot!

Xavier Cugat's Dogs

Xavier Cugat, a popular Latin American band leader during the 1930s and '40s, liked to take his Chihuahuas on stage with him. He often held a Chi in one hand while conducting his band with the other. According to a popular (and possibly true) story, he once dressed a Chi like a baby, complete with a bonnet, so he could smuggle it into his hotel room.

Caranza

Owen Wister, author of *The Virginian* (Scribner), owned Chihuahuas. One of his dogs was named Caranza, the Chihuahua breed's first sire of renown. Two lines of top-winning Chihuahuas, Perrito and Meron, trace their roots to Caranza.

Tulip

Paula Abdul, of *American Idol* and pop singing fame, owns three Chihuahuas; named Thumbelina, Tinkerbell (yes, another one), and Tulip. Just before the sixth season finale of *American Idol,* in May of 2007, Abdul tore cartilage in her nose, fractured her toe, and suffered multiple bruises when she took a bad tumble while trying to avoid stepping on Tulip. The dog wasn't hurt, and Abdul, although sore, finished the season. In the process, Tulip became famous!

The Midget of the AKC corral

The first Chihuahua registered with the American Kennel Club was a red-coated Chi named Midget, owned by a Texan from El Paso. That was in 1904. The Chihuahua Club of America was founded in 1923 and has thrived ever since. Mexico, however, took longer to acknowledge its own breed. It didn't register the Chihuahua breed until 1942.

Don Giovanni

Do you like to read novels about the mob? If so, would you like to read some that are suspenseful and hilarious at the same time and, best yet, have a Chihuahua as one of the characters? Then look for books by Laurence Shames. But don't expect the Chihuahua in the books to be bright, bold, or endearing. That isn't Shames's style.

The Chi, Don Giovanni, has traits undesirable in a Chihuahua. Fragile, frightened, and a veritable canine hypochondriac, he spends most of his waking seconds quivering in the arms of Bert the Shirt, an ex-Mafioso who's his elderly owner. But the Shirt has enough character for both of them, and his relationship with his ancient dog makes for funny and heartwarming reading. Alive with zany characters, packed with action, and set in colorful Key West, Florida, Shames's novels are among my favorites. Two of them, *Florida Straits* (Dell) and *Sunburn* (Backinprint.com), feature Don Giovanni on the cover.

Other Chihuahuas Associated with Celebrities

Many other Chis have mingled with the stars and deserve recognition, too:

✔ Pop singer Britney Spears had two Chihuahuas, Bit Bit and Lucky, but she placed Lucky with an assistant after the dog attacked the ankles of her then-husband, Kevin Federline.

✔ Actress Marilyn Monroe adopted a Chihuahua she named Choo Choo in 1948.

✔ Victorious Mexican General Santa Ana had his Chihuahuas with him at the Alamo. In 1836, when he was finally captured, several Chihuahuas were found in his camp.

✔ Actress Jayne Mansfield owned Chihuahuas; one of her dogs died with her during a tragic car crash in 1967.

✔ Tennis great Martina Navratilova is a Chihuahua owner, and so was former Yale football coach Herman Hickman. He had two exceptionally small dogs named Killer and Slugger.

✔ Sharon Osbourne, wife of musician Ozzy Osbourne and reality TV maven, has a Chihuahua named Martini.

✔ Other famous names linked with Chihuahuas include Madonna, Rosie O'Donnell, Lupe Velez, Billie Holiday, Vincent Price, Gertrude Stein, Mickey Rourke, Anne Heche, Christine Ebersole, and Charo.

Finally, try visualizing California Governor (as of press time) Arnold Schwarzenegger walking his Chihuahua. How about that for attractive opposites!

Index

• C •

• D •

BUSINESS, CAREERS & PERSONAL FINANCE

0-7645-9847-3

0-7645-2431-3

Also available:
- Business Plans Kit For Dummies 0-7645-9794-9
- Economics For Dummies 0-7645-5726-2
- Grant Writing For Dummies 0-7645-8416-2
- Home Buying For Dummies 0-7645-5331-3
- Managing For Dummies 0-7645-1771-6
- Marketing For Dummies 0-7645-5600-2

- Personal Finance For Dummies 0-7645-2590-5*
- Resumes For Dummies 0-7645-5471-9
- Selling For Dummies 0-7645-5363-1
- Six Sigma For Dummies 0-7645-6798-5
- Small Business Kit For Dummies 0-7645-5984-2
- Starting an eBay Business For Dummies 0-7645-6924-4
- Your Dream Career For Dummies 0-7645-9795-7

HOME & BUSINESS COMPUTER BASICS

0-470-05432-8

0-471-75421-8

Also available:
- Cleaning Windows Vista For Dummies 0-471-78293-9
- Excel 2007 For Dummies 0-470-03737-7
- Mac OS X Tiger For Dummies 0-7645-7675-5
- MacBook For Dummies 0-470-04859-X
- Macs For Dummies 0-470-04849-2
- Office 2007 For Dummies 0-470-00923-3

- Outlook 2007 For Dummies 0-470-03830-6
- PCs For Dummies 0-7645-8958-X
- Salesforce.com For Dummies 0-470-04893-X
- Upgrading & Fixing Laptops For Dummies 0-7645-8959-8
- Word 2007 For Dummies 0-470-03658-3
- Quicken 2007 For Dummies 0-470-04600-7

FOOD, HOME, GARDEN, HOBBIES, MUSIC & PETS

0-7645-8404-9

0-7645-9904-6

Also available:
- Candy Making For Dummies 0-7645-9734-5
- Card Games For Dummies 0-7645-9910-0
- Crocheting For Dummies 0-7645-4151-X
- Dog Training For Dummies 0-7645-8418-9
- Healthy Carb Cookbook For Dummies 0-7645-8476-6

- Home Maintenance For Dummies 0-7645-5215-5
- Horses For Dummies 0-7645-9797-3
- Jewelry Making & Beading For Dummies 0-7645-2571-9
- Orchids For Dummies 0-7645-6759-4
- Puppies For Dummies 0-7645-5255-4
- Rock Guitar For Dummies 0-7645-5356-9
- Sewing For Dummies 0-7645-6847-7
- Singing For Dummies 0-7645-2475-5

INTERNET & DIGITAL MEDIA

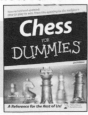

0-470-04529-9

0-470-04894-8

Also available:
- Blogging For Dummies 0-471-77084-1
- Digital Photography For Dummies 0-7645-9802-3
- Digital Photography All-in-One Desk Reference For Dummies 0-470-03743-1
- Digital SLR Cameras and Photography For Dummies 0-7645-9803-1
- eBay Business All-in-One Desk Reference For Dummies 0-7645-8438-3

- HDTV For Dummies 0-470-09673-X
- Home Entertainment PCs For Dummies 0-470-05523-5
- MySpace For Dummies 0-470-09529-6
- Search Engine Optimization For Dummies 0-471-97998-8
- Skype For Dummies 0-470-04891-3
- The Internet For Dummies 0-7645-8996-2
- Wiring Your Digital Home For Dummies 0-471-91830-X

WILEY

SPORTS, FITNESS, PARENTING, RELIGION & SPIRITUALITY

0-471-76871-5

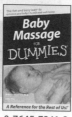

0-7645-7841-3

Also available:

- Catholicism For Dummies
  0-7645-5391-7
- Exercise Balls For Dummies
  0-7645-5623-1
- Fitness For Dummies 0-7645-7851-0
- Football For Dummies 0-7645-3936-1
- Judaism For Dummies 0-7645-5299-6
- Potty Training For Dummies
  0-7645-5417-4

- Buddhism For Dummies
  0-7645-5359-3
- Pregnancy For Dummies
  0-7645-4483-7 †
- Ten Minute Tone-Ups For Dummies
  0-7645-7207-5
- NASCAR For Dummies 0-7645-7681-X
- Religion For Dummies 0-7645-5264-3
- Soccer For Dummies 0-7645-5229-5
- Women in the Bible For Dummies
  0-7645-8475-8

TRAVEL

0-7645-7749-2

0-7645-6945-7

Also available:

- Alaska For Dummies 0-7645-7746-8
- Cruise Vacations For Dummies
  0-7645-6941-4
- England For Dummies 0-7645-4276-1
- Europe For Dummies 0-7645-7529-5
- Germany For Dummies
  0-7645-7823-5
- Hawaii For Dummies 0-7645-7402-7

- Italy For Dummies 0-7645-7386-1
- Las Vegas For Dummies
  0-7645-7382-9
- London For Dummies 0-7645-4277-X
- Paris For Dummies 0-7645-7630-5
- RV Vacations For Dummies
  0-7645-4442-X
- Walt Disney World & Orlando
  For Dummies 0-7645-9660-8

GRAPHICS, DESIGN & WEB DEVELOPMENT

0-7645-8815-X

0-7645-9571-7

Also available:

- 3D Game Animation For Dummies
  0-7645-8789-7
- AutoCAD 2006 For Dummies
  0-7645-8925-3
- Building a Web Site For Dummies
  0-7645-7144-3
- Creating Web Pages For Dummies
  0-470-08030-2
- Creating Web Pages All-in-One Desk
  Reference For Dummies
  0-7645-4345-8
- Dreamweaver 8 For Dummies
  0-7645-9649-7

- InDesign CS2 For Dummies
  0-7645-9572-5
- Macromedia Flash 8 For Dummies
  0-7645-9691-8
- Photoshop CS2 and Digital
  Photography For Dummies
  0-7645-9580-6
- Photoshop Elements 4 For Dummies
  0-471-77483-9
- Syndicating Web Sites with RSS Feeds
  For Dummies
  0-7645-8848-6
- Yahoo! SiteBuilder For Dummies
  0-7645-9800-7

NETWORKING, SECURITY, PROGRAMMING & DATABASES

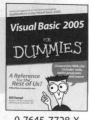

0-7645-7728-X

0-471-74940-0

Also available:

- Access 2007 For Dummies
  0-470-04612-0
- ASP.NET 2 For Dummies
  0-7645-7907-X
- C# 2005 For Dummies
  0-7645-9704-3
- Hacking For Dummies
  0-470-05235-X
- Hacking Wireless Networks
  For Dummies
  0-7645-9730-2
- Java For Dummies
  0-470-08716-1

- Microsoft SQL Server 2005
  For Dummies 0-7645-7755-7
- Networking All-in-One Desk
  Reference For Dummies
  0-7645-9939-9
- Preventing Identity Theft For Dummies
  0-7645-7336-5
- Telecom For Dummies
  0-471-77085-X
- Visual Studio 2005 All-in-One Desk
  Reference For Dummies
  0-7645-9775-2
- XML For Dummies
  0-7645-8845-1

HEALTH & SELF-HELP

0-7645-8450-2   0-7645-4149-8

Also available:

Bipolar Disorder For Dummies
0-7645-8451-0

Chemotherapy and Radiation
For Dummies 0-7645-7832-4

Controlling Cholesterol For Dummies
0-7645-5440-9

Diabetes For Dummies
0-7645-6820-5* †

Divorce For Dummies
0-7645-8417-0 †

Fibromyalgia For Dummies
0-7645-5441-7

Low-Calorie Dieting For Dummies
0-7645-9905-4

Meditation For Dummies
0-471-77774-9

Osteoporosis For Dummies
0-7645-7621-6

Overcoming Anxiety For Dummies
0-7645-5447-6

Reiki For Dummies
0-7645-9907-0

Stress Management For Dummies
0-7645-5144-2

EDUCATION, HISTORY, REFERENCE & TEST PREPARATION

0-7645-8381-6   0-7645-9554-7

Also available:

The ACT For Dummies 0-7645-9652-7

Algebra For Dummies 0-7645-5325-9

Algebra Workbook For Dummies
0-7645-8467-7

Astronomy For Dummies
0-7645-8465-0

Calculus For Dummies 0-7645-2498-4

Chemistry For Dummies
0-7645-5430-1

Forensics For Dummies
0-7645-5580-4

Freemasons For Dummies
0-7645-9796-5

French For Dummies 0-7645-5193-0

Geometry For Dummies
0-7645-5324-0

Organic Chemistry I For Dummies
0-7645-6902-3

The SAT I For Dummies
0-7645-7193-1

Spanish For Dummies 0-7645-5194-9

Statistics For Dummies
0-7645-5423-9

Get smart @ dummies.com®

- Find a full list of Dummies titles
- Look into loads of FREE on-site articles
- Sign up for FREE eTips e-mailed to you weekly
- See what other products carry the Dummies name
- Shop directly from the Dummies bookstore
- Enter to win new prizes every month!

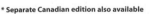